D1263785

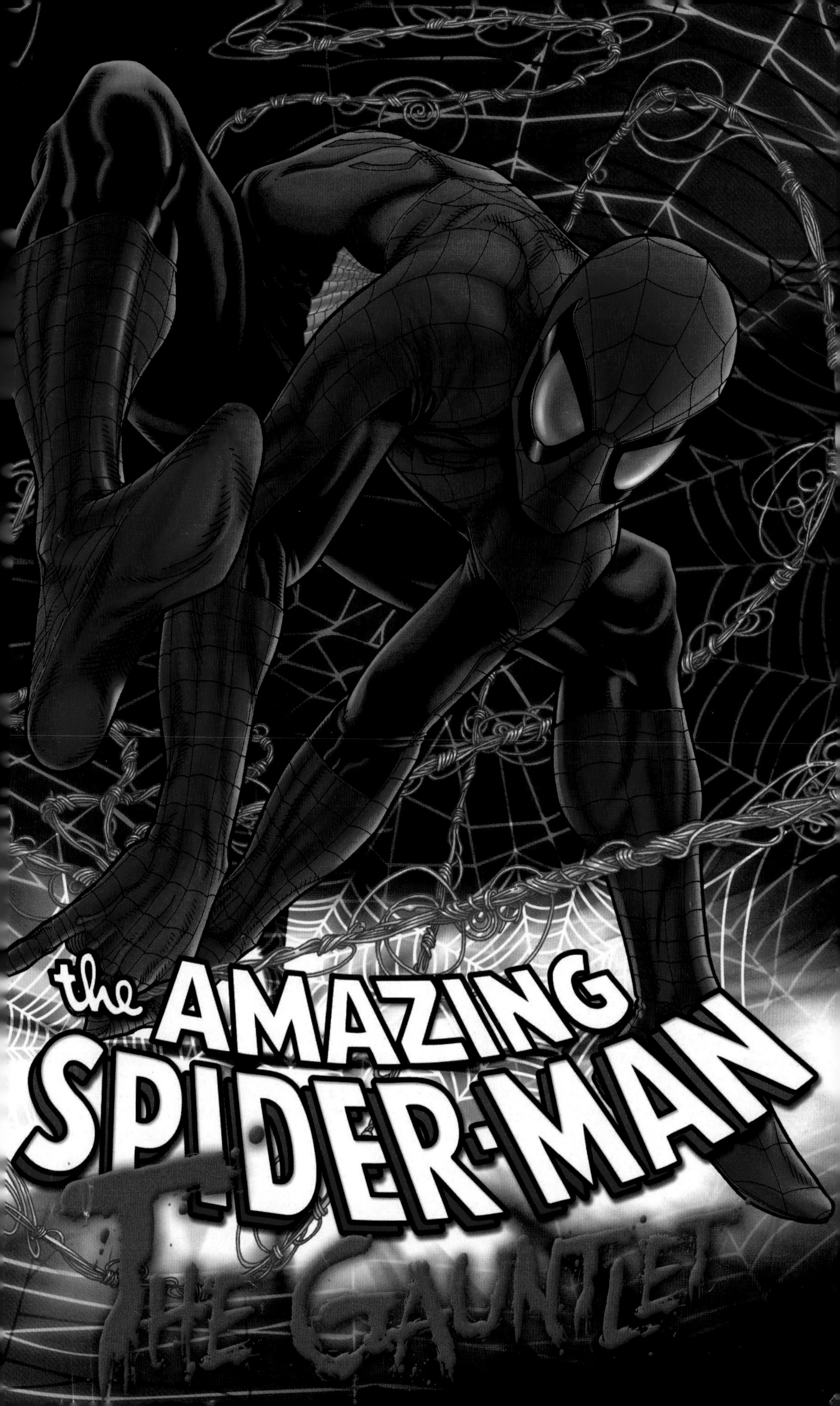
the AMAZING
SPIDER-MAN
THE GAUNTLET

the AMAZING SPIDER-MAN
THE GAUNTLET

VULTURE & MORBIUS

"THE IRRITABLE J. JONAH JAMESON"
Writer: **TOM PEYER**
Artist: **JAVIER RODRIGUEZ**
Letterer: **JARED K. FLETCHER**

ISSUE #622
Writers: **FRED VAN LENTE & GREG WEISMAN**
Artists: **JOE QUINONES & LUKE ROSS**
Colorist: **JOE QUINONES & ROB SCHWAGER**
Letterer: **VC'S JOE CARAMAGNA**

ISSUE #623-624
Writer: **MARK WAID** WITH **TOM PEYER**
Artist: **PAUL AZACETA** WITH **JAVIER RODRIGUEZ**
Colorist: **ANDRES MOSSA**
Letterer: **VC'S JOE CARAMAGNA**

ISSUE #625
Writer: **JOE KELLY**
Penciler: **MAX FIUMARA**
Colorist: **FABIO D'AURIA**
Letterer: **VC'S JOE CARAMAGNA**

"GAUNTLET ORIGINS: VULTURE"
Writer: **FRED VAN LENTE**
Artist: **FRANCIS PORTELA**
Colorist: **CHRIS SOTOMAYOR**
Letterer: **RUS WOOTON**

Web-Heads: **BOB GALE, JOE KELLY, DAN SLOTT, FRED VAN LENTE, MARK WAID & ZEB WELLS**
Assistant Editor: **THOMAS BRENNAN** • Editor: **STEPHEN WACKER** • Executive Editor: **TOM BREVOORT**

Collection Editor: **JENNIFER GRÜNWALD** • Assistant Editor: **ALEX STARBUCK**
Associate Editor: **JOHN DENNING** • Editor, Special Projects: **MARK D. BEAZLEY**
Senior Editor, Special Projects: **JEFF YOUNGQUIST** • Senior Vice President of Sales: **DAVID GABRIEL**

Editor in Chief: **JOE QUESADA** • Publisher: **DAN BUCKLEY** • Executive Producer: **ALAN FINE**

SPIDER-MAN: THE GAUNTLET VOL. 3 — VULTURE & MORBIUS. Contains material originally published in magazine form as AMAZING SPIDER-MAN #622-625, and WEB OF SPIDER-MAN #2 and #6. First printing 2010. Hardcover ISBN# 978-0-7851-4611-7. Softcover ISBN# 978-0-7851-4612-4. Published by MARVEL WORLDWIDE, INC., a subsidiary of MARVEL ENTERTAINMENT, LLC. OFFICE OF PUBLICATION: 417 5th Avenue, New York, NY 10016. Copyright © 2009 and 2010 Marvel Characters, Inc. All rights reserved. Hardcover: $19.99 per copy in the U.S. (GST #R127032852). Softcover: $14.99 per copy in the U.S. (GST #R127032852). Canadian Agreement #40668537. All characters featured in this issue and the distinctive names and likenesses thereof, and all related indicia are trademarks of Marvel Characters, Inc. No similarity between any of the names, characters, persons, and/or institutions in this magazine with those of any living or dead person or institution is intended, and any such similarity which may exist is purely coincidental. **Printed in the U.S.A.** ALAN FINE, EVP - Office of the President, Marvel Worldwide, Inc. and EVP & CMO Marvel Characters B.V.; DAN BUCKLEY, Chief Executive Officer and Publisher - Print, Animation & Digital Media; JIM SOKOLOWSKI, Chief Operating Officer; DAVID GABRIEL, SVP of Publishing Sales & Circulation; DAVID BOGART, SVP of Business Affairs & Talent Management; MICHAEL PASCIULLO, VP Merchandising & Communications; JIM O'KEEFE, VP of Operations & Logistics; DAN CARR, Executive Director of Publishing Technology; JUSTIN F. GABRIE, Director of Publishing & Editorial Operations; SUSAN CRESPI, Editorial Operations Manager; ALEX MORALES, Publishing Operations Manager; STAN LEE, Chairman Emeritus. For information regarding advertising in Marvel Comics or on Marvel.com, please contact Ron Stern, VP of Business Development, at rstern@marvel.com. For Marvel subscription inquiries, please call 800-217-9158. **Manufactured between 4/5/10 and 5/5/10 (hardcover), and 4/5/10 and 10/6/10 (softcover), by R.R. DONNELLEY, INC., SALEM, VA, USA.**
10 9 8 7 6 5 4 3 2 1

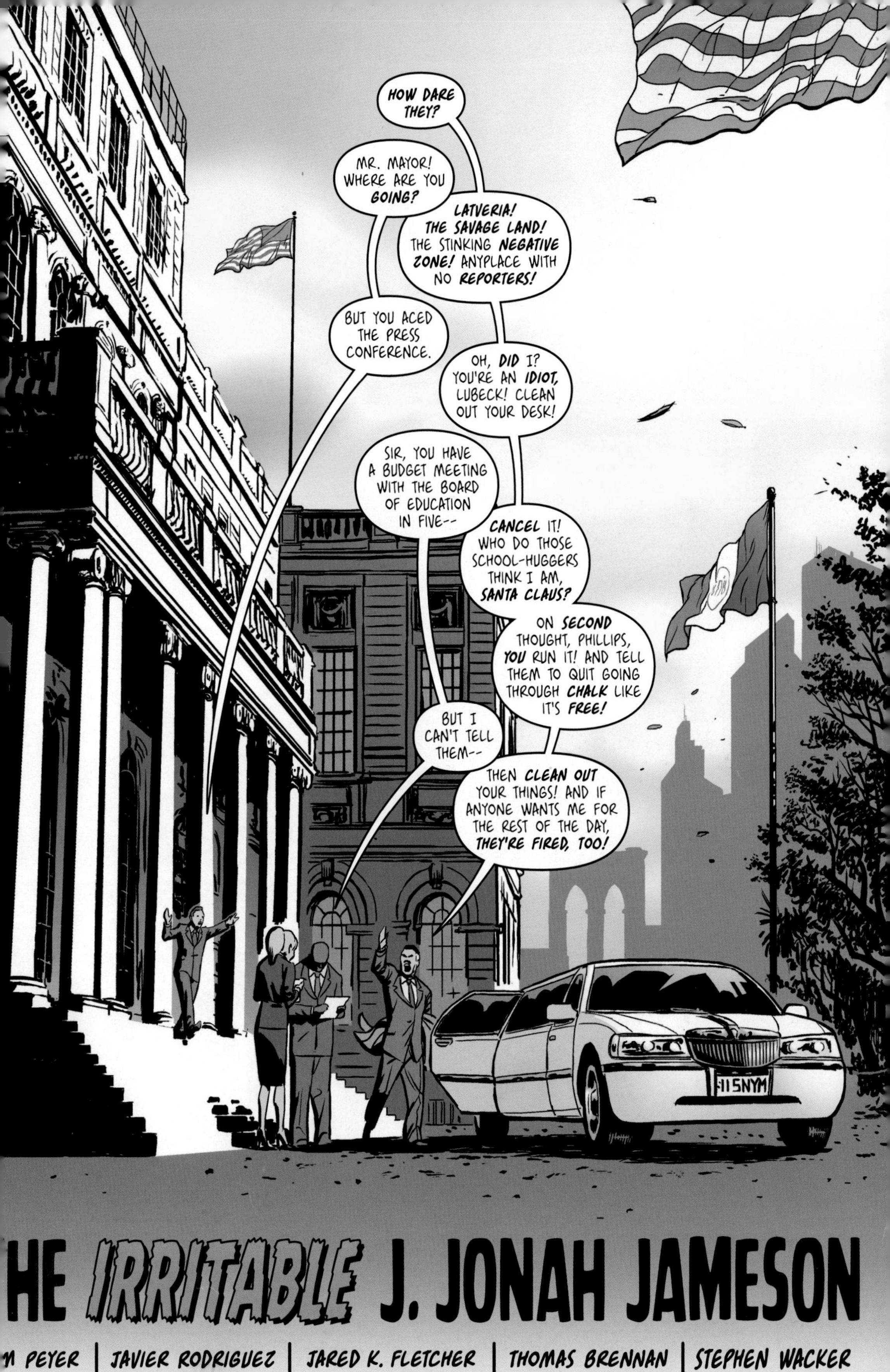
HOW DARE THEY?
MR. MAYOR! WHERE ARE YOU GOING?
LATVERIA! THE SAVAGE LAND! THE STINKING NEGATIVE ZONE! ANYPLACE WITH NO REPORTERS!
BUT YOU ACED THE PRESS CONFERENCE.
OH, DID I? YOU'RE AN IDIOT, LUBECK! CLEAN OUT YOUR DESK!
SIR, YOU HAVE A BUDGET MEETING WITH THE BOARD OF EDUCATION IN FIVE--
CANCEL IT! WHO DO THOSE SCHOOL-HUGGERS THINK I AM, SANTA CLAUS?
ON SECOND THOUGHT, PHILLIPS, YOU RUN IT! AND TELL THEM TO QUIT GOING THROUGH CHALK LIKE IT'S FREE!
BUT I CAN'T TELL THEM--
THEN CLEAN OUT YOUR THINGS! AND IF ANYONE WANTS ME FOR THE REST OF THE DAY, THEY'RE FIRED, TOO!
115NYM

HE IRRITABLE J. JONAH JAMESON

M PEYER WRITER | JAVIER RODRIGUEZ ARTIST | JARED K. FLETCHER LETTERS | THOMAS BRENNAN ASST. EDITOR | STEPHEN WACKER J.J.J. LITE

TOM BREVOORT EXECUTIVE EDITOR | JOE QUESADA EDITOR IN CHIEF | DAN BUCKLEY PUBLISHER | ALAN FINE EXECUTIVE PRODUCER

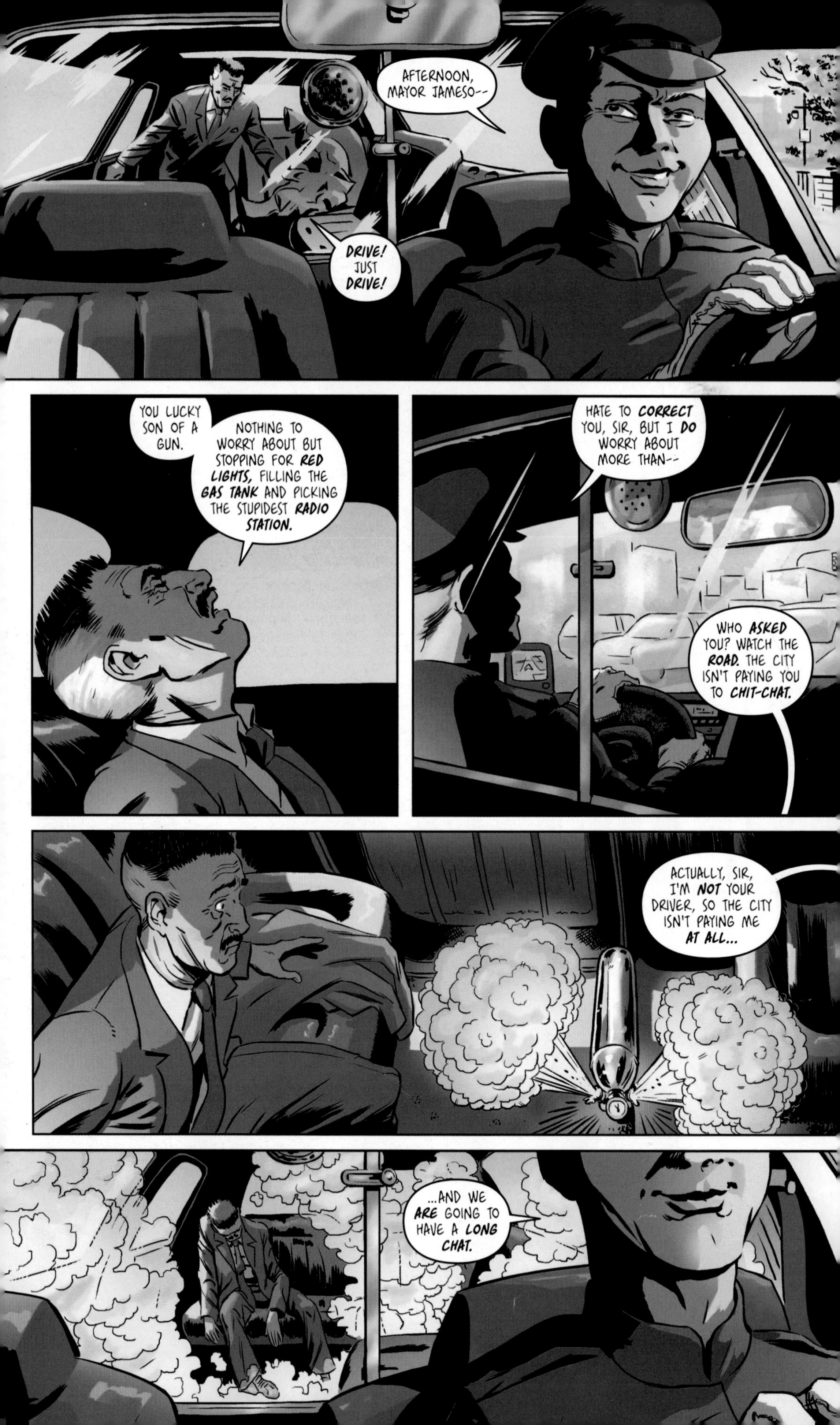
AFTERNOON, MAYOR JAMESO--
DRIVE! JUST DRIVE!
YOU LUCKY SON OF A GUN.
NOTHING TO WORRY ABOUT BUT STOPPING FOR RED LIGHTS, FILLING THE GAS TANK AND PICKING THE STUPIDEST RADIO STATION.
HATE TO CORRECT YOU, SIR, BUT I DO WORRY ABOUT MORE THAN--
WHO ASKED YOU? WATCH THE ROAD. THE CITY ISN'T PAYING YOU TO CHIT-CHAT.
ACTUALLY, SIR, I'M NOT YOUR DRIVER, SO THE CITY ISN'T PAYING ME AT ALL...
...AND WE ARE GOING TO HAVE A LONG CHAT.

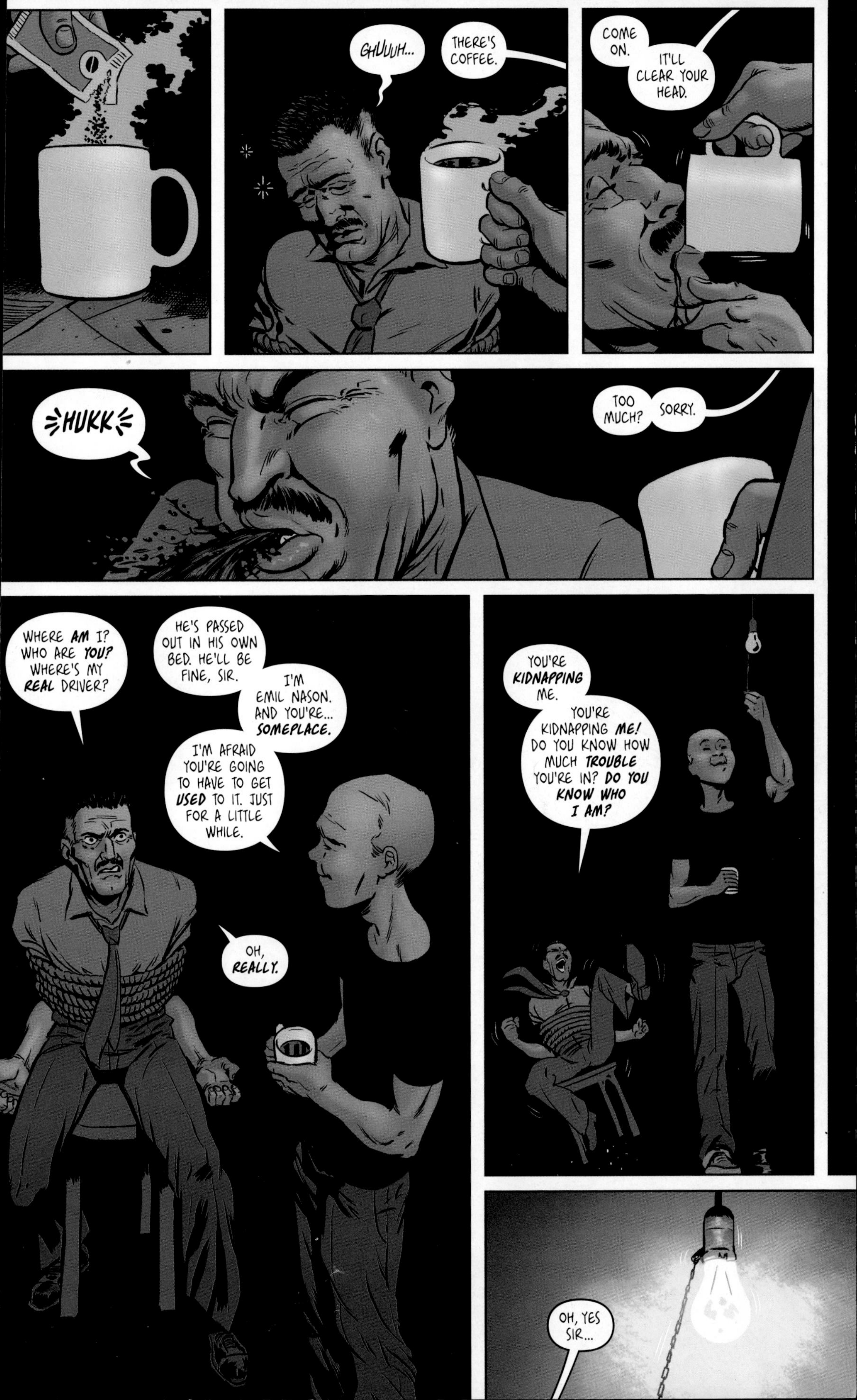
GHUUUH...
THERE'S COFFEE.
COME ON.
IT'LL CLEAR YOUR HEAD.
HUKK
TOO MUCH?
SORRY.
WHERE AM I? WHO ARE YOU? WHERE'S MY REAL DRIVER?
HE'S PASSED OUT IN HIS OWN BED. HE'LL BE FINE, SIR.
I'M EMIL NASON. AND YOU'RE... SOMEPLACE.
I'M AFRAID YOU'RE GOING TO HAVE TO GET USED TO IT. JUST FOR A LITTLE WHILE.
OH, REALLY.
YOU'RE KIDNAPPING ME.
YOU'RE KIDNAPPING ME! DO YOU KNOW HOW MUCH TROUBLE YOU'RE IN? DO YOU KNOW WHO I AM?
OH, YES SIR...

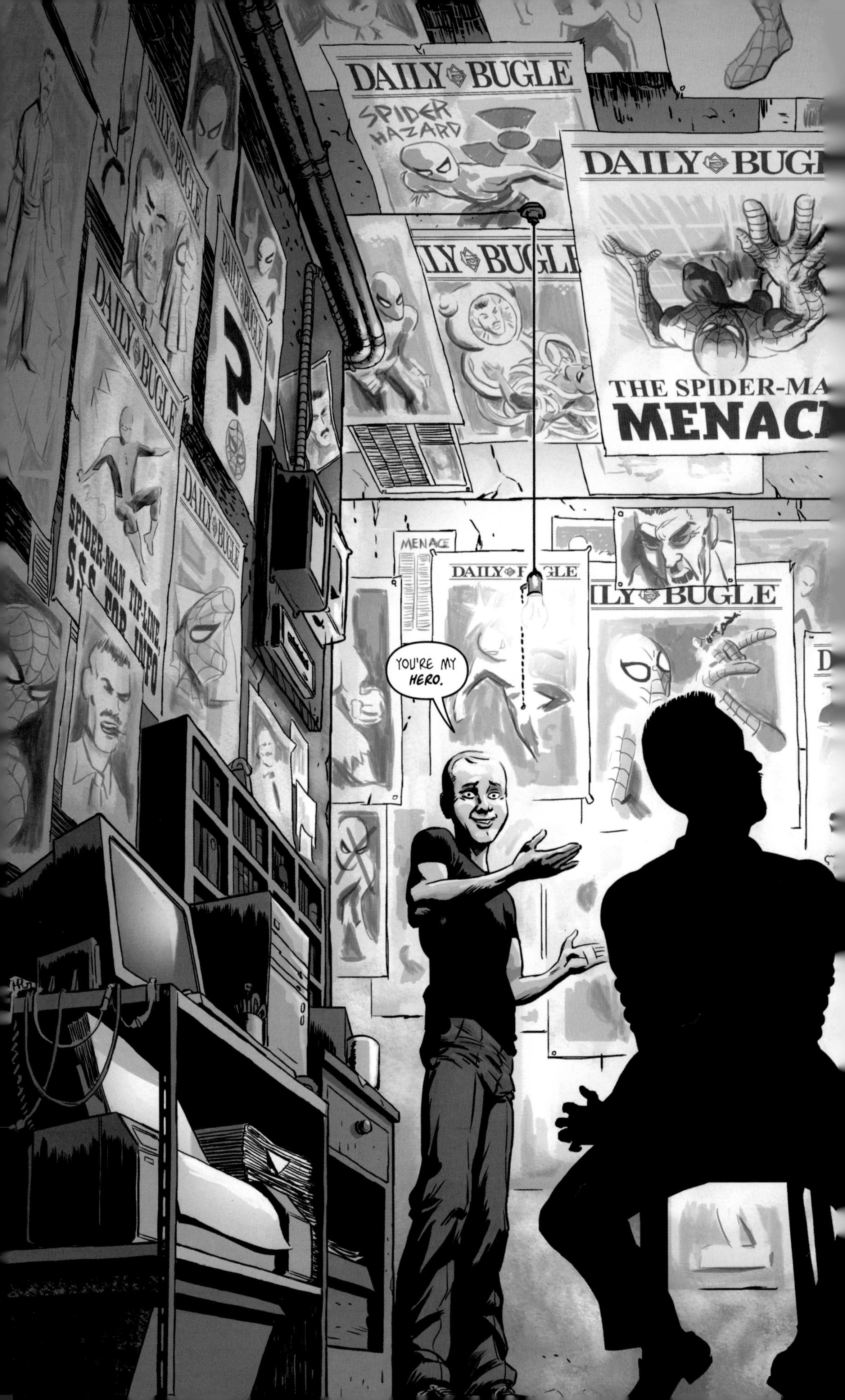
DAILY BUGLE
SPIDER HAZARD
DAILY BUGLE
DAILY BUGLE
SPIDER-MAN TIP-LINE $$$ FOR INFO
MENACE
YOU'RE MY HERO.

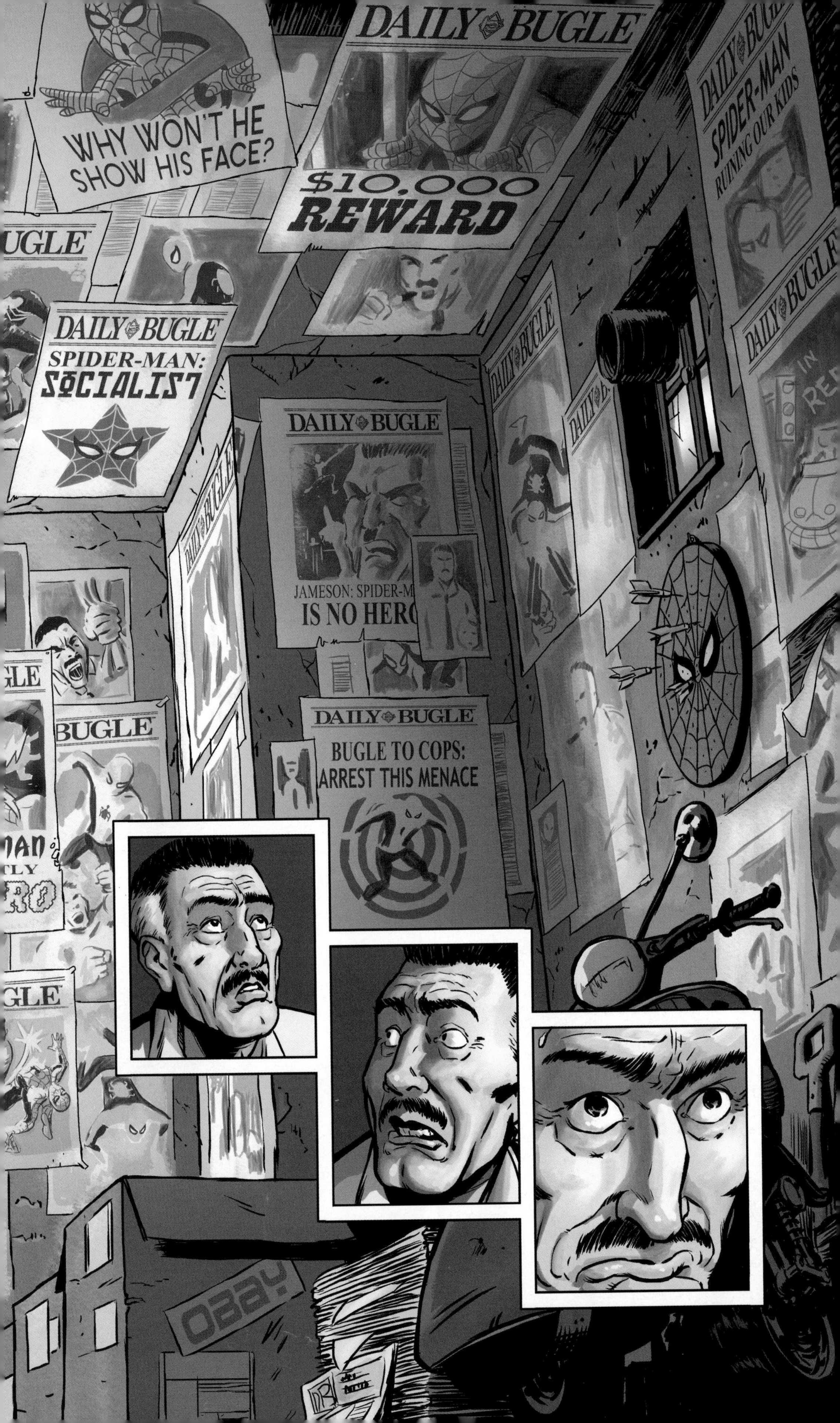

WHY WON'T HE SHOW HIS FACE?
DAILY BUGLE
$10,000 REWARD
DAILY BUGLE
SPIDER-MAN RUINING OUR KIDS
UGLE
DAILY BUGLE
SPIDER-MAN: SOCIALIST
DAILY BUGLE
DAILY BUGLE
JAMESON: SPIDER-M
IS NO HERO
DAILY BUGLE
BUGLE TO COPS: ARREST THIS MENACE
BUGLE
GLE

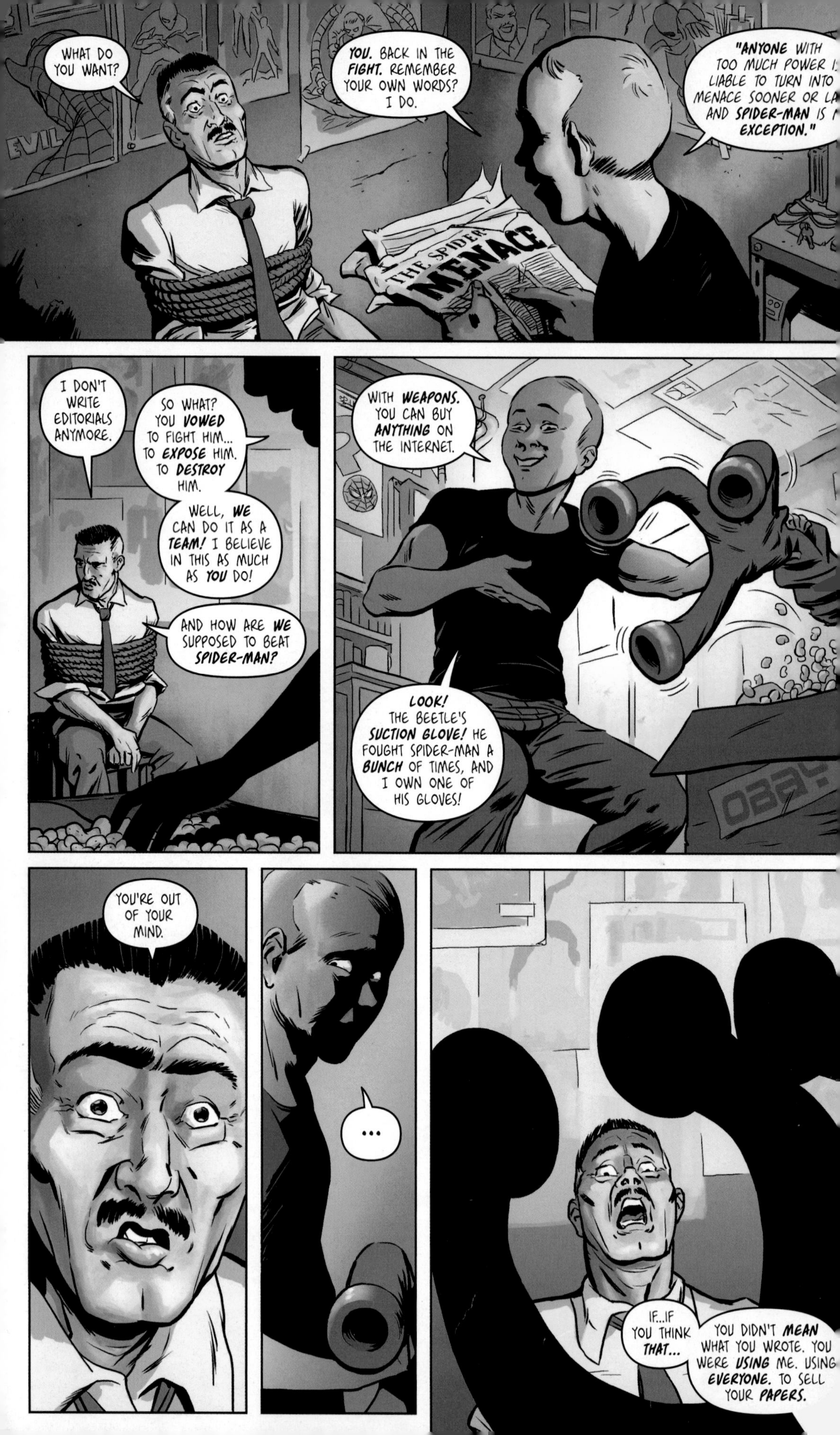
EVIL
WHAT DO YOU WANT?
YOU. BACK IN THE FIGHT. REMEMBER YOUR OWN WORDS? I DO.
"ANYONE WITH TOO MUCH POWER IS LIABLE TO TURN INTO A MENACE SOONER OR LATER AND SPIDER-MAN IS NO EXCEPTION."
THE SPIDER MENACE
I DON'T WRITE EDITORIALS ANYMORE.
SO WHAT? YOU VOWED TO FIGHT HIM... TO EXPOSE HIM. TO DESTROY HIM.
WELL, WE CAN DO IT AS A TEAM! I BELIEVE IN THIS AS MUCH AS YOU DO!
AND HOW ARE WE SUPPOSED TO BEAT SPIDER-MAN?
WITH WEAPONS. YOU CAN BUY ANYTHING ON THE INTERNET.
LOOK! THE BEETLE'S SUCTION GLOVE! HE FOUGHT SPIDER-MAN A BUNCH OF TIMES, AND I OWN ONE OF HIS GLOVES!
YOU'RE OUT OF YOUR MIND.
...
IF...IF YOU THINK THAT...
YOU DIDN'T MEAN WHAT YOU WROTE. YOU WERE USING ME. USING EVERYONE. TO SELL YOUR PAPERS.

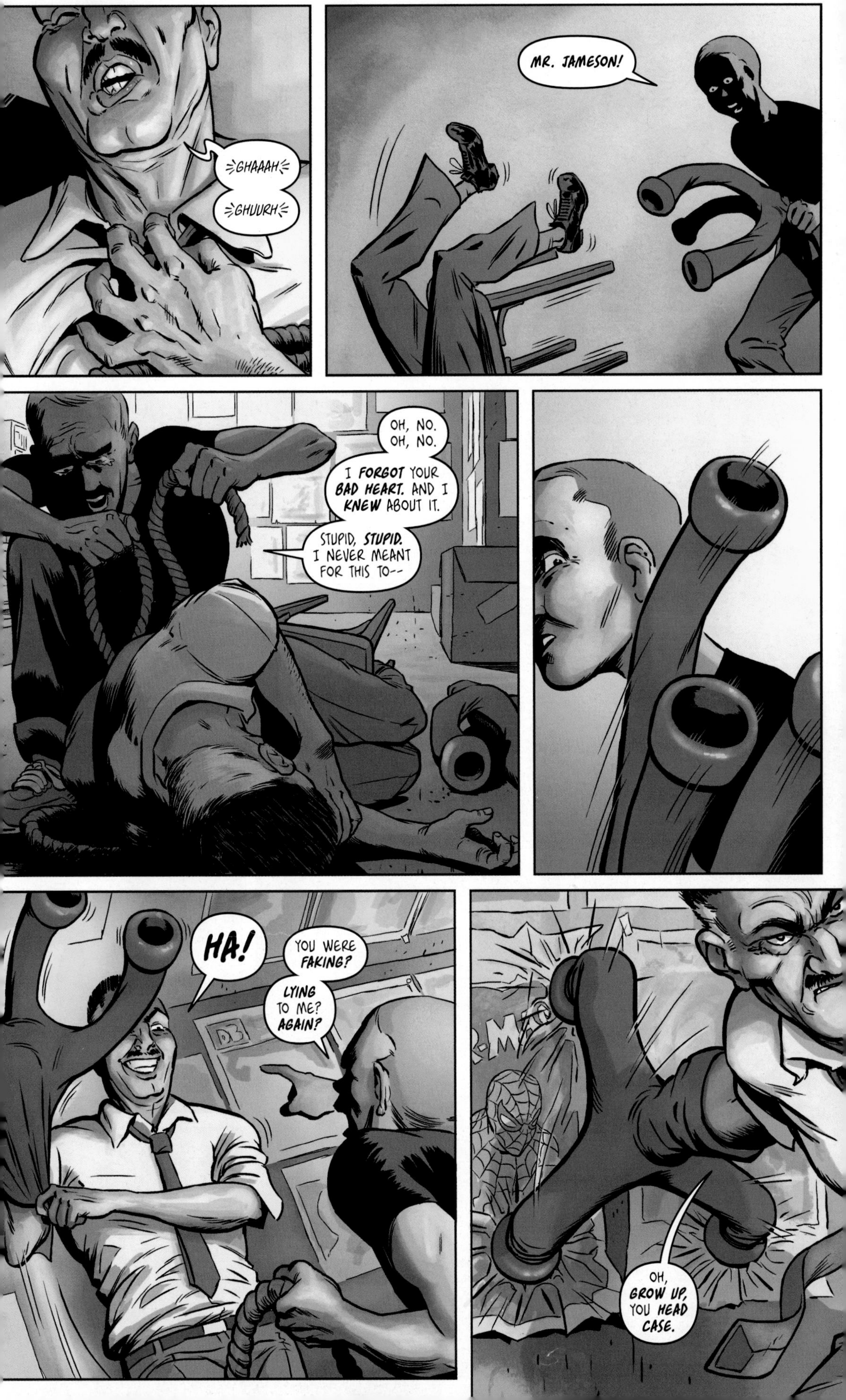
GHAAAH
GHUURH
MR. JAMESON!
OH, NO. OH, NO.
I FORGOT YOUR BAD HEART. AND I KNEW ABOUT IT.
STUPID, STUPID. I NEVER MEANT FOR THIS TO--
HA!
YOU WERE FAKING?
LYING TO ME? AGAIN?
OH, GROW UP, YOU HEAD CASE.

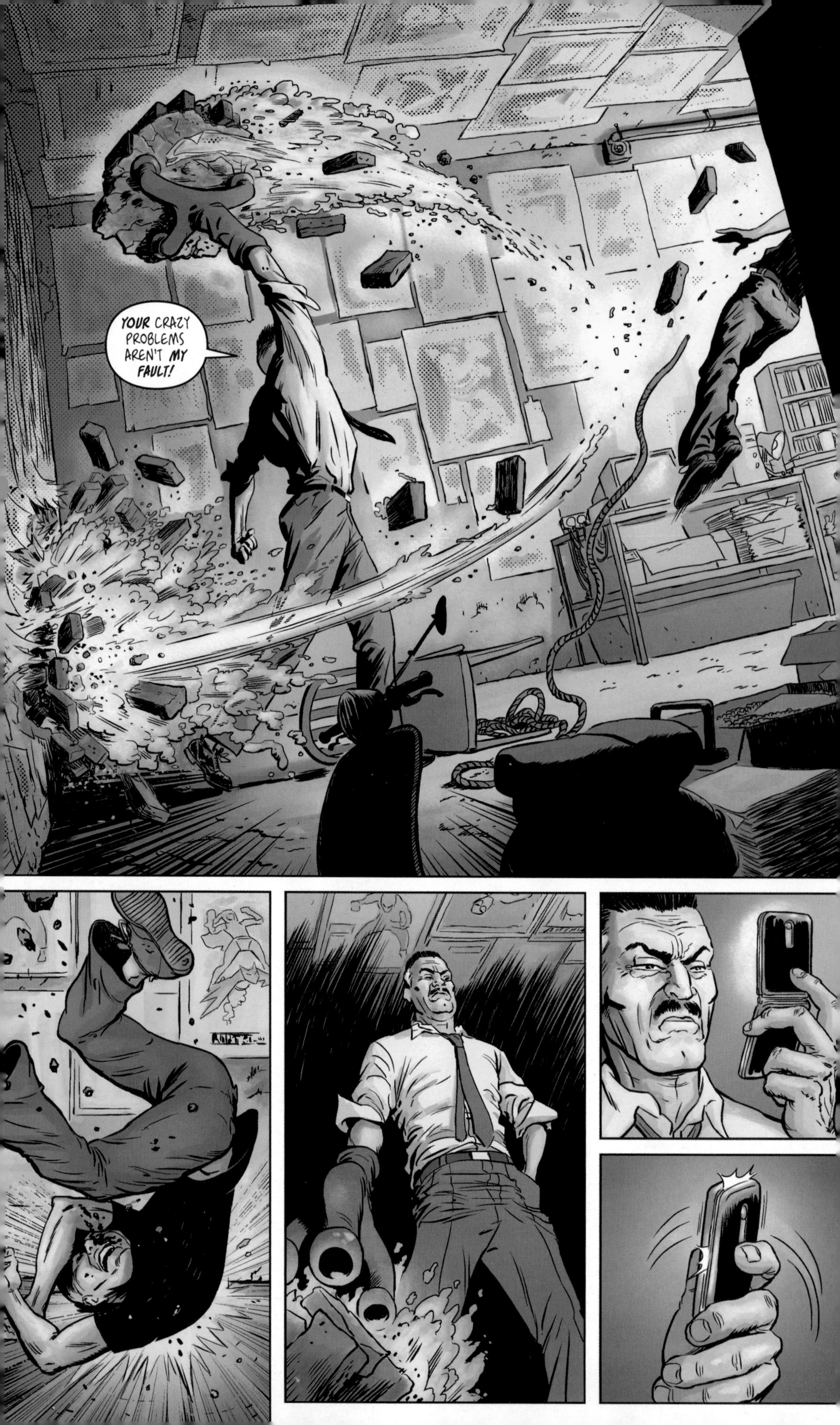
YOUR CRAZY PROBLEMS AREN'T MY FAULT!

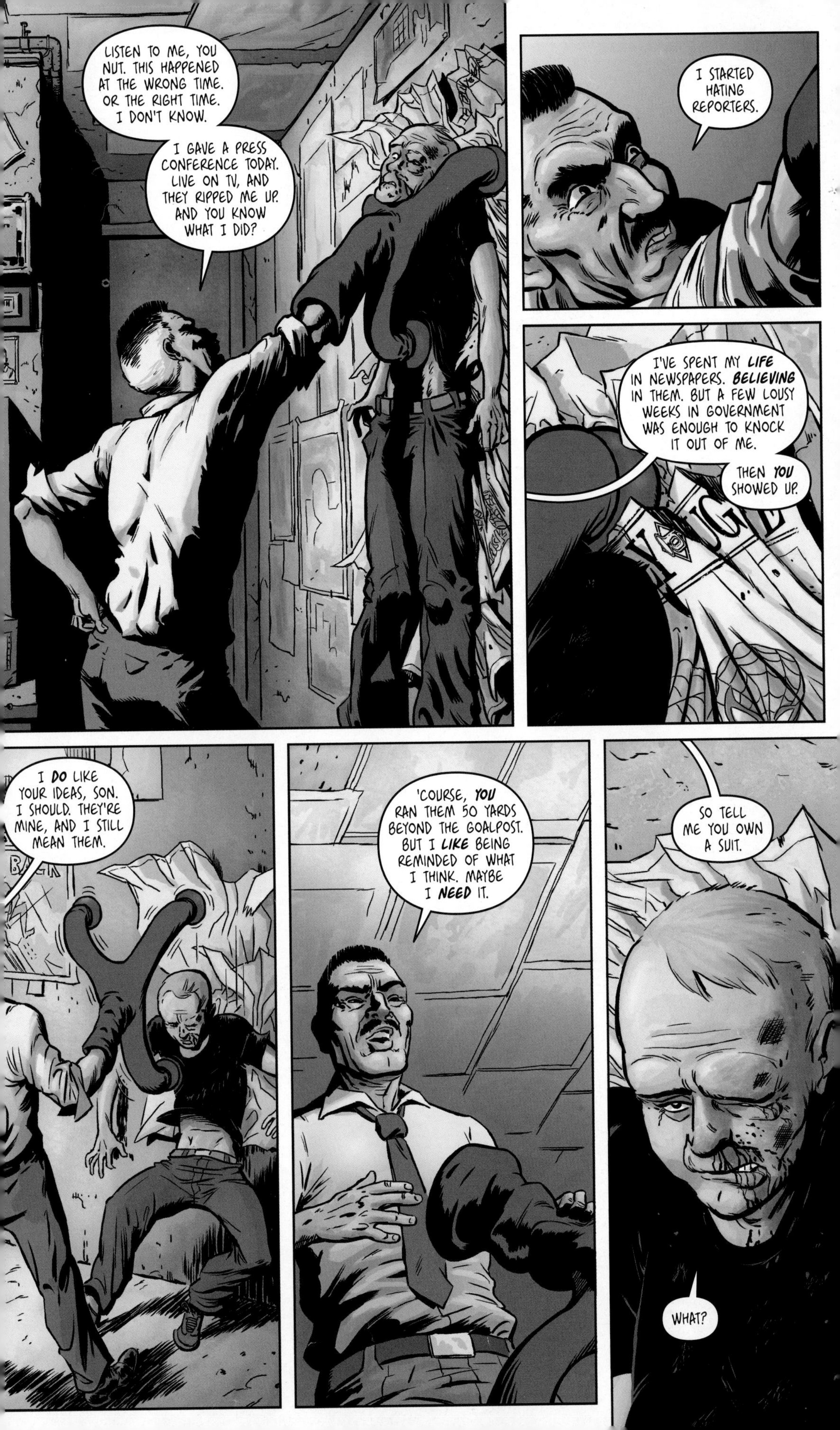
LISTEN TO ME, YOU NUT. THIS HAPPENED AT THE WRONG TIME. OR THE RIGHT TIME. I DON'T KNOW.
I GAVE A PRESS CONFERENCE TODAY. LIVE ON TV, AND THEY RIPPED ME UP. AND YOU KNOW WHAT I DID?
I STARTED HATING REPORTERS.
I'VE SPENT MY LIFE IN NEWSPAPERS. BELIEVING IN THEM. BUT A FEW LOUSY WEEKS IN GOVERNMENT WAS ENOUGH TO KNOCK IT OUT OF ME.
THEN YOU SHOWED UP.
I DO LIKE YOUR IDEAS, SON. I SHOULD. THEY'RE MINE, AND I STILL MEAN THEM.
'COURSE, YOU RAN THEM 50 YARDS BEYOND THE GOALPOST. BUT I LIKE BEING REMINDED OF WHAT I THINK. MAYBE I NEED IT.
SO TELL ME YOU OWN A SUIT.
WHAT?

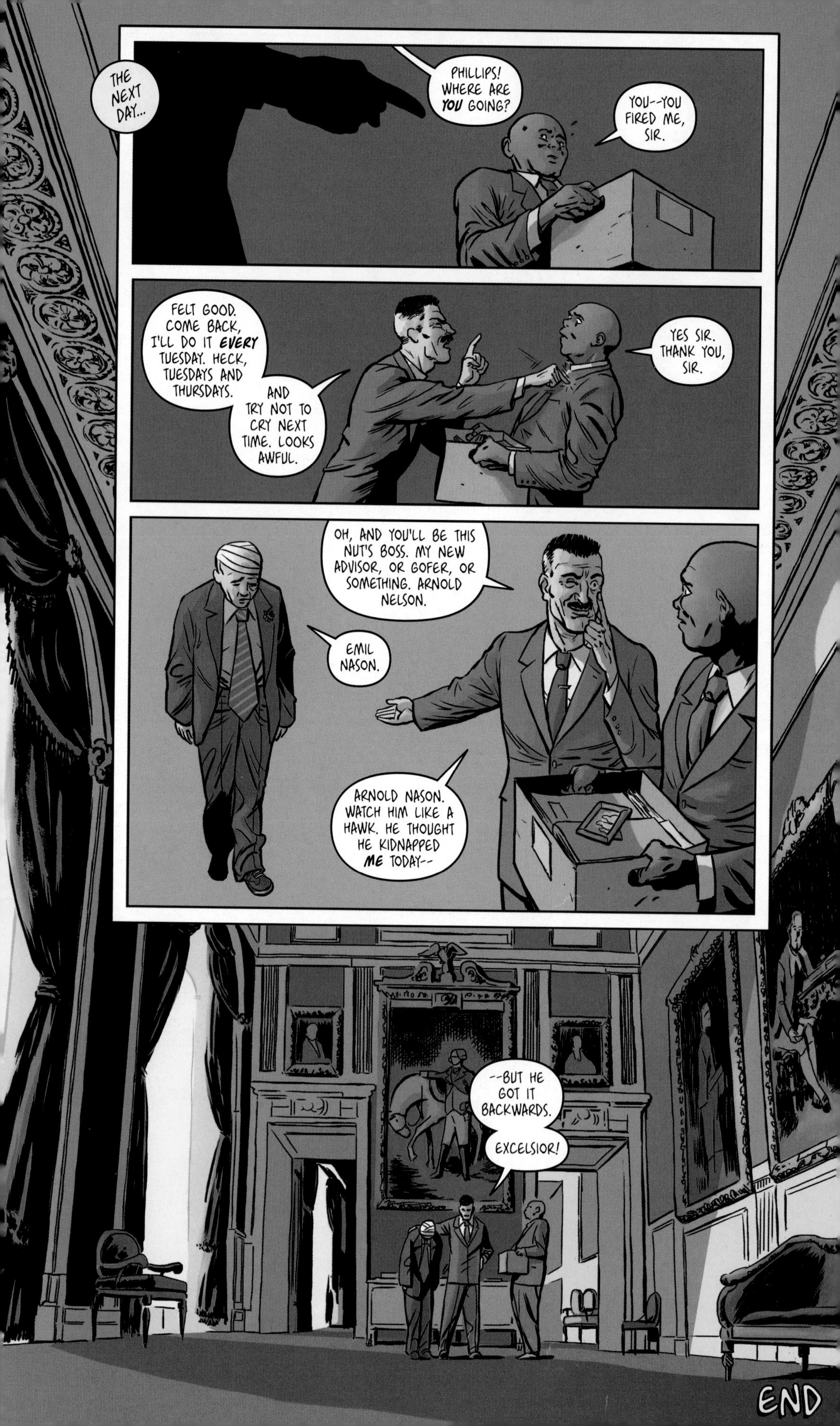
THE NEXT DAY...
PHILLIPS! WHERE ARE YOU GOING?
YOU--YOU FIRED ME, SIR.
FELT GOOD. COME BACK, I'LL DO IT EVERY TUESDAY. HECK, TUESDAYS AND THURSDAYS.
AND TRY NOT TO CRY NEXT TIME. LOOKS AWFUL.
YES SIR. THANK YOU, SIR.
OH, AND YOU'LL BE THIS NUT'S BOSS. MY NEW ADVISOR, OR GOFER, OR SOMETHING. ARNOLD NELSON.
EMIL NASON.
ARNOLD NASON. WATCH HIM LIKE A HAWK. HE THOUGHT HE KIDNAPPED ME TODAY--
--BUT HE GOT IT BACKWARDS.
EXCELSIOR!
END

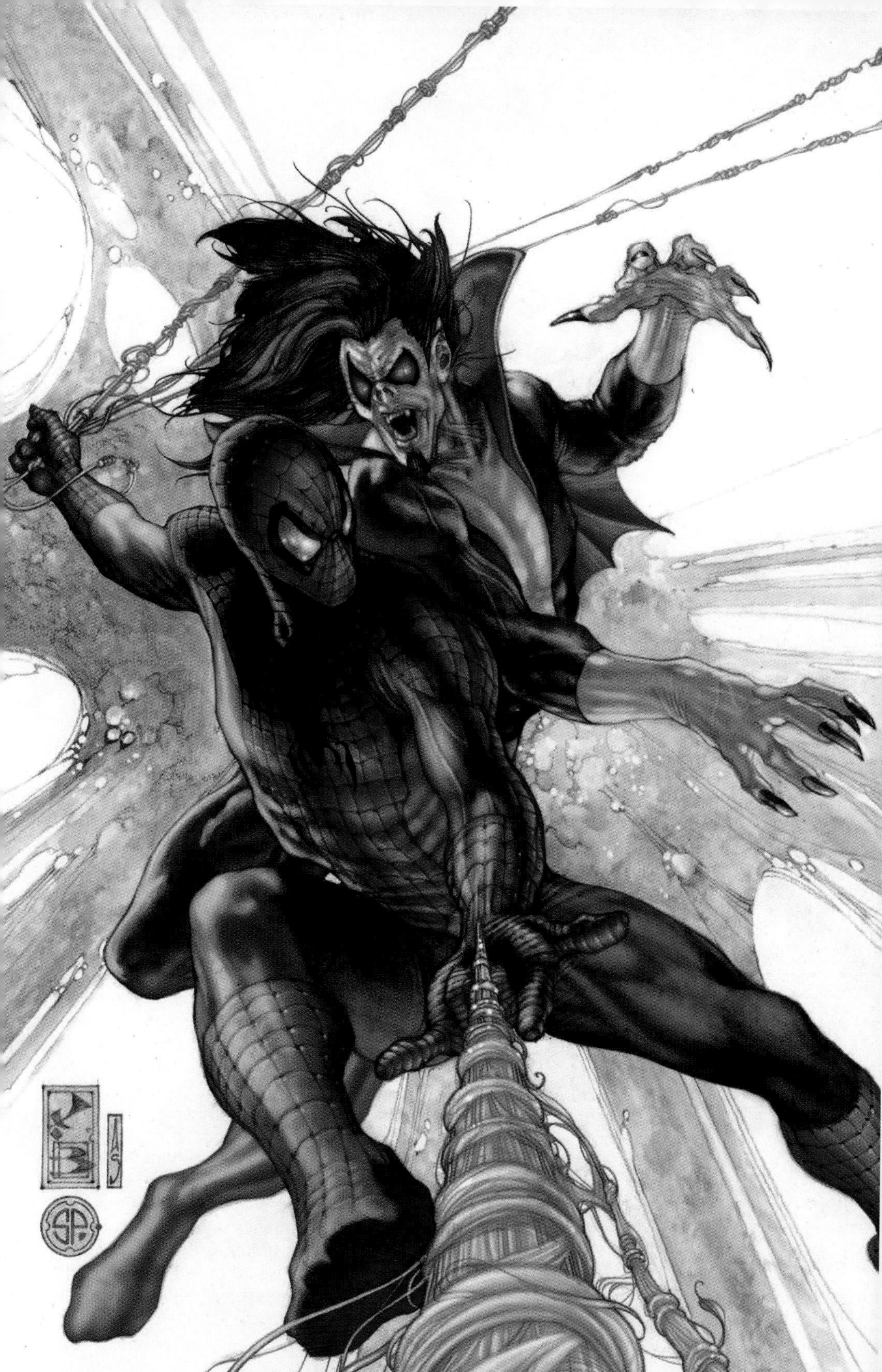

SPIDER-MAN #622
& SIMONE PERUZZI

Simone Bianchi & Simone Perruzzi – Cover

Tom Brennan – Asst. Editor
Stephen Wacker – Editor
Tom Brevoort – Executive Editor
Joe Quesada – Editor in Chief
Dan Buckley – Publisher
Alan Fine – Executive Producer
Gale, Kelly, Slott, Van Lente, Waid & Wells – Web-Heads

FLASH THOMPSON REMAINS NEW YORK'S MOST POPULAR BACHELOR AND HERO – but how does the injured veteran feel to be at home – away from the action and alone in his daily struggle? more…

IS MR. NEGATIVE'S GRIP ON CHINATOWN SLIPPING? Between Spider-Man's renewed efforts to foil Mr. Negative's operations and Martin Li's do-gooder spirit influencing the community, the man in black may be on his way out! more…

THE CITY'S MOST LITERALLY-NAMED CAT BURGLAR SPOTTED OUTSIDE GRACIE'S MANSION – the New York City Mayor's residence! Why was she there? Reports may surprise... more…

Michael Morbius, the Greek biochemist whose experiments to cu himself of a rare blood disease left him infected with vampirism, h long had his history intertwined with the Amazing Spider-Man -- both adversaries and uneasy allies. Although he is a vampire affect with blood lust, Morbius's humanity has stayed true and he's manag to (mostly) hold to a noble course, defending so-called Monsters society.

But you know what vampires like a lot? Blood. And Spidey recer had a whole bunch of his stolen by the enigmatic Mr. Negative, a cri lord empowered by the dark force. The blood was put into Negativ signature weapon -- the Devil's Breath, a gas which, when encod with DNA from blood samples -- can kill anyone of that DNA's blo line. With the help of his colleague-with-benefits, Black Cat, Spic rescued his blood sample from Negative's grasp. His strictly mas on relationship with Black Cat has gotten progressively complicate While she's often opposing the forces of greed and corruption, sh a thief -- something Spidey's conscience can't abide. And his grow attraction to his friend, CSI sleuth Carlie Cooper, could put his d identity in some tricky spots...

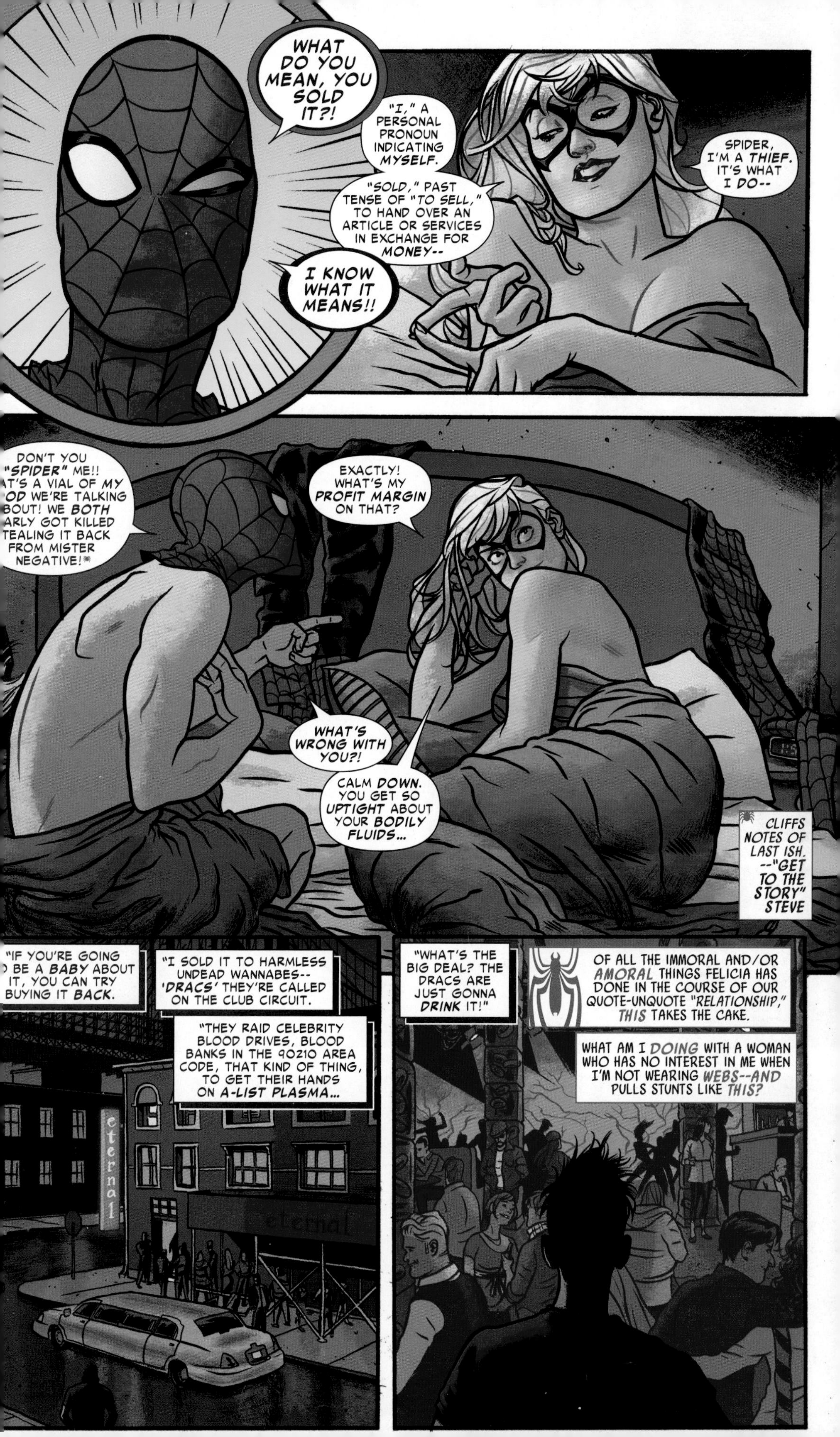
WHAT DO YOU MEAN, YOU SOLD IT?!
"I," A PERSONAL PRONOUN INDICATING MYSELF.
"SOLD," PAST TENSE OF "TO SELL," TO HAND OVER AN ARTICLE OR SERVICES IN EXCHANGE FOR MONEY--
I KNOW WHAT IT MEANS!!
SPIDER, I'M A THIEF. IT'S WHAT I DO--
DON'T YOU "SPIDER" ME!! AT'S A VIAL OF MY OD WE'RE TALKING BOUT! WE BOTH ARLY GOT KILLED TEALING IT BACK FROM MISTER NEGATIVE!
EXACTLY! WHAT'S MY PROFIT MARGIN ON THAT?
WHAT'S WRONG WITH YOU?!
CALM DOWN. YOU GET SO UPTIGHT ABOUT YOUR BODILY FLUIDS...
CLIFFS NOTES OF LAST ISH. --"GET TO THE STORY" STEVE
"IF YOU'RE GOING BE A BABY ABOUT IT, YOU CAN TRY BUYING IT BACK.
"I SOLD IT TO HARMLESS UNDEAD WANNABES-- 'DRACS' THEY'RE CALLED ON THE CLUB CIRCUIT.
"THEY RAID CELEBRITY BLOOD DRIVES, BLOOD BANKS IN THE 90210 AREA CODE, THAT KIND OF THING, TO GET THEIR HANDS ON A-LIST PLASMA...
eternal
eternal
"WHAT'S THE BIG DEAL? THE DRACS ARE JUST GONNA DRINK IT!"
OF ALL THE IMMORAL AND/OR AMORAL THINGS FELICIA HAS DONE IN THE COURSE OF OUR QUOTE-UNQUOTE "RELATIONSHIP," THIS TAKES THE CAKE.
WHAT AM I DOING WITH A WOMAN WHO HAS NO INTEREST IN ME WHEN I'M NOT WEARING WEBS--AND PULLS STUNTS LIKE THIS?

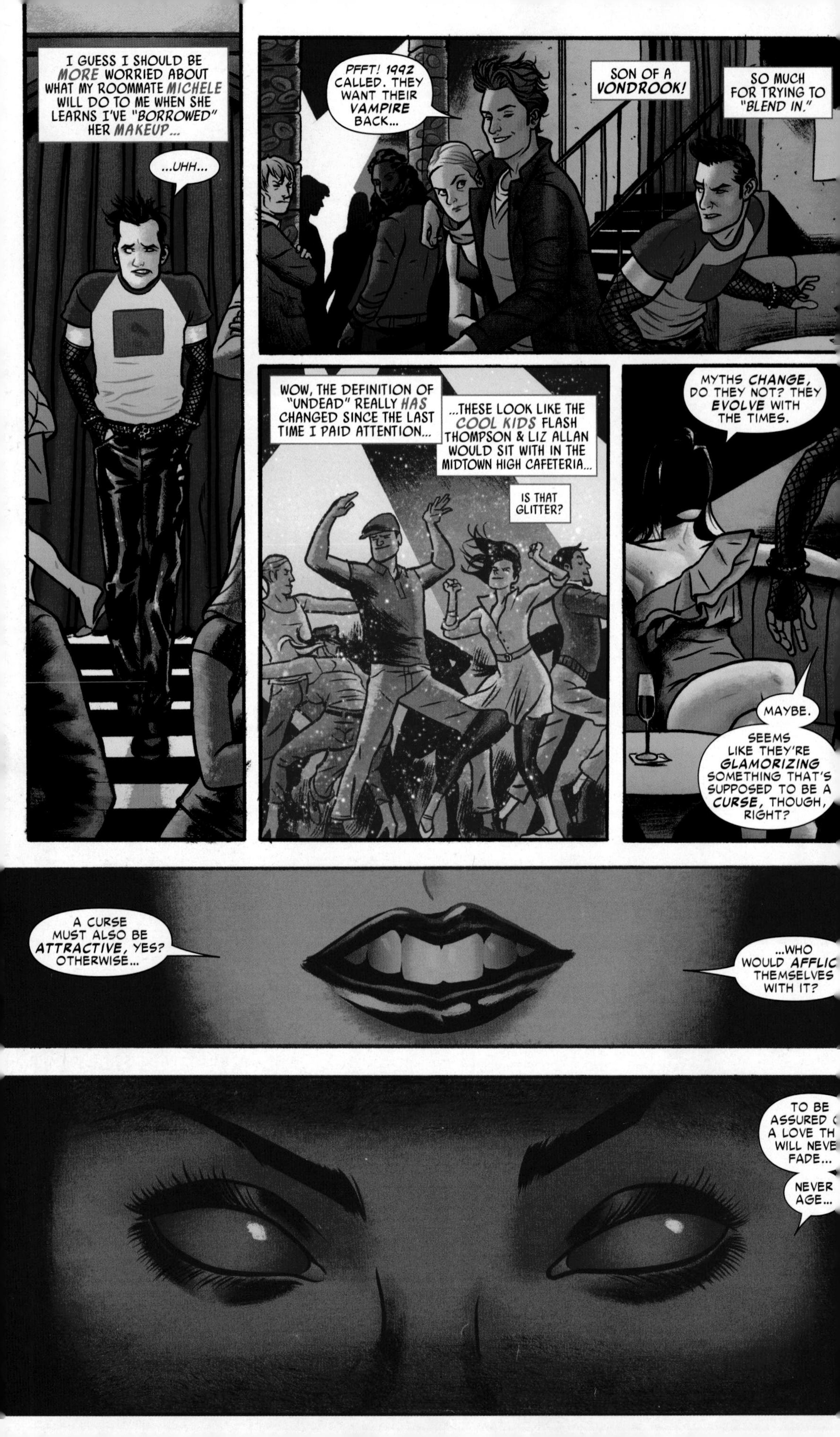
I GUESS I SHOULD BE MORE WORRIED ABOUT WHAT MY ROOMMATE MICHELE WILL DO TO ME WHEN SHE LEARNS I'VE "BORROWED" HER MAKEUP...
...UHH...
PFFT! 1992 CALLED. THEY WANT THEIR VAMPIRE BACK...
SON OF A VONDROOK!
SO MUCH FOR TRYING TO "BLEND IN."
WOW, THE DEFINITION OF "UNDEAD" REALLY HAS CHANGED SINCE THE LAST TIME I PAID ATTENTION...
...THESE LOOK LIKE THE COOL KIDS FLASH THOMPSON & LIZ ALLAN WOULD SIT WITH IN THE MIDTOWN HIGH CAFETERIA...
IS THAT GLITTER?
MYTHS CHANGE, DO THEY NOT? THEY EVOLVE WITH THE TIMES.
MAYBE.
SEEMS LIKE THEY'RE GLAMORIZING SOMETHING THAT'S SUPPOSED TO BE A CURSE, THOUGH, RIGHT?
A CURSE MUST ALSO BE ATTRACTIVE, YES? OTHERWISE...
...WHO WOULD AFFLIC THEMSELVES WITH IT?
TO BE ASSURED A LOVE TH WILL NEVE FADE...
NEVER AGE...

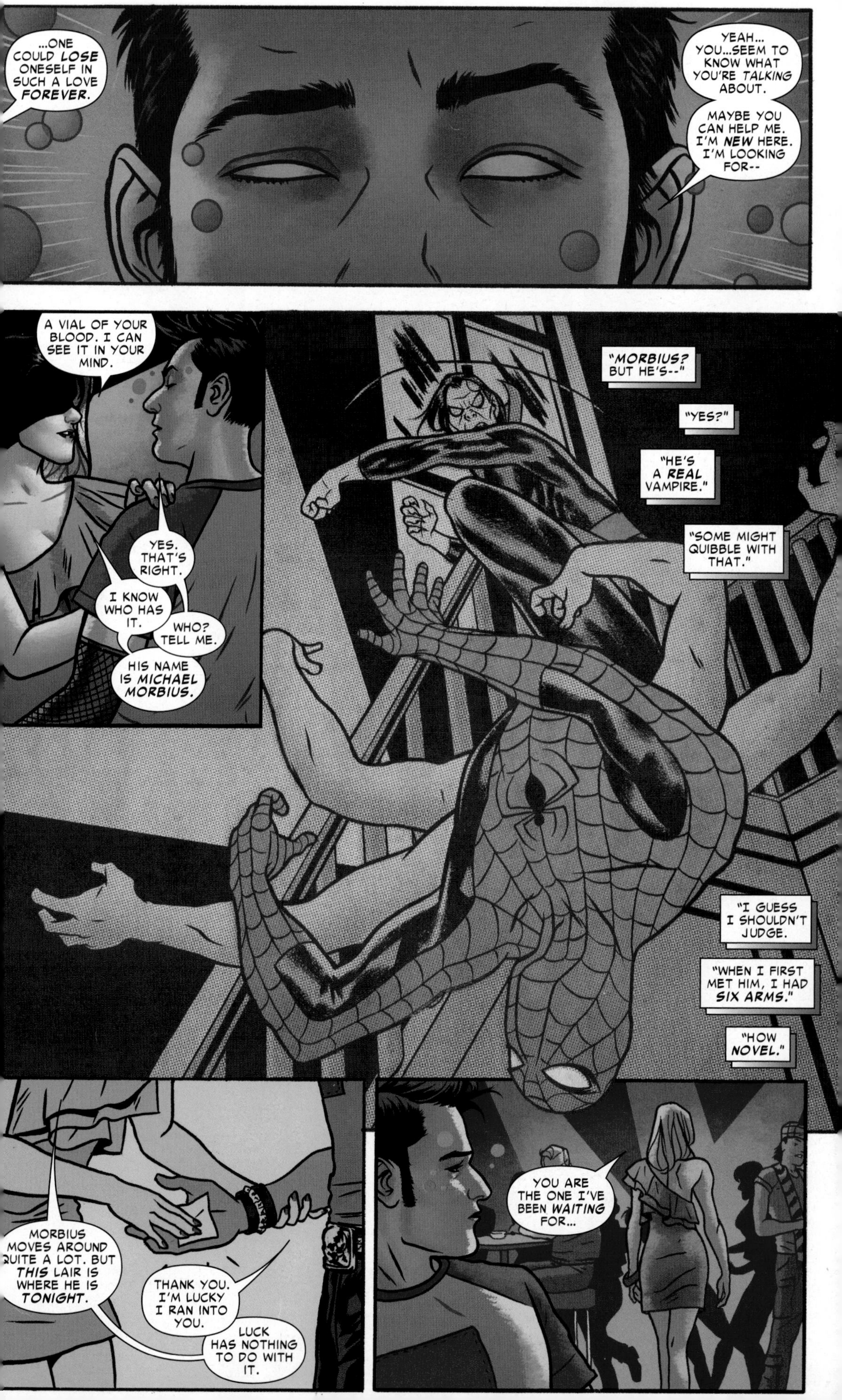
...ONE COULD *LOSE* ONESELF IN SUCH A LOVE *FOREVER*.
YEAH... YOU...SEEM TO KNOW WHAT YOU'RE *TALKING* ABOUT.
MAYBE YOU CAN HELP ME. I'M *NEW* HERE. I'M LOOKING FOR--
A VIAL OF YOUR BLOOD. I CAN SEE IT IN YOUR MIND.
YES. THAT'S RIGHT.
I KNOW WHO HAS IT.
WHO? TELL ME.
HIS NAME IS *MICHAEL MORBIUS*.
"*MORBIUS?* BUT HE'S--"
"YES?"
"HE'S A *REAL* VAMPIRE."
"SOME MIGHT QUIBBLE WITH THAT."
"I GUESS I SHOULDN'T JUDGE.
"WHEN I FIRST MET HIM, I HAD *SIX ARMS*."
"HOW *NOVEL*."
MORBIUS MOVES AROUND QUITE A LOT. BUT *THIS* LAIR IS WHERE HE IS *TONIGHT*.
THANK YOU. I'M LUCKY I RAN INTO YOU.
LUCK HAS NOTHING TO DO WITH IT.
YOU ARE THE ONE I'VE BEEN *WAITING* FOR...

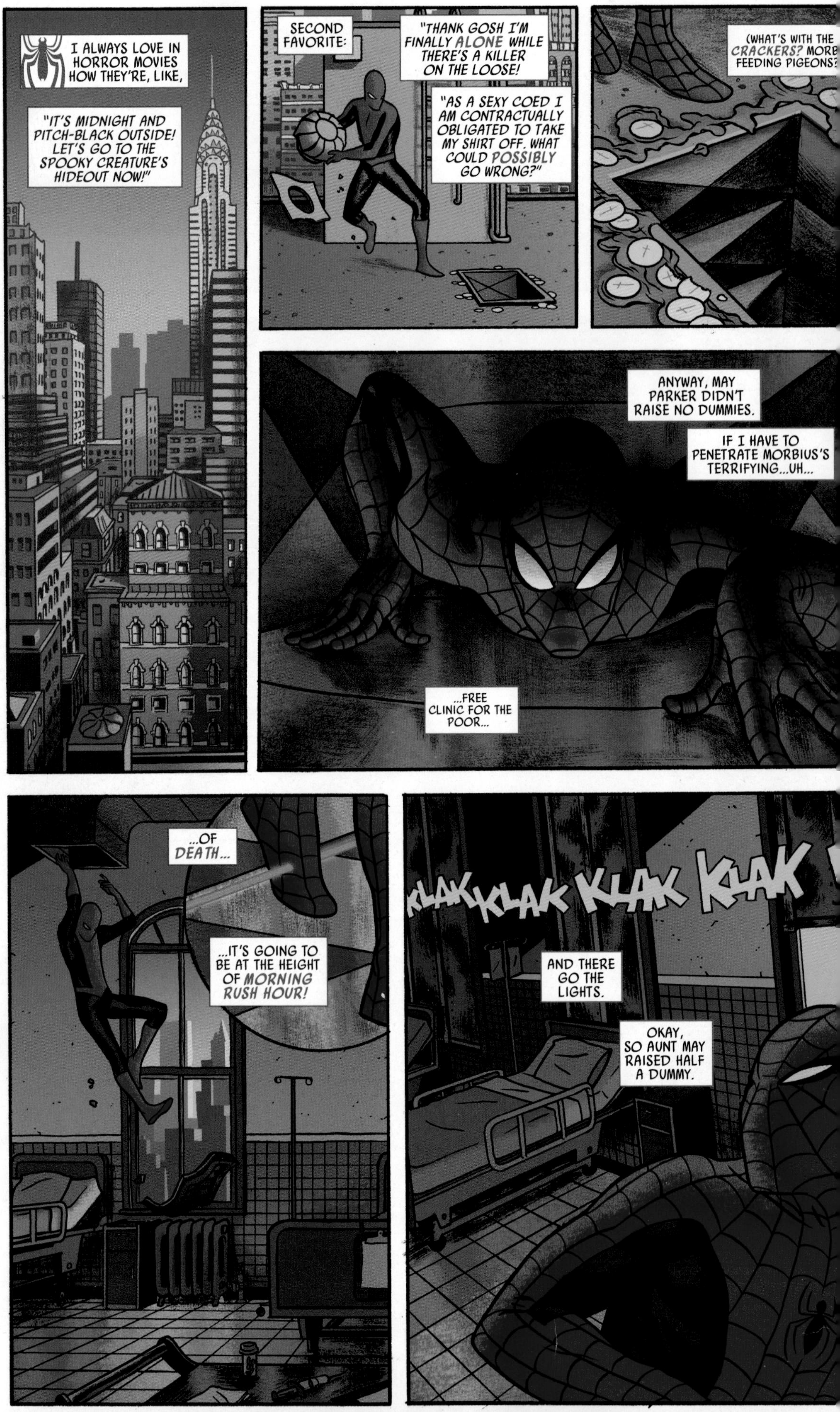
I ALWAYS LOVE IN HORROR MOVIES HOW THEY'RE, LIKE,
"IT'S MIDNIGHT AND PITCH-BLACK OUTSIDE! LET'S GO TO THE SPOOKY CREATURE'S HIDEOUT NOW!"
SECOND FAVORITE:
"THANK GOSH I'M FINALLY ALONE WHILE THERE'S A KILLER ON THE LOOSE!
"AS A SEXY COED I AM CONTRACTUALLY OBLIGATED TO TAKE MY SHIRT OFF. WHAT COULD POSSIBLY GO WRONG?"
(WHAT'S WITH THE CRACKERS? MORB FEEDING PIGEONS?
ANYWAY, MAY PARKER DIDN'T RAISE NO DUMMIES.
IF I HAVE TO PENETRATE MORBIUS'S TERRIFYING...UH...
...FREE CLINIC FOR THE POOR...
...OF DEATH...
...IT'S GOING TO BE AT THE HEIGHT OF MORNING RUSH HOUR!
KLAK KLAK KLAK KLAK
AND THERE GO THE LIGHTS.
OKAY, SO AUNT MAY RAISED HALF A DUMMY.

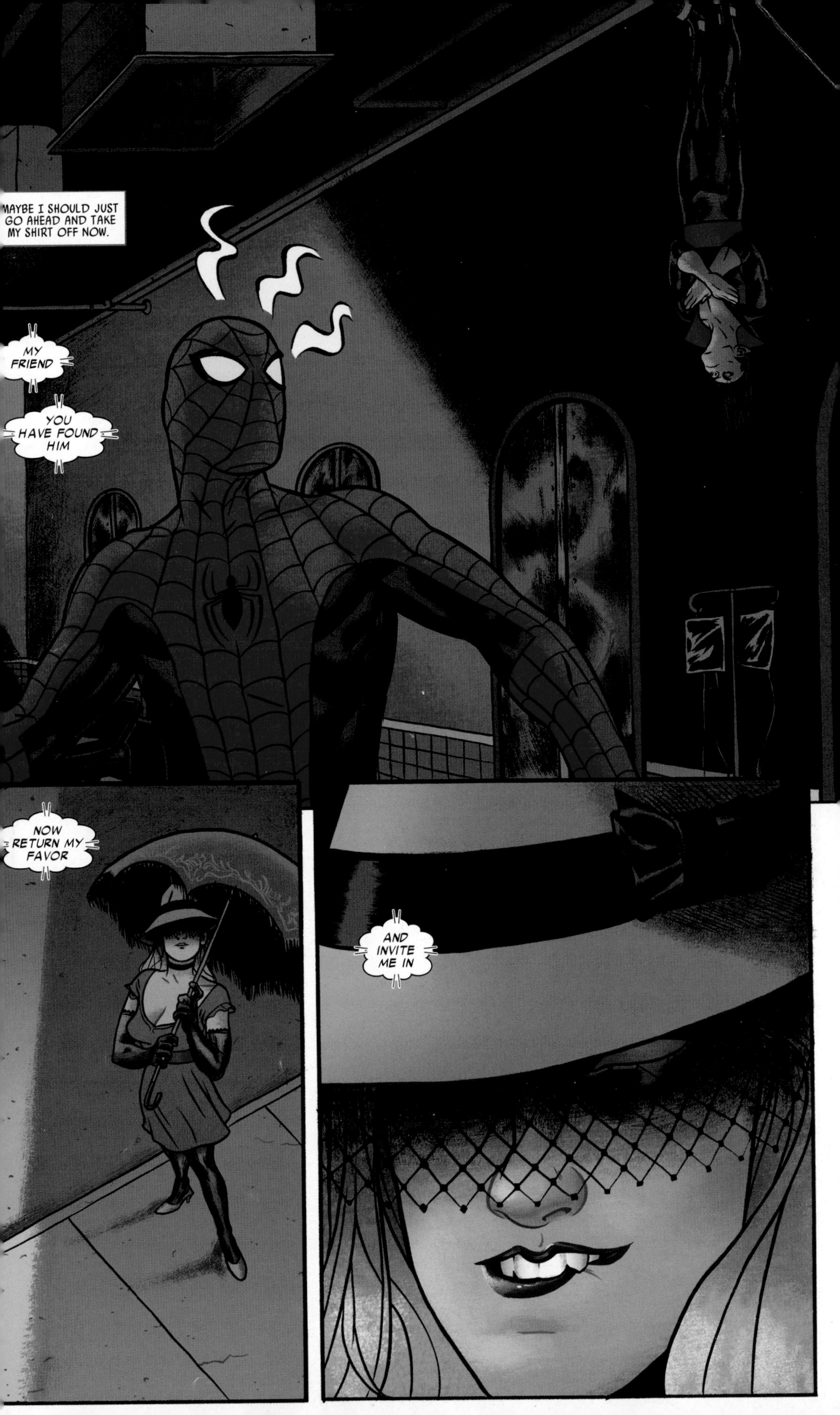
MAYBE I SHOULD JUST GO AHEAD AND TAKE MY SHIRT OFF NOW.
MY FRIEND
YOU HAVE FOUND HIM
NOW RETURN MY FAVOR
AND INVITE ME IN

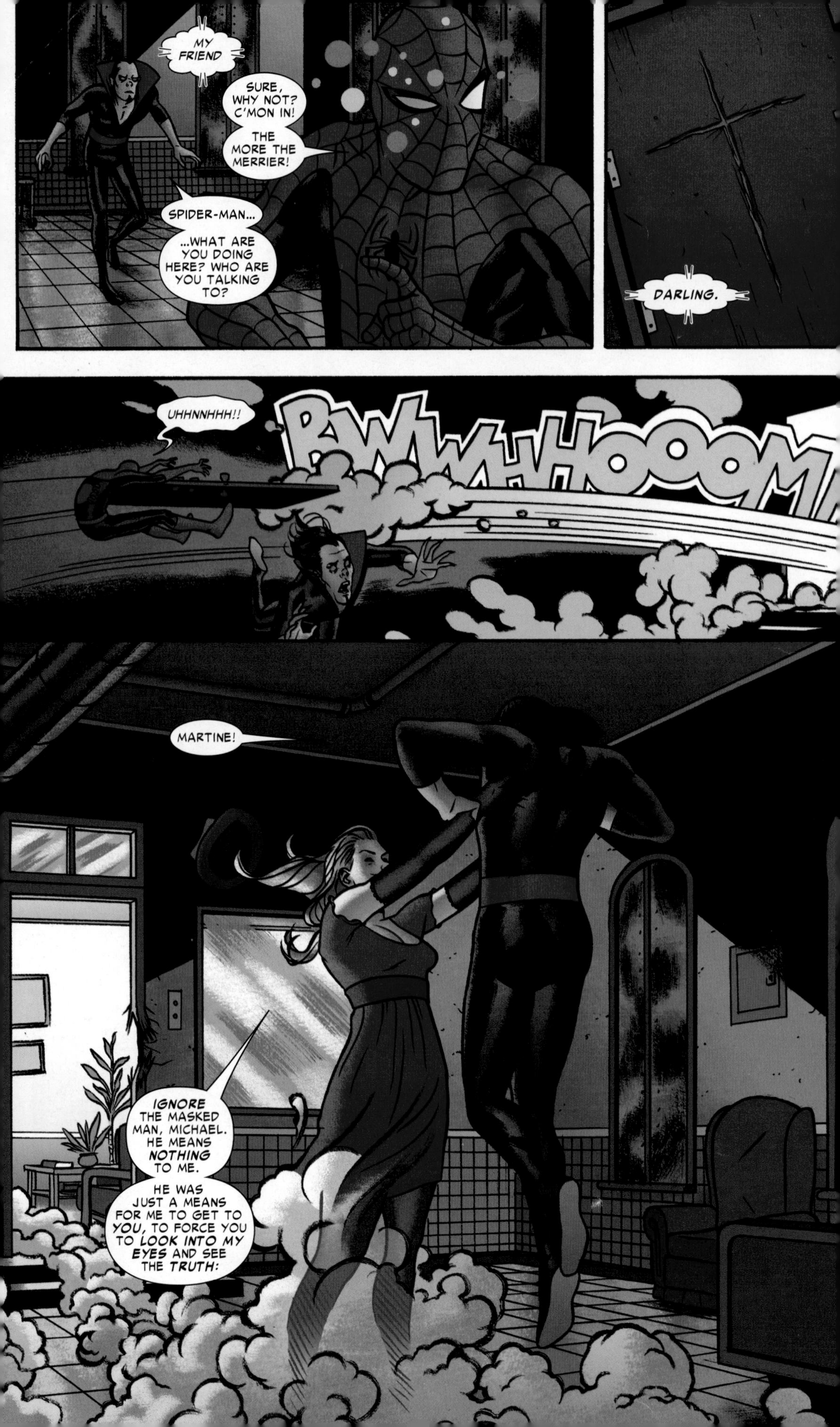
MY FRIEND
SURE, WHY NOT? C'MON IN!
THE MORE THE MERRIER!
SPIDER-MAN...
...WHAT ARE YOU DOING HERE? WHO ARE YOU TALKING TO?
DARLING.
UHHNNHHH!!
BWHHOOOM
MARTINE!
IGNORE THE MASKED MAN, MICHAEL. HE MEANS NOTHING TO ME.
HE WAS JUST A MEANS FOR ME TO GET TO YOU, TO FORCE YOU TO LOOK INTO MY EYES AND SEE THE TRUTH:

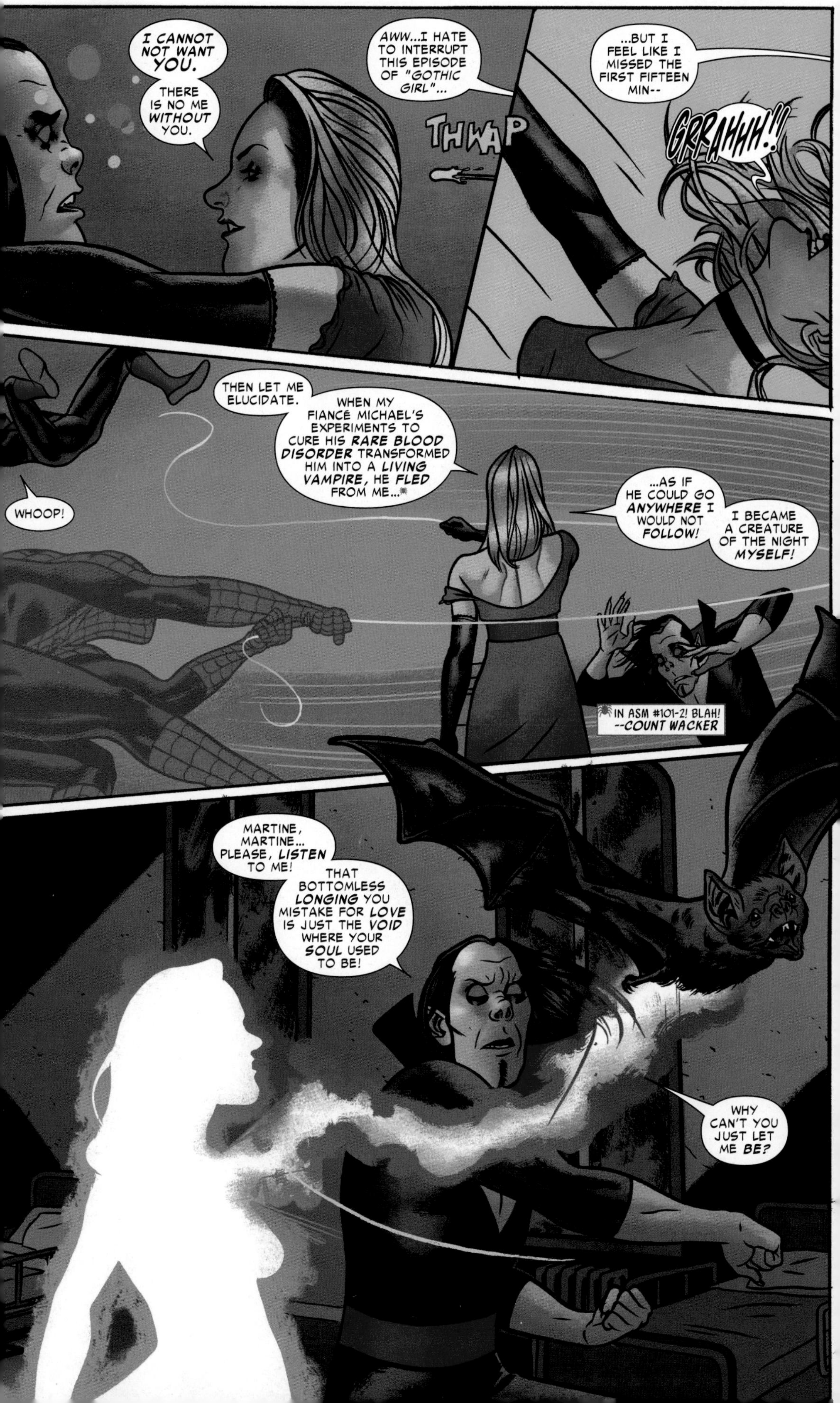
I CANNOT NOT WANT YOU.
THERE IS NO ME WITHOUT YOU.
AWW...I HATE TO INTERRUPT THIS EPISODE OF "GOTHIC GIRL"...
THWAP
...BUT I FEEL LIKE I MISSED THE FIRST FIFTEEN MIN--
GRRAHHH!!
THEN LET ME ELUCIDATE.
WHEN MY FIANCÉ MICHAEL'S EXPERIMENTS TO CURE HIS RARE BLOOD DISORDER TRANSFORMED HIM INTO A LIVING VAMPIRE, HE FLED FROM ME...
WHOOP!
...AS IF HE COULD GO ANYWHERE I WOULD NOT FOLLOW!
I BECAME A CREATURE OF THE NIGHT MYSELF!
IN ASM #101-2! BLAH! --COUNT WACKER
MARTINE, MARTINE... PLEASE, LISTEN TO ME!
THAT BOTTOMLESS LONGING YOU MISTAKE FOR LOVE IS JUST THE VOID WHERE YOUR SOUL USED TO BE!
WHY CAN'T YOU JUST LET ME BE?

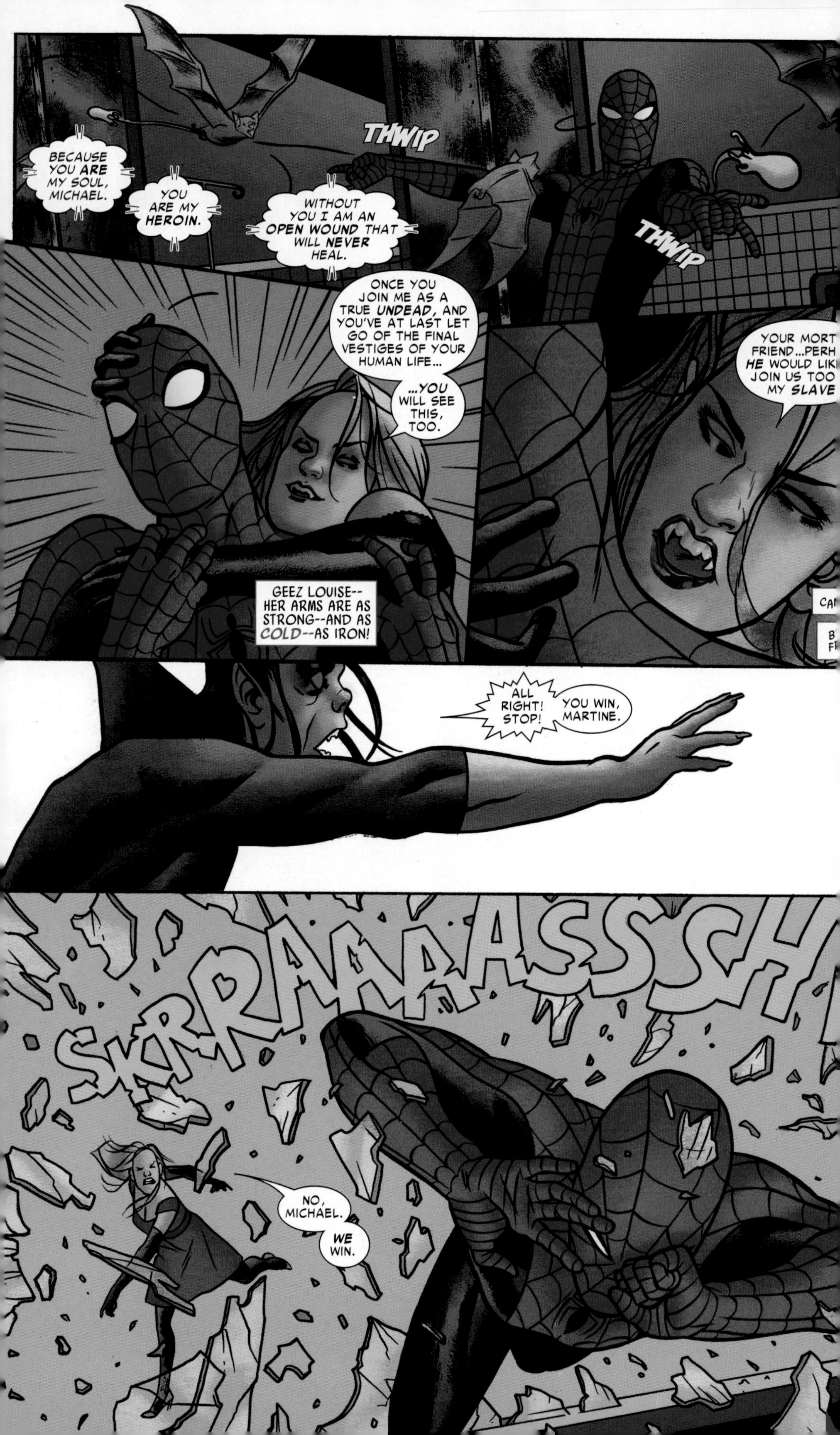
THWIP
BECAUSE YOU ARE MY SOUL, MICHAEL.
YOU ARE MY HEROIN.
WITHOUT YOU I AM AN OPEN WOUND THAT WILL NEVER HEAL.
THWIP
ONCE YOU JOIN ME AS A TRUE UNDEAD, AND YOU'VE AT LAST LET GO OF THE FINAL VESTIGES OF YOUR HUMAN LIFE...
...YOU WILL SEE THIS, TOO.
GEEZ LOUISE--HER ARMS ARE AS STRONG--AND AS COLD--AS IRON!
YOUR MORT FRIEND...PERH HE WOULD LIK JOIN US TOO MY SLAVE
ALL RIGHT! STOP!
YOU WIN, MARTINE.
SKRRAAAASSSCH
NO, MICHAEL.
WE WIN.

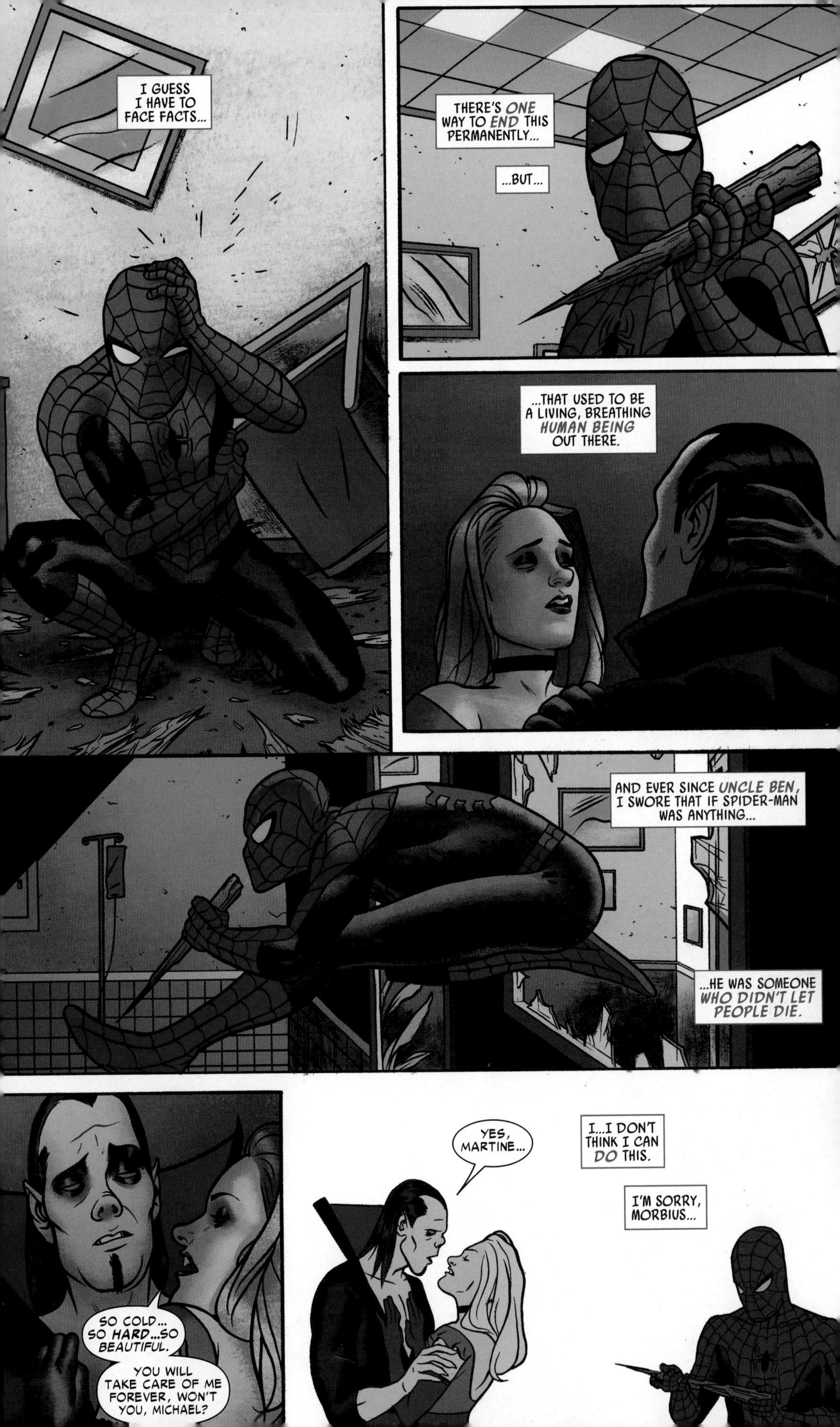
I GUESS I HAVE TO FACE FACTS...
THERE'S ONE WAY TO END THIS PERMANENTLY...
...BUT...
...THAT USED TO BE A LIVING, BREATHING HUMAN BEING OUT THERE.
AND EVER SINCE UNCLE BEN, I SWORE THAT IF SPIDER-MAN WAS ANYTHING...
...HE WAS SOMEONE WHO DIDN'T LET PEOPLE DIE.
SO COLD... SO HARD...SO BEAUTIFUL.
YOU WILL TAKE CARE OF ME FOREVER, WON'T YOU, MICHAEL?
YES, MARTINE...
I...I DON'T THINK I CAN DO THIS.
I'M SORRY, MORBIUS...

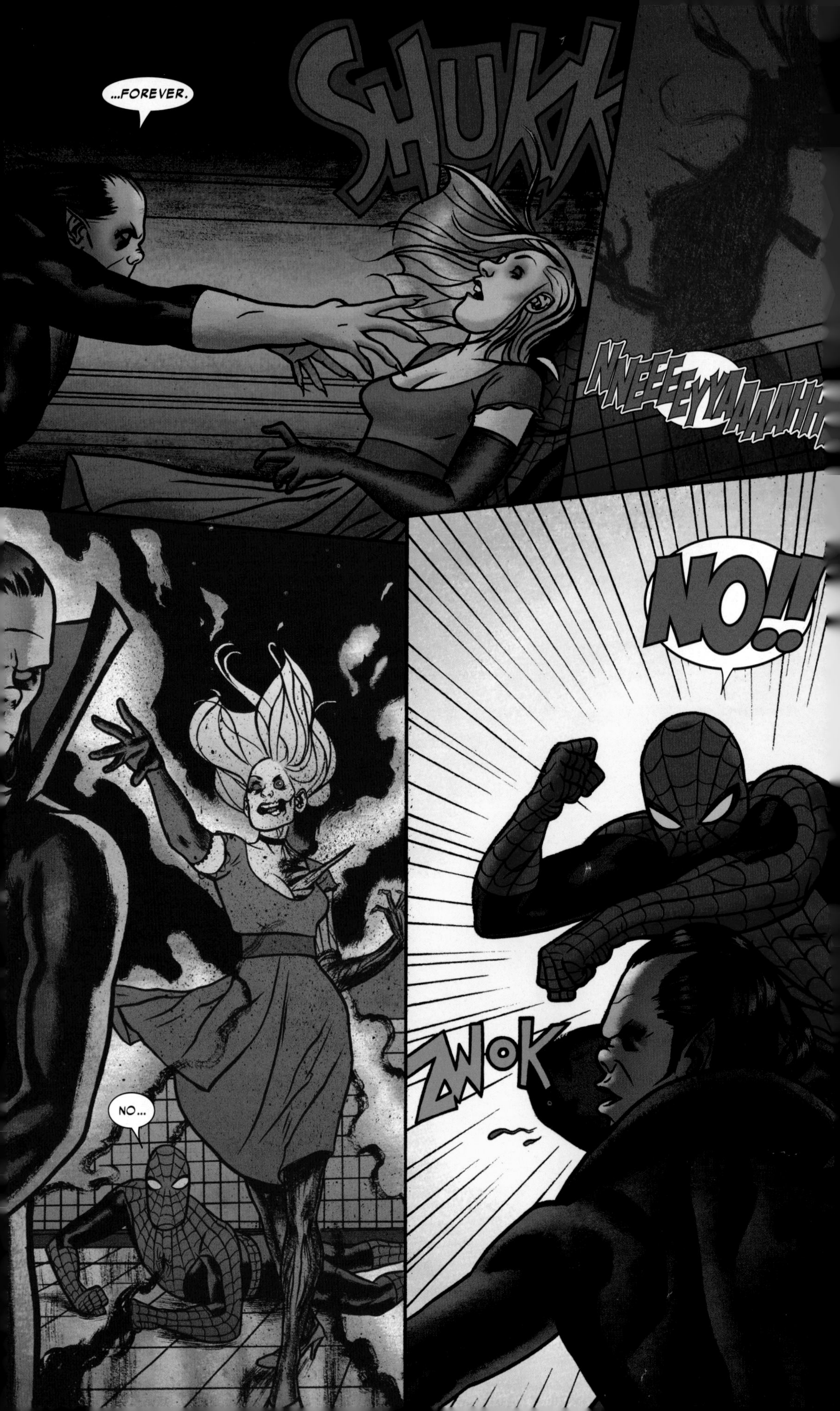
...FOREVER.
SHUKK
NNEEEEYAAAAHH
NO...
NO!!
ZWOK

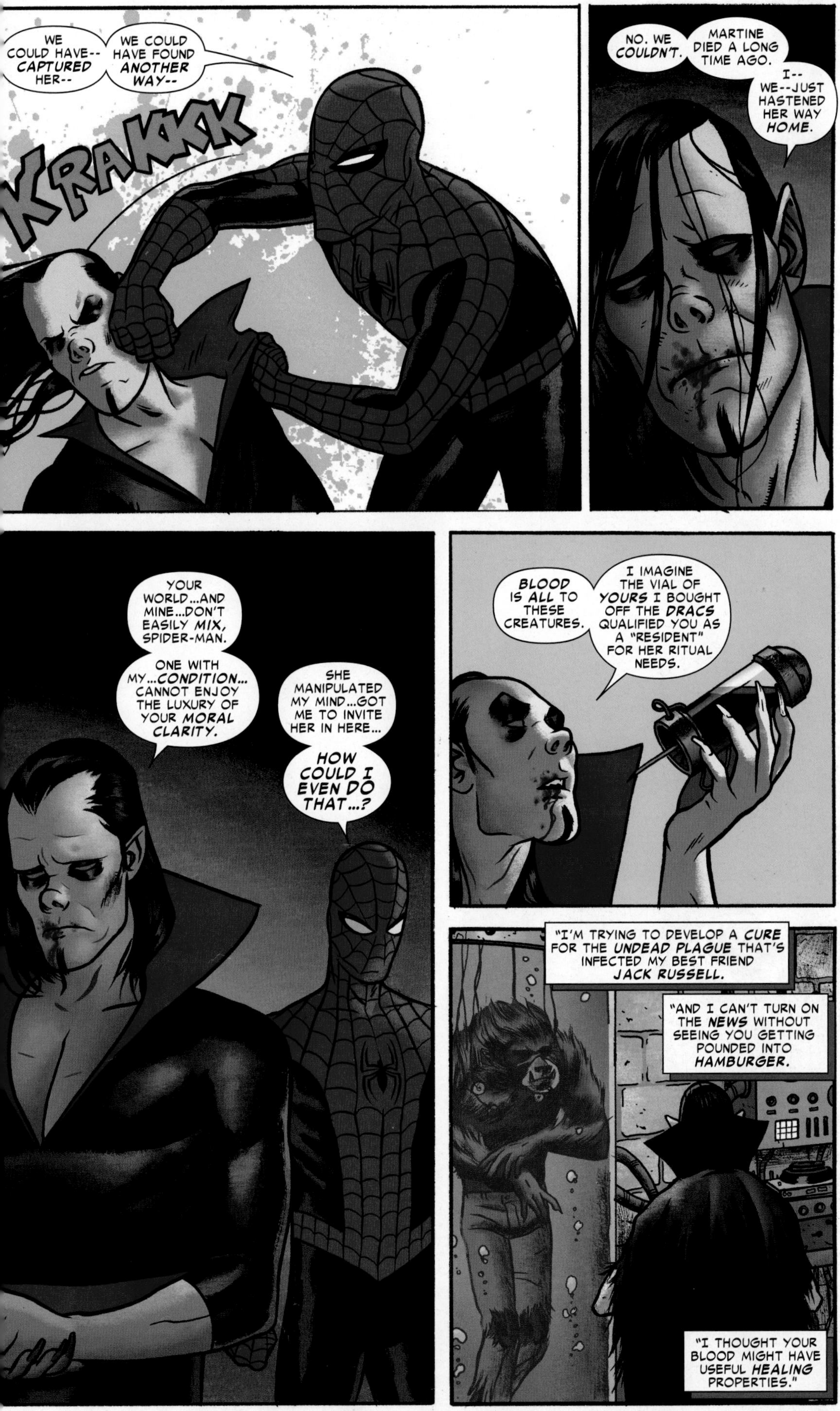
WE COULD HAVE-- CAPTURED HER--
WE COULD HAVE FOUND ANOTHER WAY--
KRAKKK
NO. WE COULDN'T.
MARTINE DIED A LONG TIME AGO.
I-- WE--JUST HASTENED HER WAY HOME.
YOUR WORLD...AND MINE...DON'T EASILY MIX, SPIDER-MAN.
ONE WITH MY...CONDITION... CANNOT ENJOY THE LUXURY OF YOUR MORAL CLARITY.
SHE MANIPULATED MY MIND...GOT ME TO INVITE HER IN HERE...
HOW COULD I EVEN DO THAT...?
BLOOD IS ALL TO THESE CREATURES.
I IMAGINE THE VIAL OF YOURS I BOUGHT OFF THE DRACS QUALIFIED YOU AS A "RESIDENT" FOR HER RITUAL NEEDS.
"I'M TRYING TO DEVELOP A CURE FOR THE UNDEAD PLAGUE THAT'S INFECTED MY BEST FRIEND JACK RUSSELL.
"AND I CAN'T TURN ON THE NEWS WITHOUT SEEING YOU GETTING POUNDED INTO HAMBURGER.
"I THOUGHT YOUR BLOOD MIGHT HAVE USEFUL HEALING PROPERTIES."

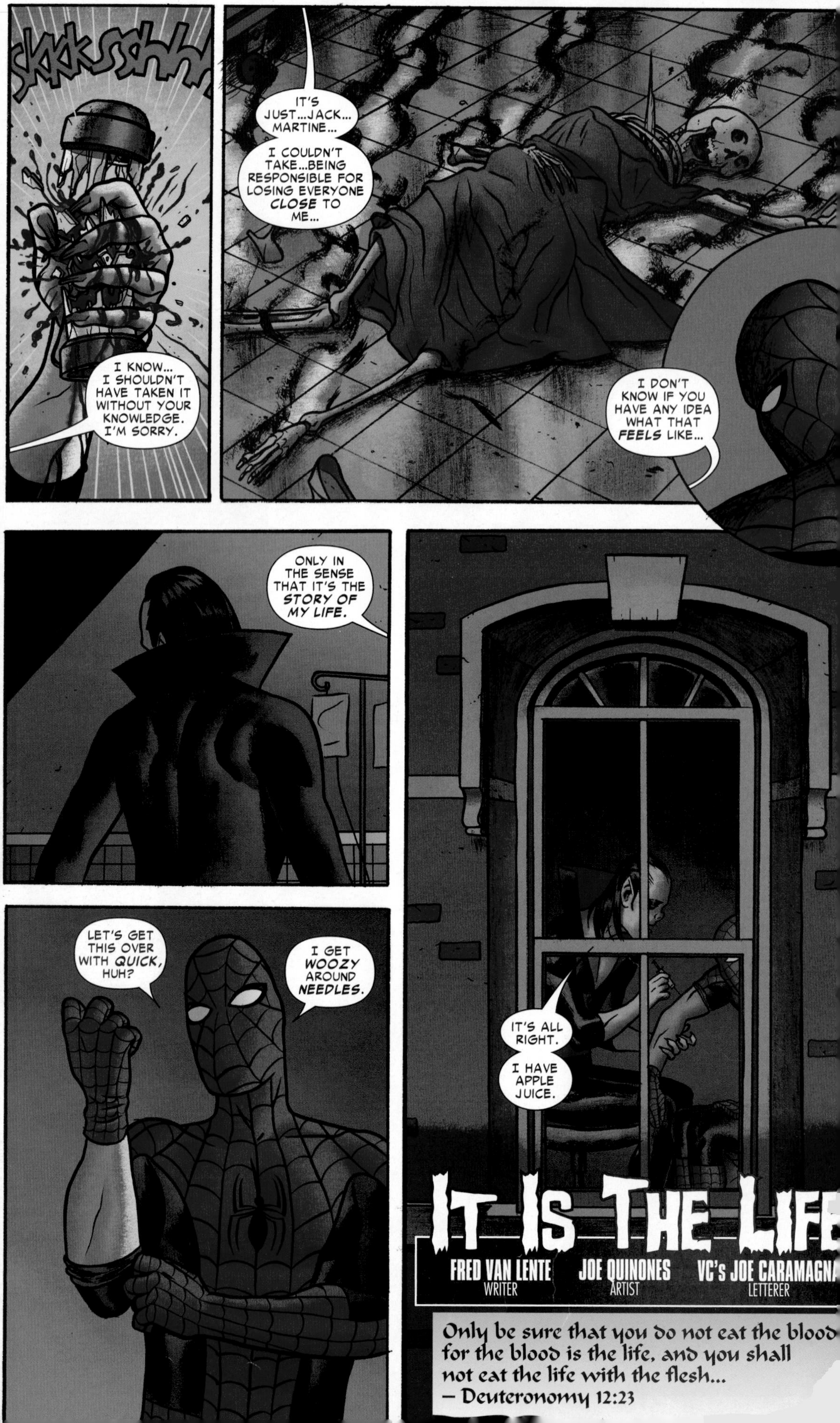
SKKKSSHHH
IT'S JUST...JACK... MARTINE...
I COULDN'T TAKE...BEING RESPONSIBLE FOR LOSING EVERYONE CLOSE TO ME...
I KNOW... I SHOULDN'T HAVE TAKEN IT WITHOUT YOUR KNOWLEDGE. I'M SORRY.
I DON'T KNOW IF YOU HAVE ANY IDEA WHAT THAT FEELS LIKE...
ONLY IN THE SENSE THAT IT'S THE STORY OF MY LIFE.
LET'S GET THIS OVER WITH QUICK, HUH?
I GET WOOZY AROUND NEEDLES.
IT'S ALL RIGHT.
I HAVE APPLE JUICE.
IT IS THE LIFE
FRED VAN LENTE WRITER
JOE QUINONES ARTIST
VC's JOE CARAMAGNA LETTERER
Only be sure that you do not eat the blood for the blood is the life, and you shall not eat the life with the flesh...
– Deuteronomy 12:23

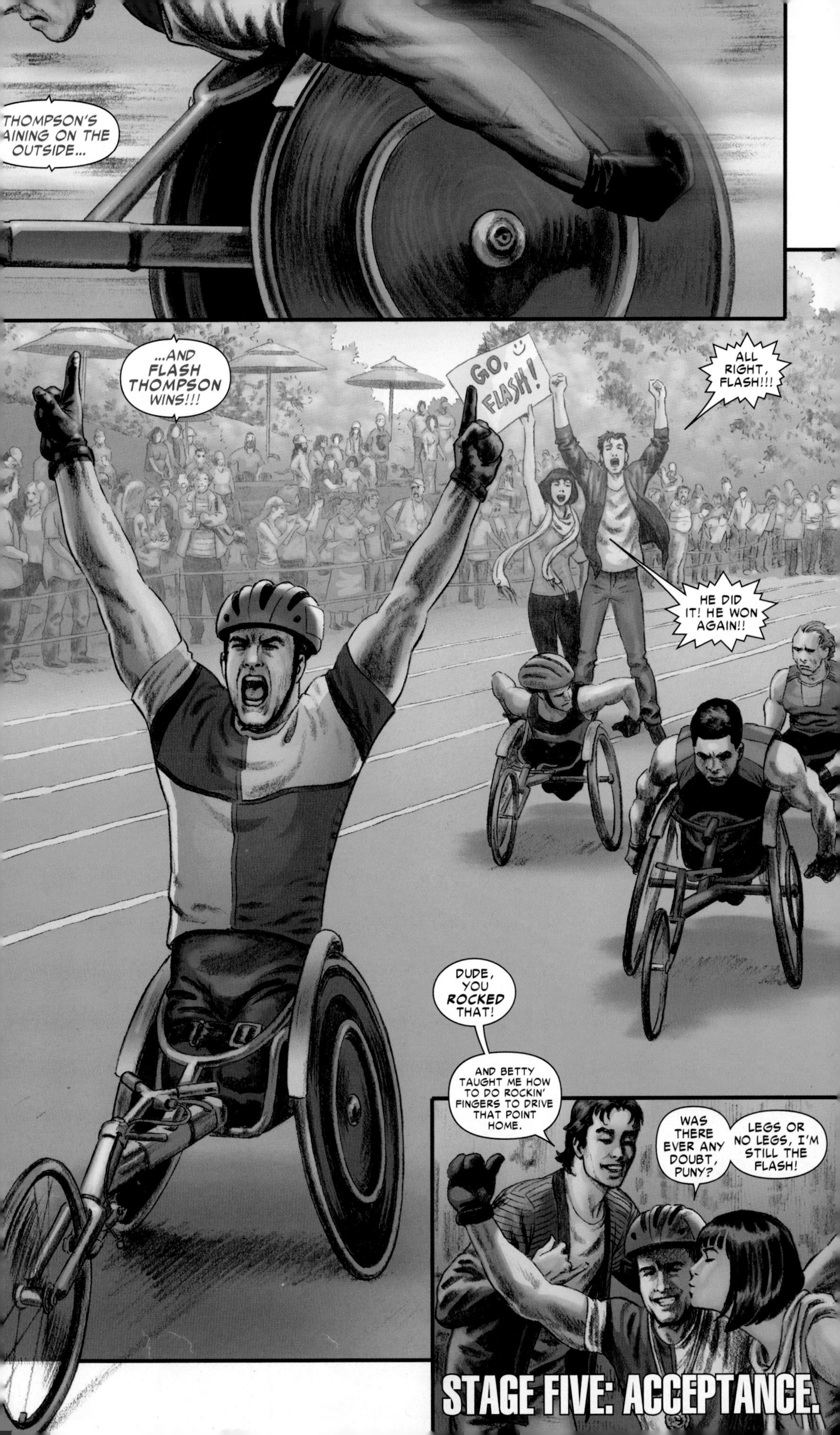
THOMPSON'S
AINING ON THE
OUTSIDE...
...AND
FLASH
THOMPSON
WINS!!!
GO, FLASH!
ALL
RIGHT,
FLASH!!!
HE DID
IT! HE WON
AGAIN!!
DUDE,
YOU
ROCKED
THAT!
AND BETTY
TAUGHT ME HOW
TO DO ROCKIN'
FINGERS TO DRIVE
THAT POINT
HOME.
WAS
THERE
EVER ANY
DOUBT,
PUNY?
LEGS OR
NO LEGS, I'M
STILL THE
FLASH!
STAGE FIVE: ACCEPTANCE.

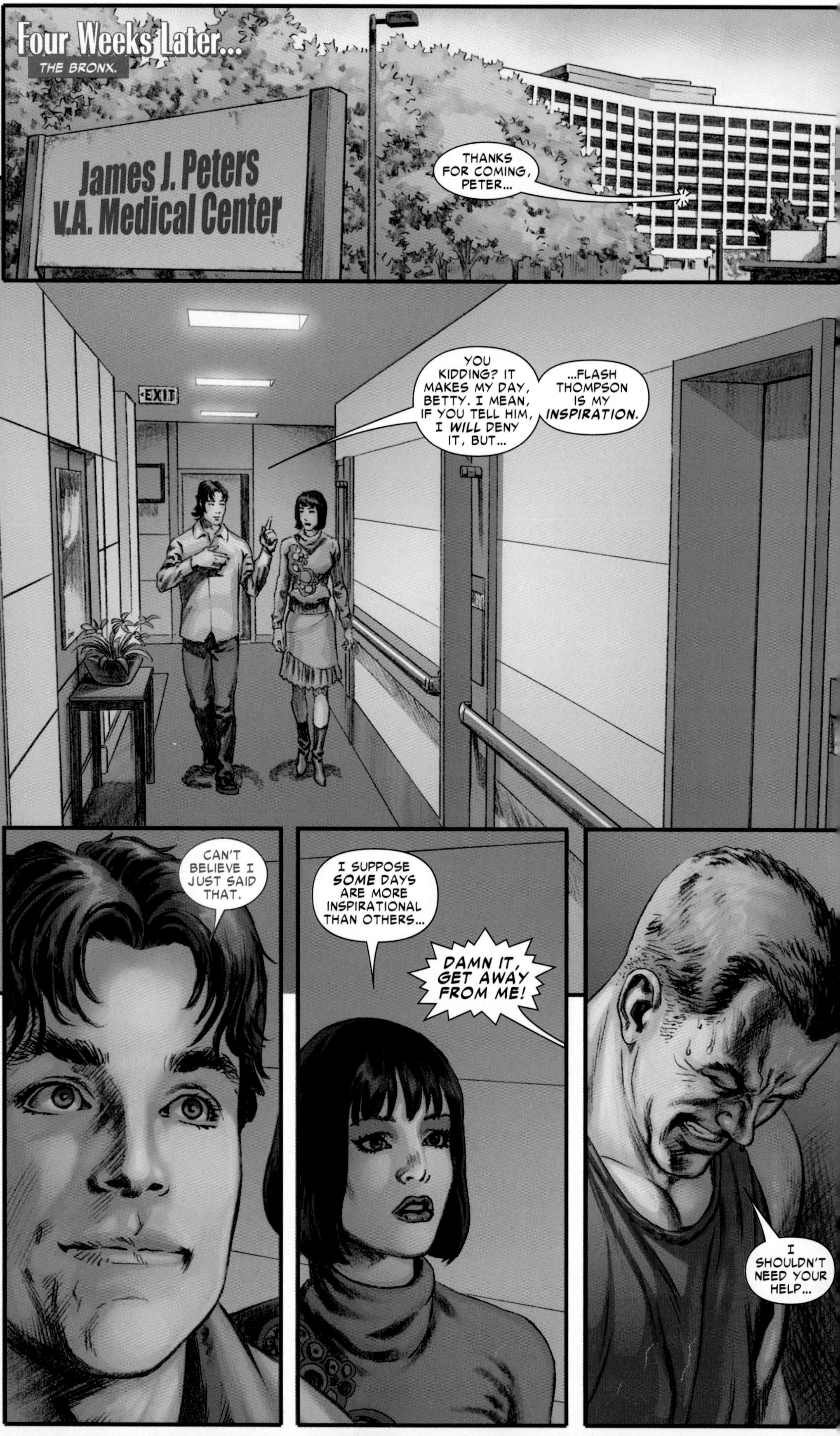
Four Weeks Later...
THE BRONX.
James J. Peters
V.A. Medical Center
THANKS FOR COMING, PETER...
EXIT
YOU KIDDING? IT MAKES MY DAY, BETTY. I MEAN, IF YOU TELL HIM, I WILL DENY IT, BUT...
...FLASH THOMPSON IS MY INSPIRATION.
CAN'T BELIEVE I JUST SAID THAT.
I SUPPOSE SOME DAYS ARE MORE INSPIRATIONAL THAN OTHERS...
DAMN IT, GET AWAY FROM ME!
I SHOULDN'T NEED YOUR HELP...

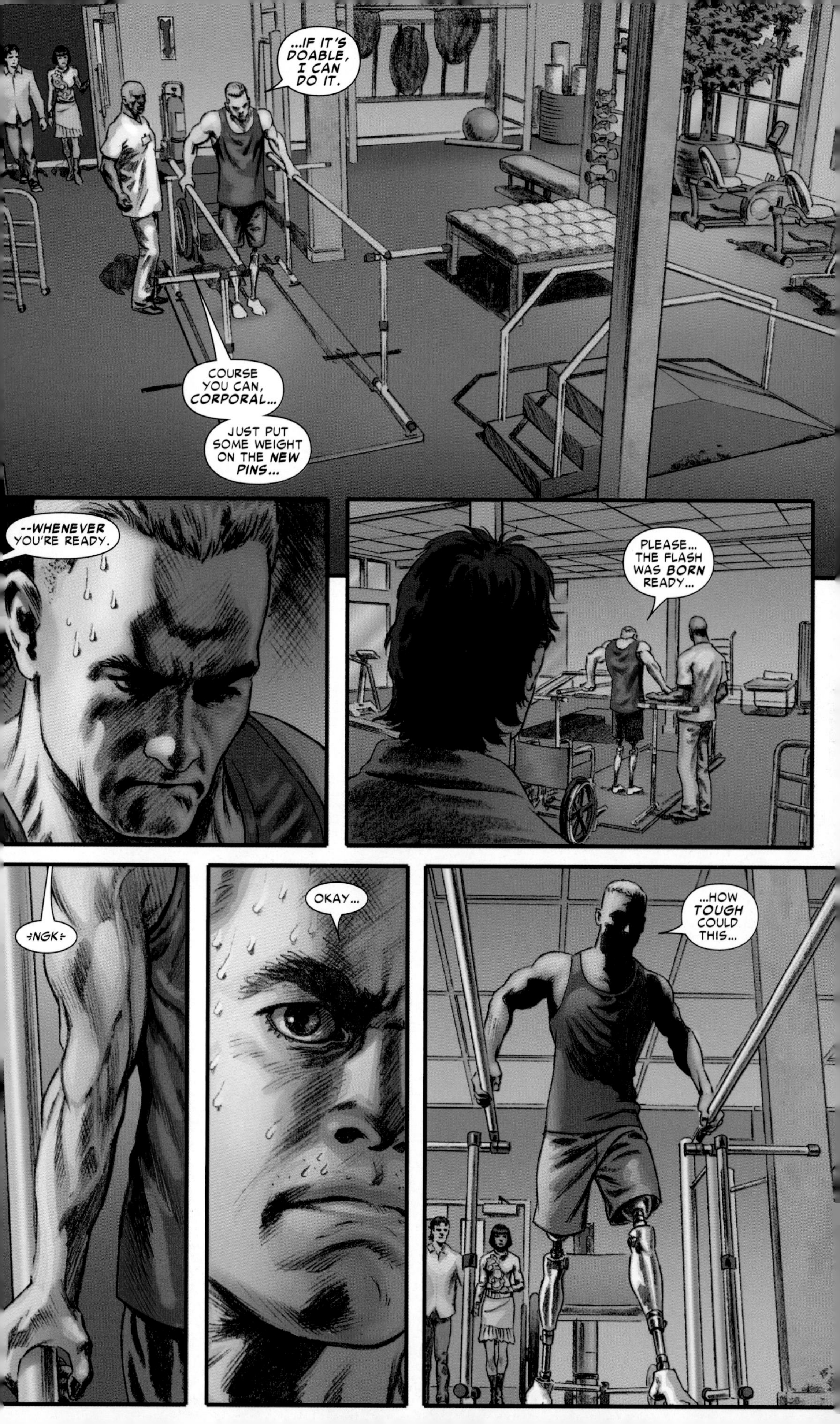
...IF IT'S DOABLE, I CAN DO IT.
COURSE YOU CAN, CORPORAL...
JUST PUT SOME WEIGHT ON THE NEW PINS...
--WHENEVER YOU'RE READY.
PLEASE... THE FLASH WAS BORN READY...
NGK
OKAY...
...HOW TOUGH COULD THIS...

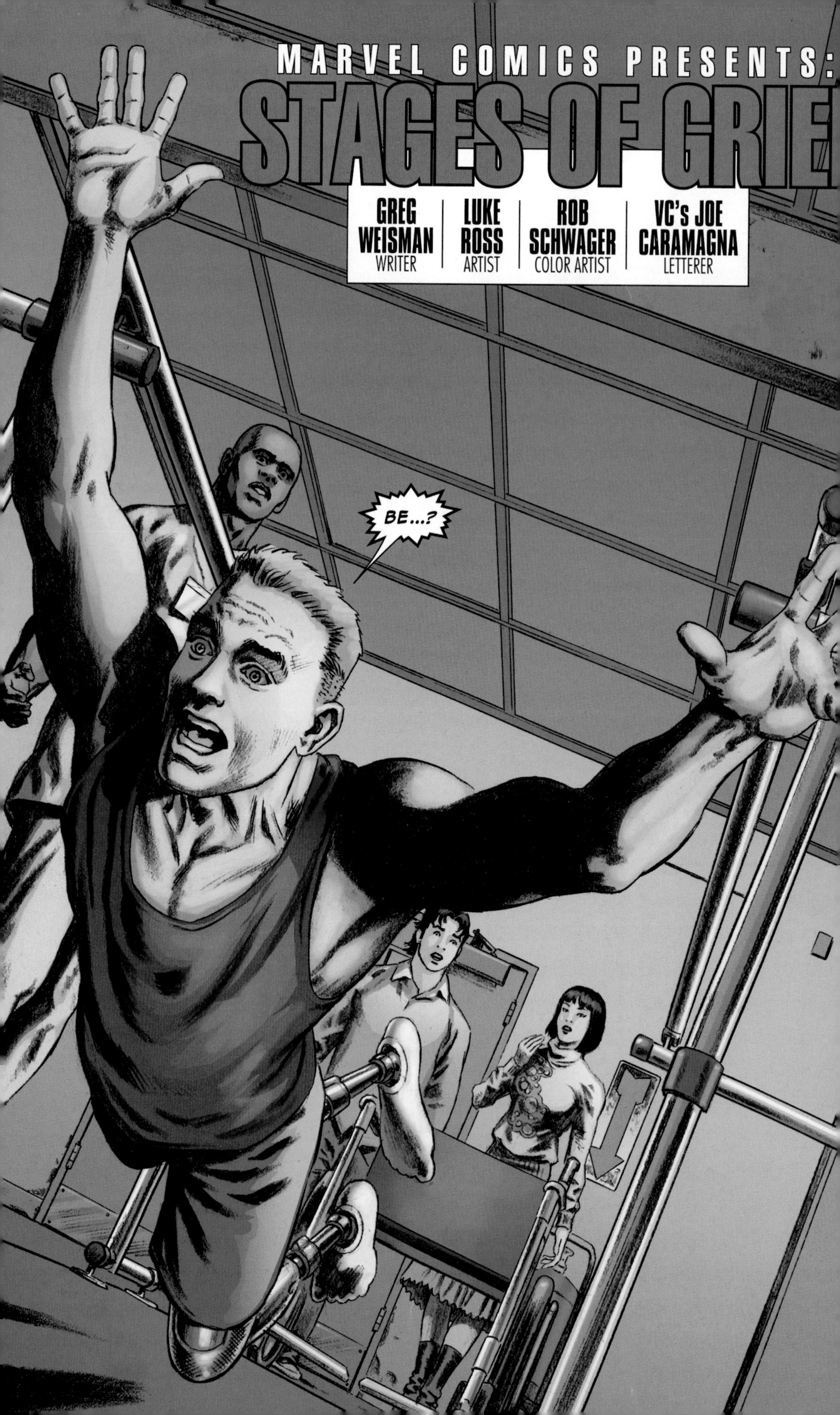

MARVEL COMICS PRESENTS:
STAGES OF GRIEF
GREG WEISMAN WRITER
LUKE ROSS ARTIST
ROB SCHWAGER COLOR ARTIST
VC's JOE CARAMAGNA LETTERER
BE...?

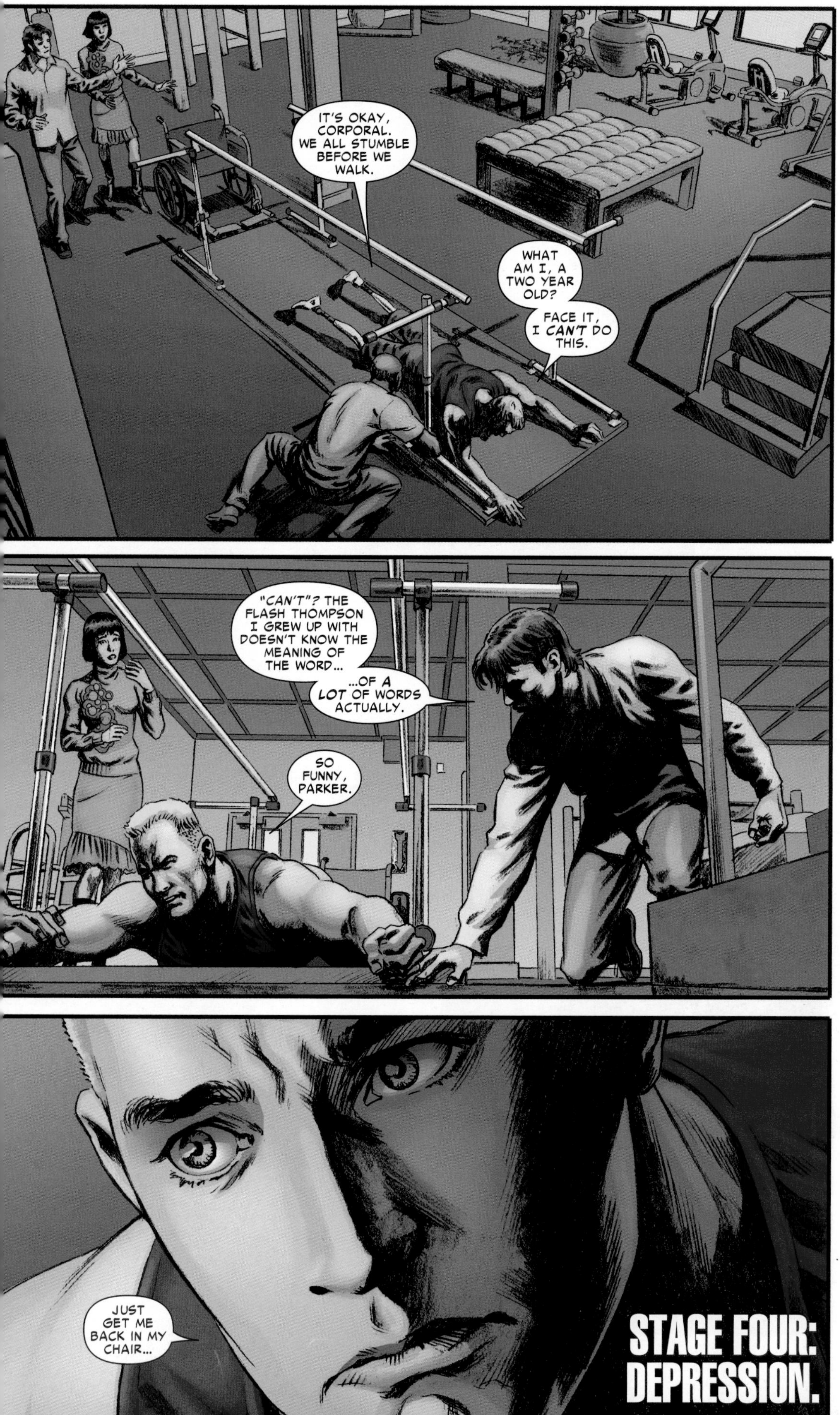
IT'S OKAY, CORPORAL. WE ALL STUMBLE BEFORE WE WALK.
WHAT AM I, A TWO YEAR OLD?
FACE IT, I CAN'T DO THIS.
"CAN'T"? THE FLASH THOMPSON I GREW UP WITH DOESN'T KNOW THE MEANING OF THE WORD...
...OF A LOT OF WORDS ACTUALLY.
SO FUNNY, PARKER.
JUST GET ME BACK IN MY CHAIR...
STAGE FOUR: DEPRESSION.

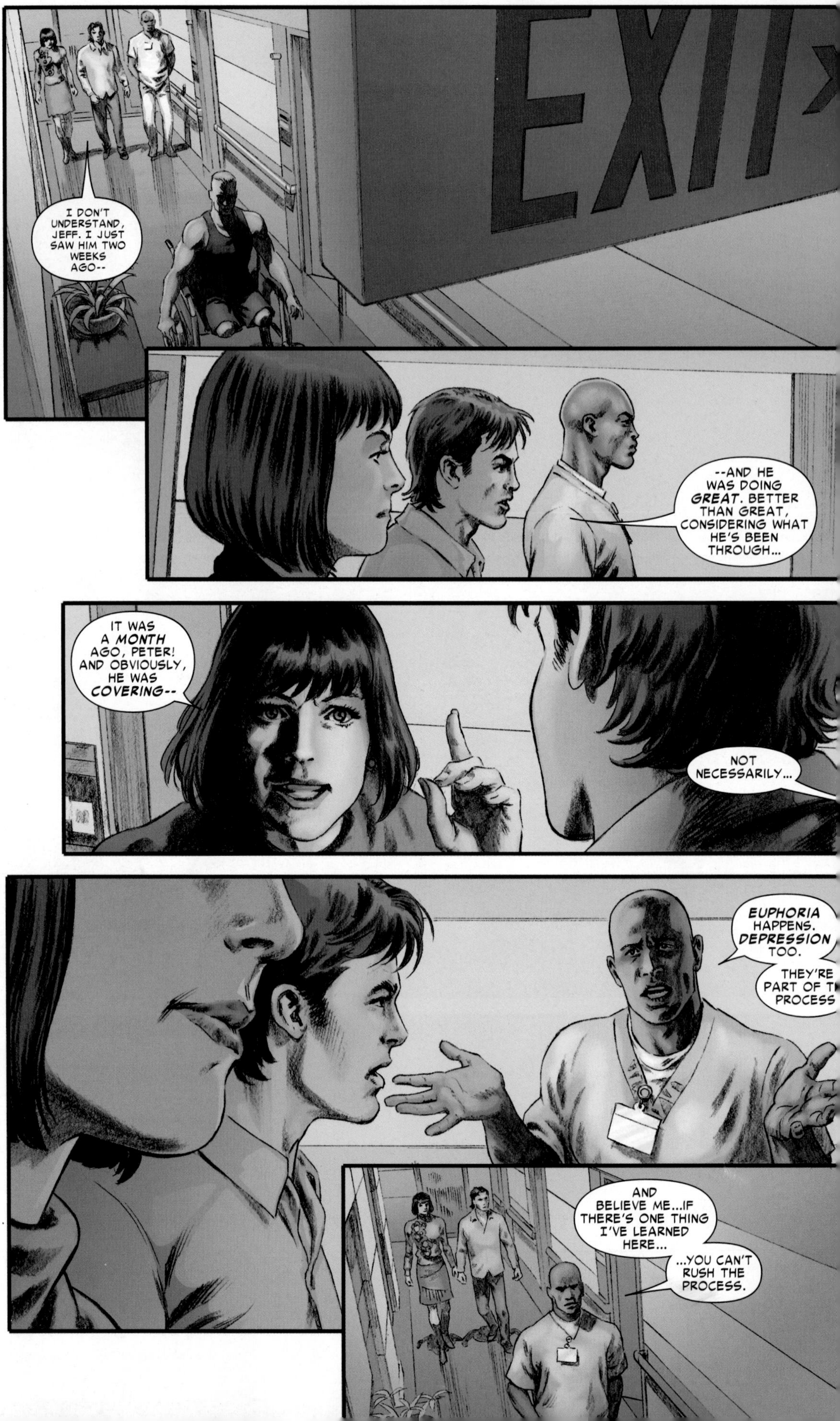
EXIT
I DON'T UNDERSTAND, JEFF. I JUST SAW HIM TWO WEEKS AGO--
--AND HE WAS DOING GREAT. BETTER THAN GREAT, CONSIDERING WHAT HE'S BEEN THROUGH...
IT WAS A MONTH AGO, PETER! AND OBVIOUSLY, HE WAS COVERING--
NOT NECESSARILY...
EUPHORIA HAPPENS. DEPRESSION TOO.
THEY'RE PART OF T PROCESS
AND BELIEVE ME...IF THERE'S ONE THING I'VE LEARNED HERE...
...YOU CAN'T RUSH THE PROCESS.

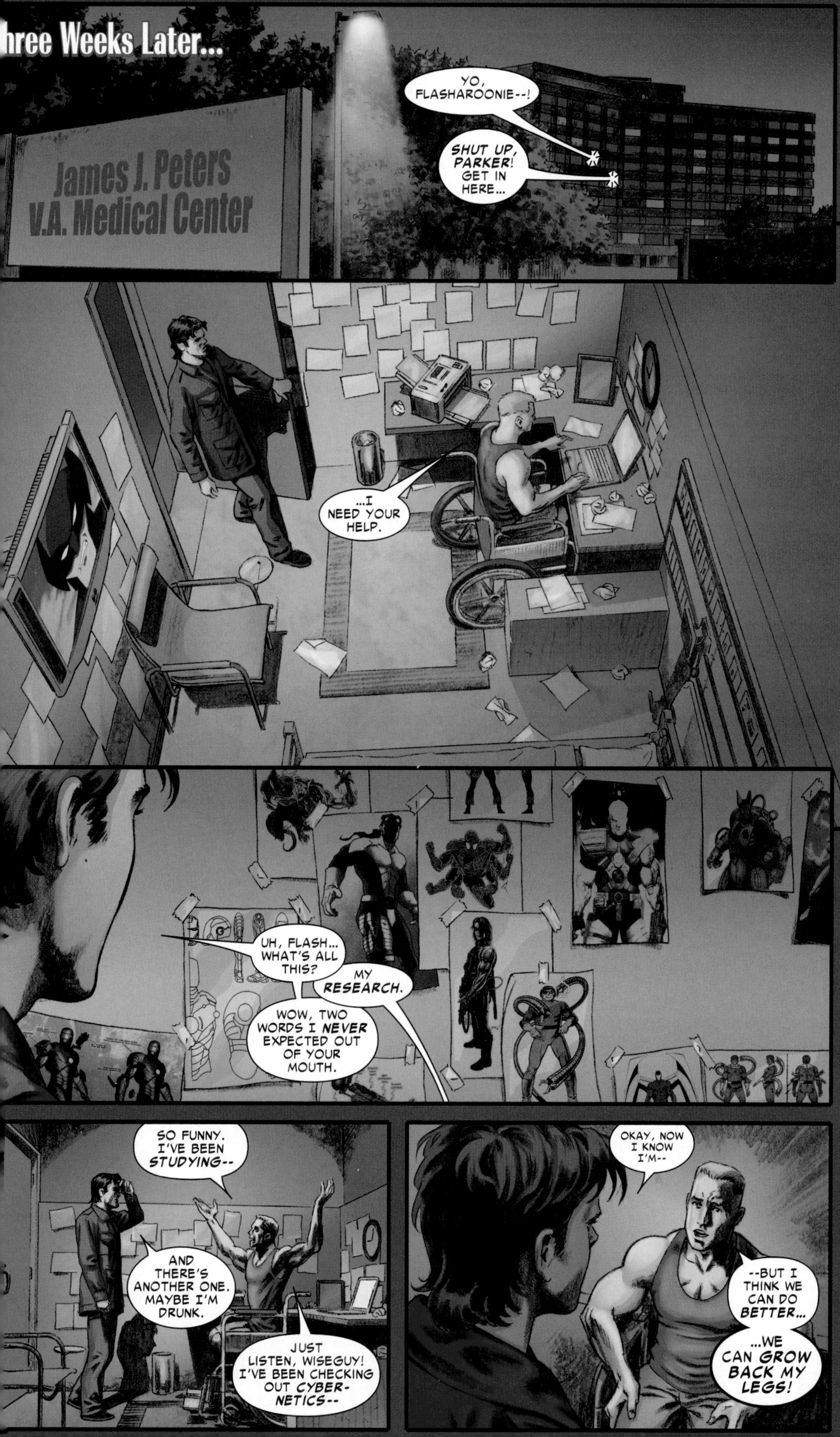
hree Weeks Later...
James J. Peters
V.A. Medical Center
YO, FLASHAROONIE--!
SHUT UP, PARKER! GET IN HERE...
...I NEED YOUR HELP.
UH, FLASH... WHAT'S ALL THIS?
MY RESEARCH.
WOW, TWO WORDS I NEVER EXPECTED OUT OF YOUR MOUTH.
SO FUNNY. I'VE BEEN STUDYING--
AND THERE'S ANOTHER ONE. MAYBE I'M DRUNK.
JUST LISTEN, WISEGUY! I'VE BEEN CHECKING OUT CYBER-NETICS--
OKAY, NOW I KNOW I'M--
--BUT I THINK WE CAN DO BETTER...
...WE CAN GROW BACK MY LEGS!

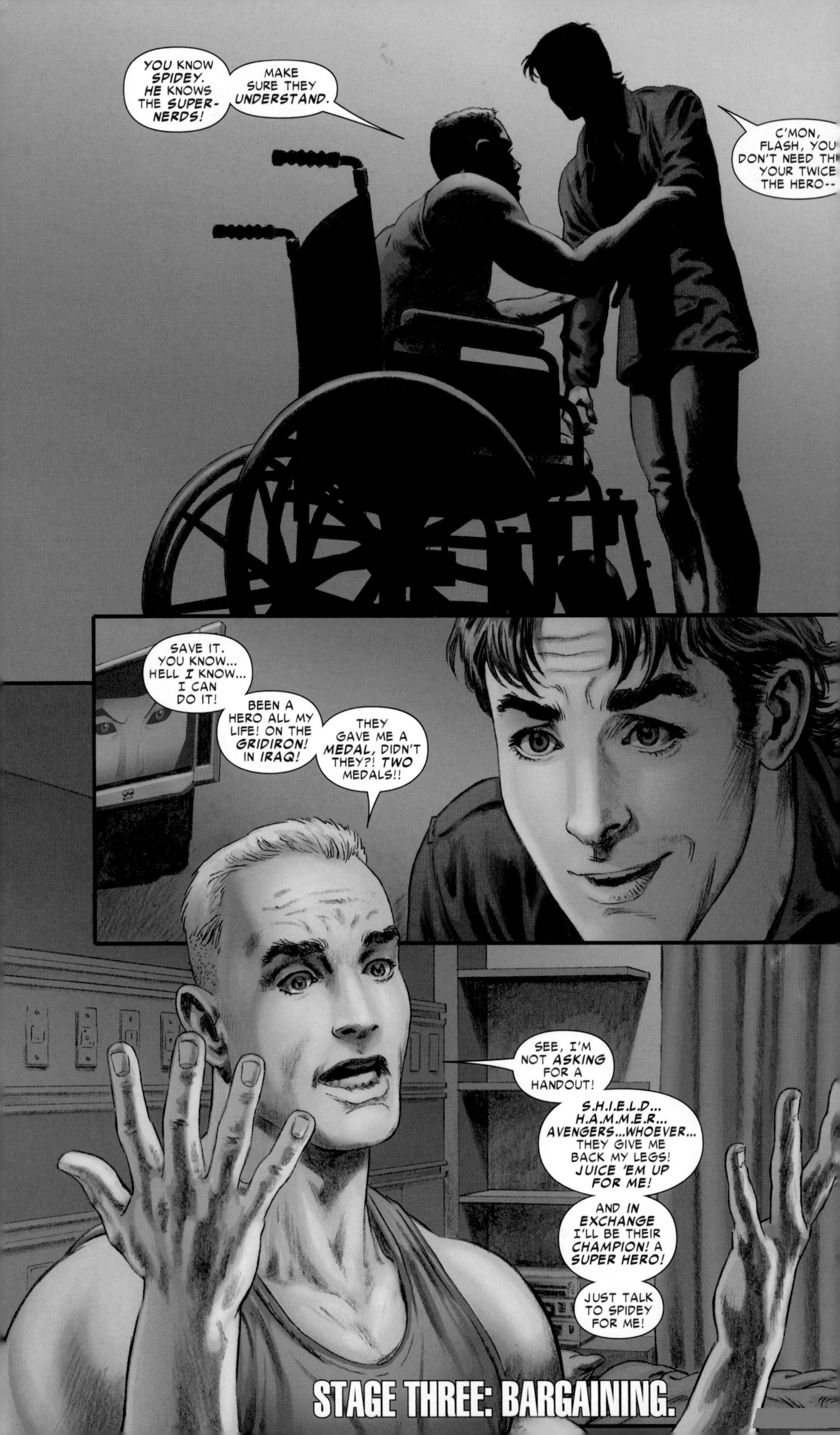

YOU KNOW SPIDEY. HE KNOWS THE SUPER-NERDS!
MAKE SURE THEY UNDERSTAND.
C'MON, FLASH, YOU DON'T NEED TH YOUR TWICE THE HERO--
SAVE IT. YOU KNOW... HELL I KNOW... I CAN DO IT!
BEEN A HERO ALL MY LIFE! ON THE GRIDIRON! IN IRAQ!
THEY GAVE ME A MEDAL, DIDN'T THEY?! TWO MEDALS!!
SEE, I'M NOT ASKING FOR A HANDOUT!
S.H.I.E.L.D... H.A.M.M.E.R... AVENGERS...WHOEVER... THEY GIVE ME BACK MY LEGS! JUICE 'EM UP FOR ME!
AND IN EXCHANGE I'LL BE THEIR CHAMPION! A SUPER HERO!
JUST TALK TO SPIDEY FOR ME!
STAGE THREE: BARGAINING.

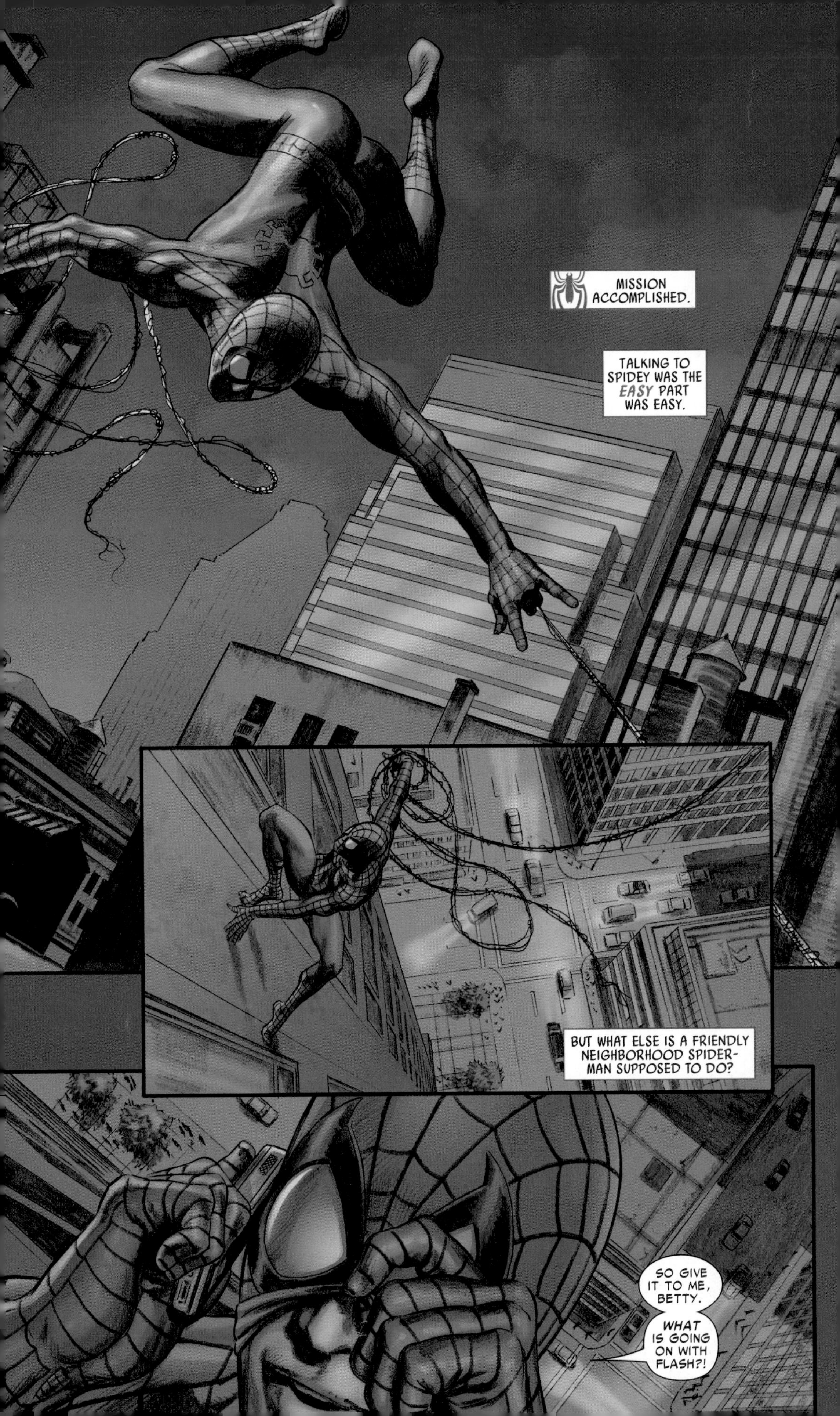
MISSION ACCOMPLISHED.
TALKING TO SPIDEY WAS THE *EASY* PART WAS EASY.
BUT WHAT ELSE IS A FRIENDLY NEIGHBORHOOD SPIDER-MAN SUPPOSED TO DO?
SO GIVE IT TO ME, BETTY.
WHAT IS GOING ON WITH FLASH?!

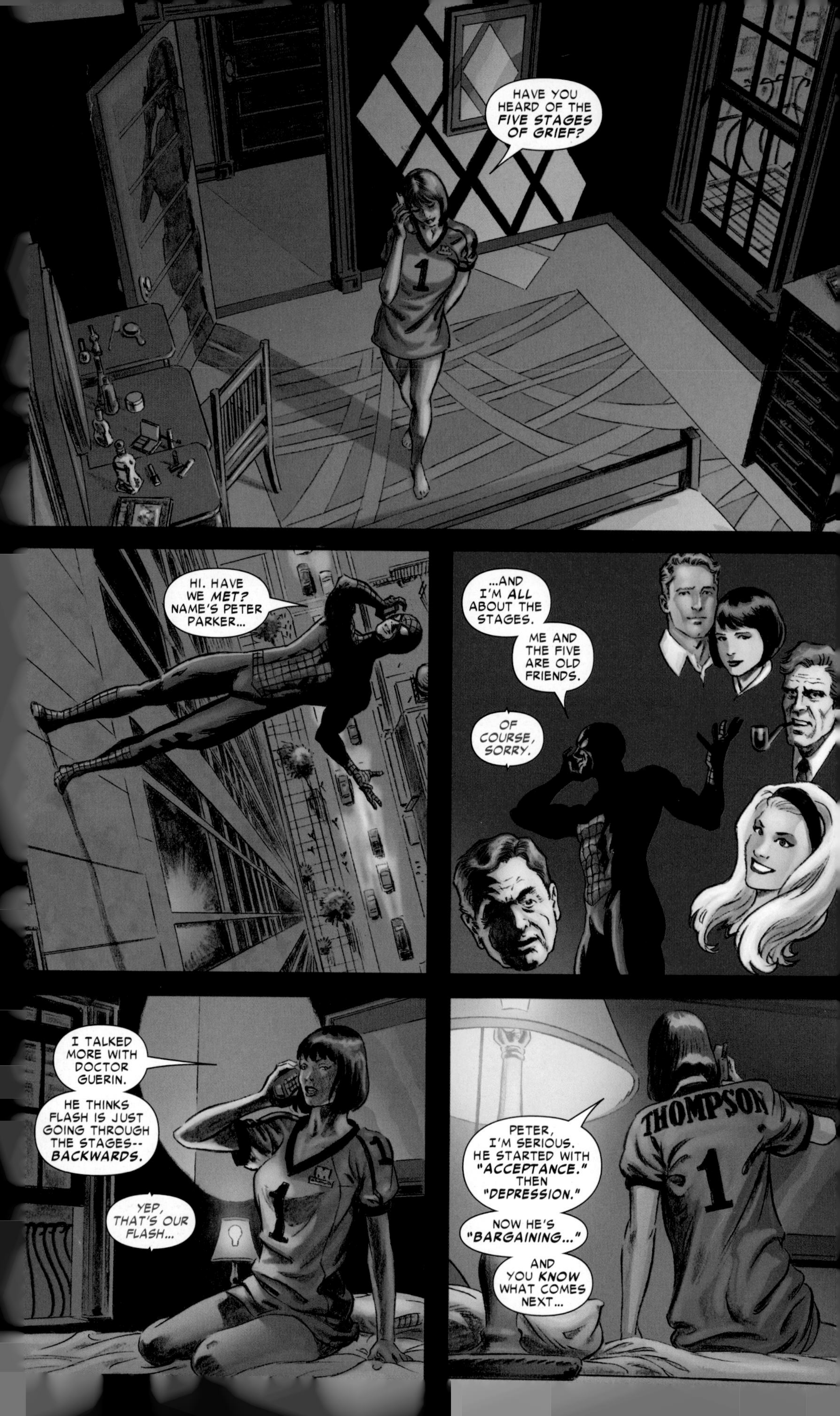
HAVE YOU HEARD OF THE *FIVE STAGES OF GRIEF?*
HI. HAVE WE *MET?* NAME'S PETER PARKER...
...AND I'M **ALL** ABOUT THE STAGES.
ME AND THE FIVE ARE OLD FRIENDS.
OF COURSE, SORRY.
I TALKED MORE WITH DOCTOR GUERIN.
HE THINKS FLASH IS JUST GOING THROUGH THE STAGES-- ***BACKWARDS.***
YEP, THAT'S OUR FLASH...
THOMPSON
1
PETER, I'M SERIOUS. HE STARTED WITH **"*ACCEPTANCE.*"** THEN **"*DEPRESSION.*"**
NOW HE'S **"*BARGAINING...*"**
AND YOU **KNOW** WHAT COMES NEXT...

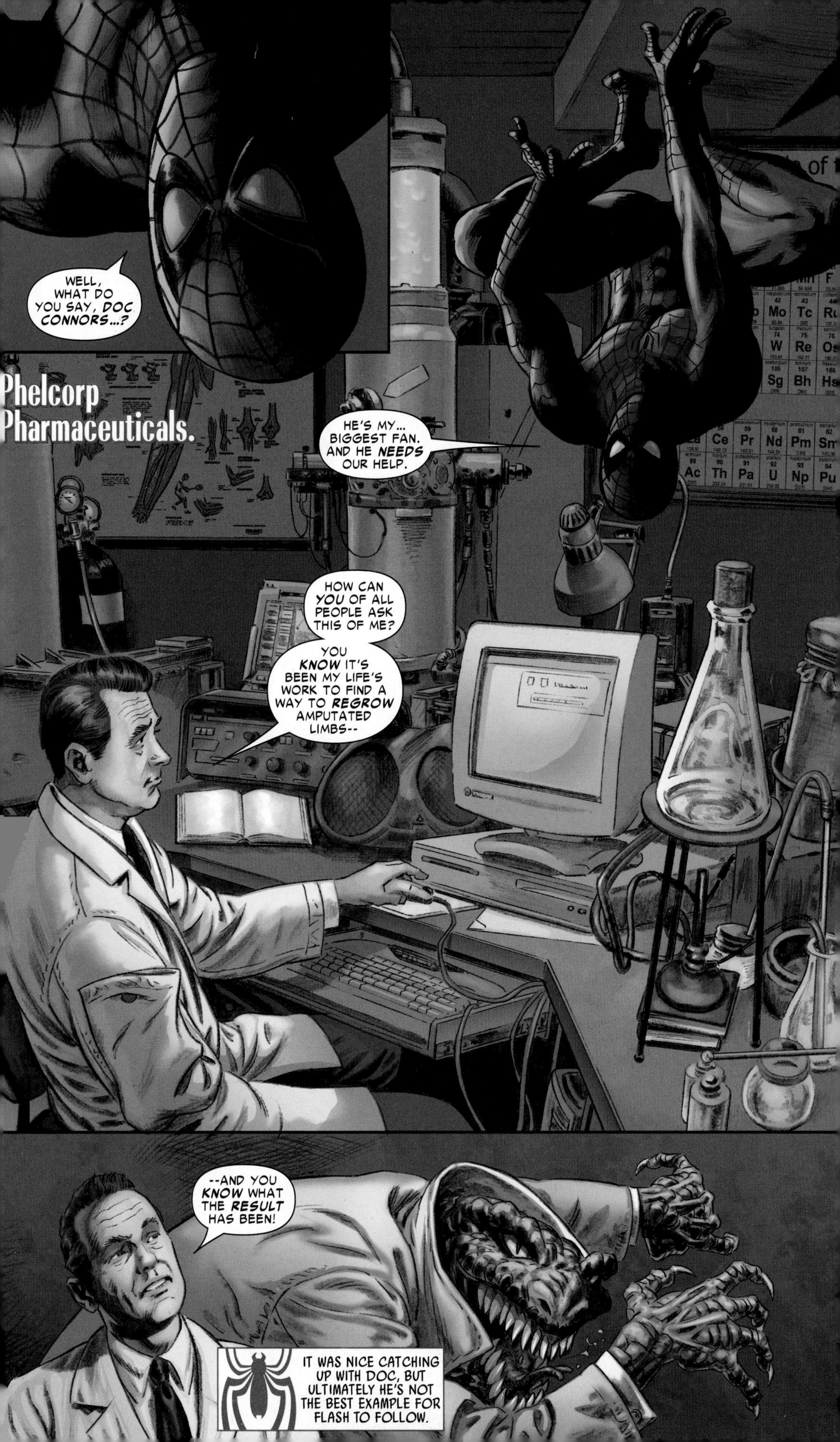
WELL, WHAT DO YOU SAY, DOC CONNORS...?
Phelcorp Pharmaceuticals.
HE'S MY... BIGGEST FAN. AND HE NEEDS OUR HELP.
HOW CAN YOU OF ALL PEOPLE ASK THIS OF ME?
YOU KNOW IT'S BEEN MY LIFE'S WORK TO FIND A WAY TO REGROW AMPUTATED LIMBS--
--AND YOU KNOW WHAT THE RESULT HAS BEEN!
IT WAS NICE CATCHING UP WITH DOC, BUT ULTIMATELY HE'S NOT THE BEST EXAMPLE FOR FLASH TO FOLLOW.

Internet Bubble Laundry.

ON THE FIRST FLOOR OF PETER PARKER'S APARTMENT BUILDING.

C'MON THINK!

...AND MJ AND I HAVE SEPARATE ROOMS. SHE'S LIKE A SISTER, YA KNOW?

IT'S FINE, HARRY. REALLY. I'M FINE WITH IT. WE'VE BOTH MOVED ON.

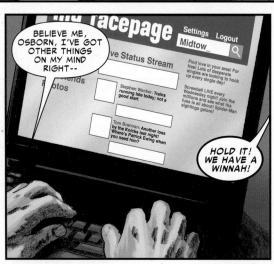

BELIEVE ME, OSBORN, I'VE GOT OTHER THINGS ON MY MIND RIGHT--

facepage

Settings   Logout

Midtow_

ve Status Stream

Find love in your area! For free! Lots of desperate singles are looking to hook up every single day!

Stephen Wacker: Trains running late today; not a good start

Screwball LIVE every Wednesday night! Join the millions and see what the fuss is all about! Spider-Man sightings galore!

Tom Brennan: Another loss by the Knicks last night! Where's Patrick Ewing when you need him?

HOLD IT! WE HAVE A WINNAH!

TOLD YOU I COULD TRACK HER DOWN FIRST.

REALLY? YOU FOUND HER?

AND YOU WON'T *BELIEVE* WHAT SHE DOES FOR A LIVING NOW. IT'S PERFECT.

♪ ...IF YA LIKED IT, THEN YA SHOULDA PUT A RING ON IT... ♪

THAT'S MY PHONE!

HOLD THAT THOUGHT, HARRY...

HELLO?

OH, HI. UH...THANKS FOR CALLING ME BACK.

IT MEANS A LOT TO--

TO FLASH. RIGHT. EXACT WHAT I WAS GOING TO SAY...

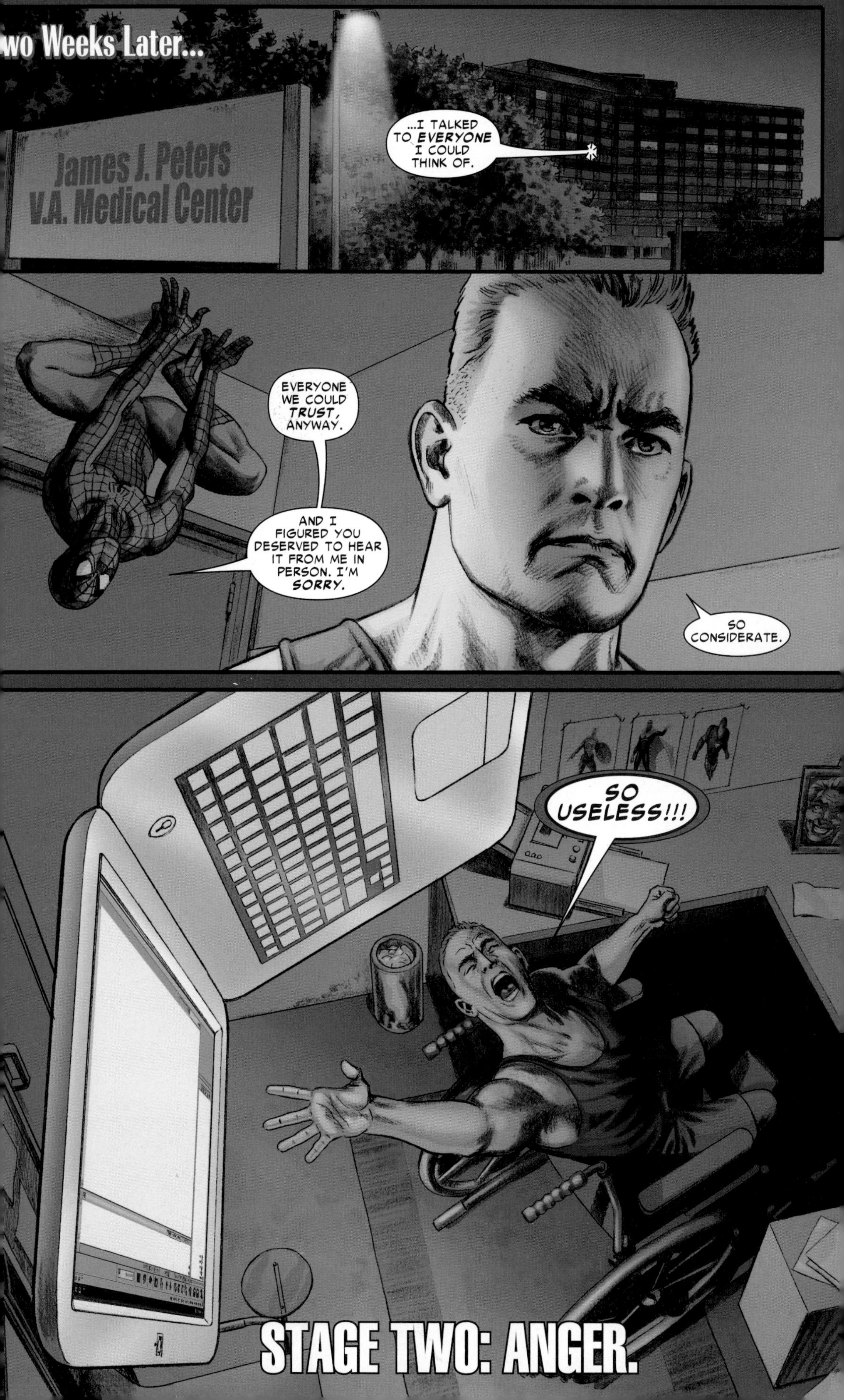
wo Weeks Later...
James J. Peters
V.A. Medical Center
...I TALKED TO EVERYONE I COULD THINK OF.
EVERYONE WE COULD TRUST, ANYWAY.
AND I FIGURED YOU DESERVED TO HEAR IT FROM ME IN PERSON. I'M SORRY.
SO CONSIDERATE.
SO USELESS!!!
STAGE TWO: ANGER.

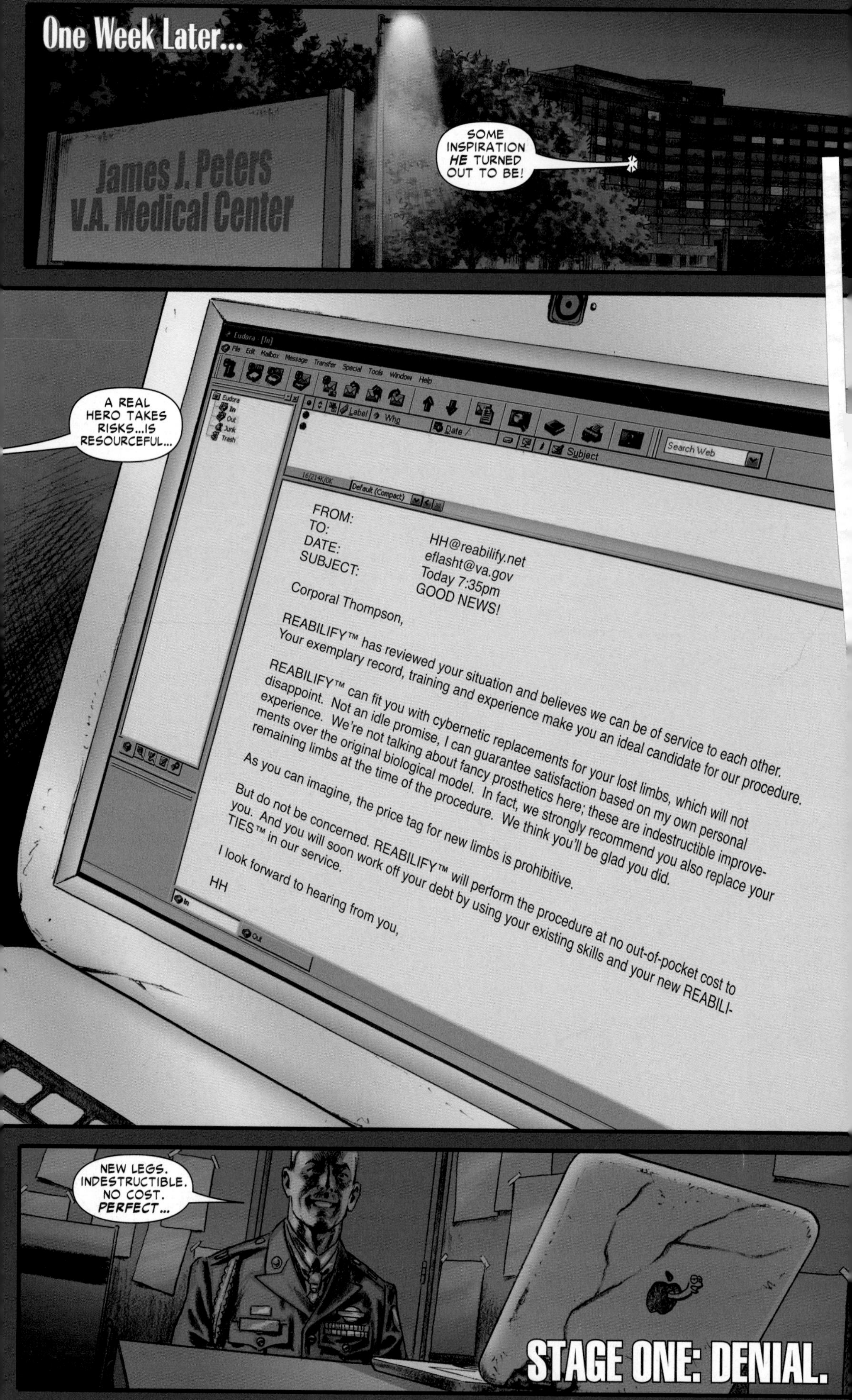
One Week Later...
James J. Peters
V.A. Medical Center
SOME INSPIRATION HE TURNED OUT TO BE!
A REAL HERO TAKES RISKS...IS RESOURCEFUL...
Eudora - [In]
File Edit Mailbox Message Transfer Special Tools Window Help
Eudora
In
Out
Junk
Trash
Label
Who
Date
Subject
Search Web
Default (Compact)
FROM: HH@reabilify.net
TO: eflasht@va.gov
DATE: Today 7:35pm
SUBJECT: GOOD NEWS!
Corporal Thompson,
REABILIFY™ has reviewed your situation and believes we can be of service to each other. Your exemplary record, training and experience make you an ideal candidate for our procedure.
REABILIFY™ can fit you with cybernetic replacements for your lost limbs, which will not disappoint. Not an idle promise, I can guarantee satisfaction based on my own personal experience. We're not talking about fancy prosthetics here; these are indestructible improvements over the original biological model. In fact, we strongly recommend you also replace your remaining limbs at the time of the procedure. We think you'll be glad you did.
As you can imagine, the price tag for new limbs is prohibitive.
But do not be concerned. REABILIFY™ will perform the procedure at no out-of-pocket cost to you. And you will soon work off your debt by using your existing skills and your new REABILITIES™ in our service.
I look forward to hearing from you,
HH
In
Out
NEW LEGS. INDESTRUCTIBLE. NO COST. PERFECT...
STAGE ONE: DENIAL.

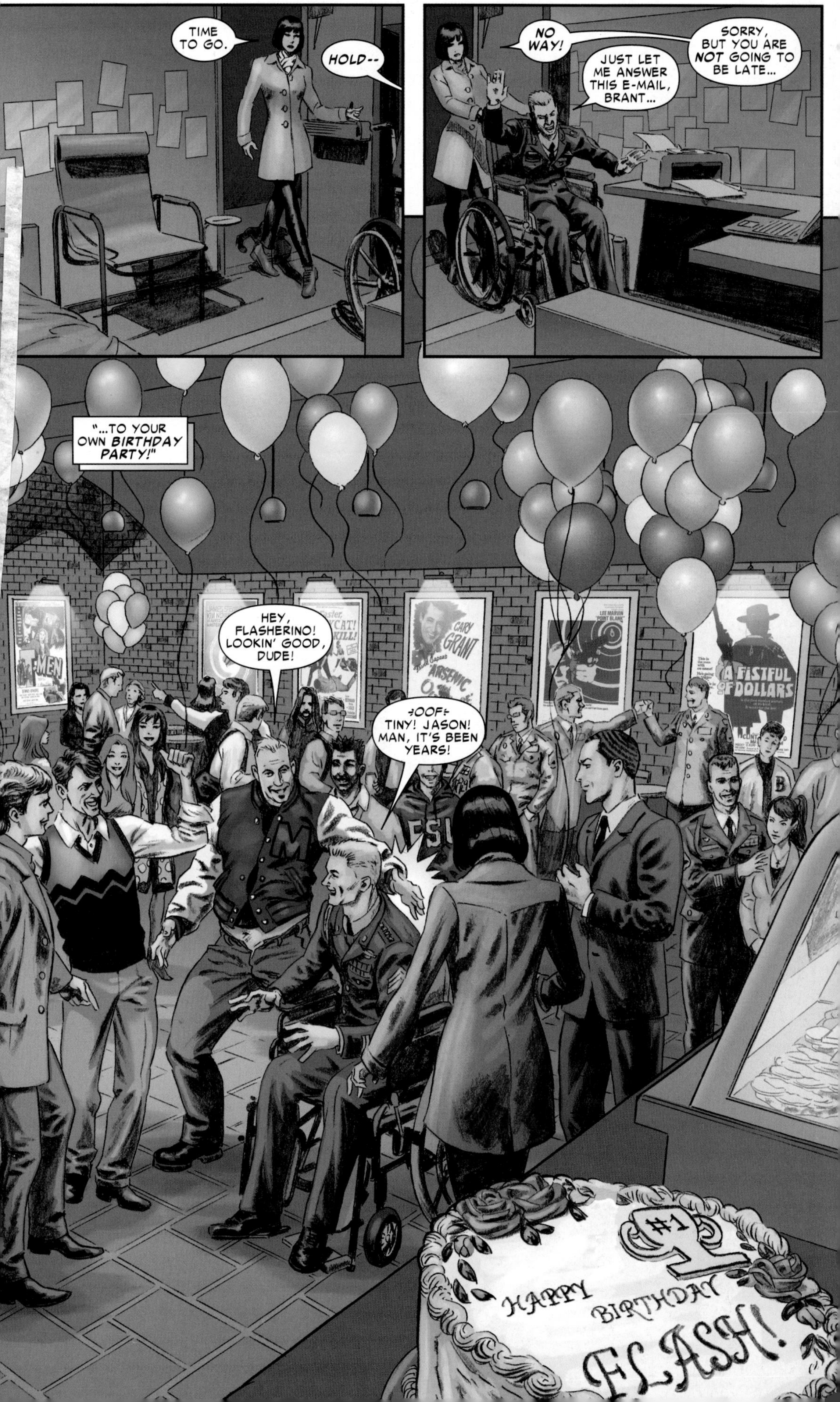
TIME TO GO.
HOLD--
NO WAY!
JUST LET ME ANSWER THIS E-MAIL, BRANT...
SORRY, BUT YOU ARE NOT GOING TO BE LATE...
"...TO YOUR OWN BIRTHDAY PARTY!"
HEY, FLASHERINO! LOOKIN' GOOD, DUDE!
OOF
TINY! JASON! MAN, IT'S BEEN YEARS!
T-MEN
CARY GRANT
ARSENIC
LEE MARVIN
"POINT BLANK"
A FISTFUL OF DOLLARS
#1
HAPPY BIRTHDAY FLASH!

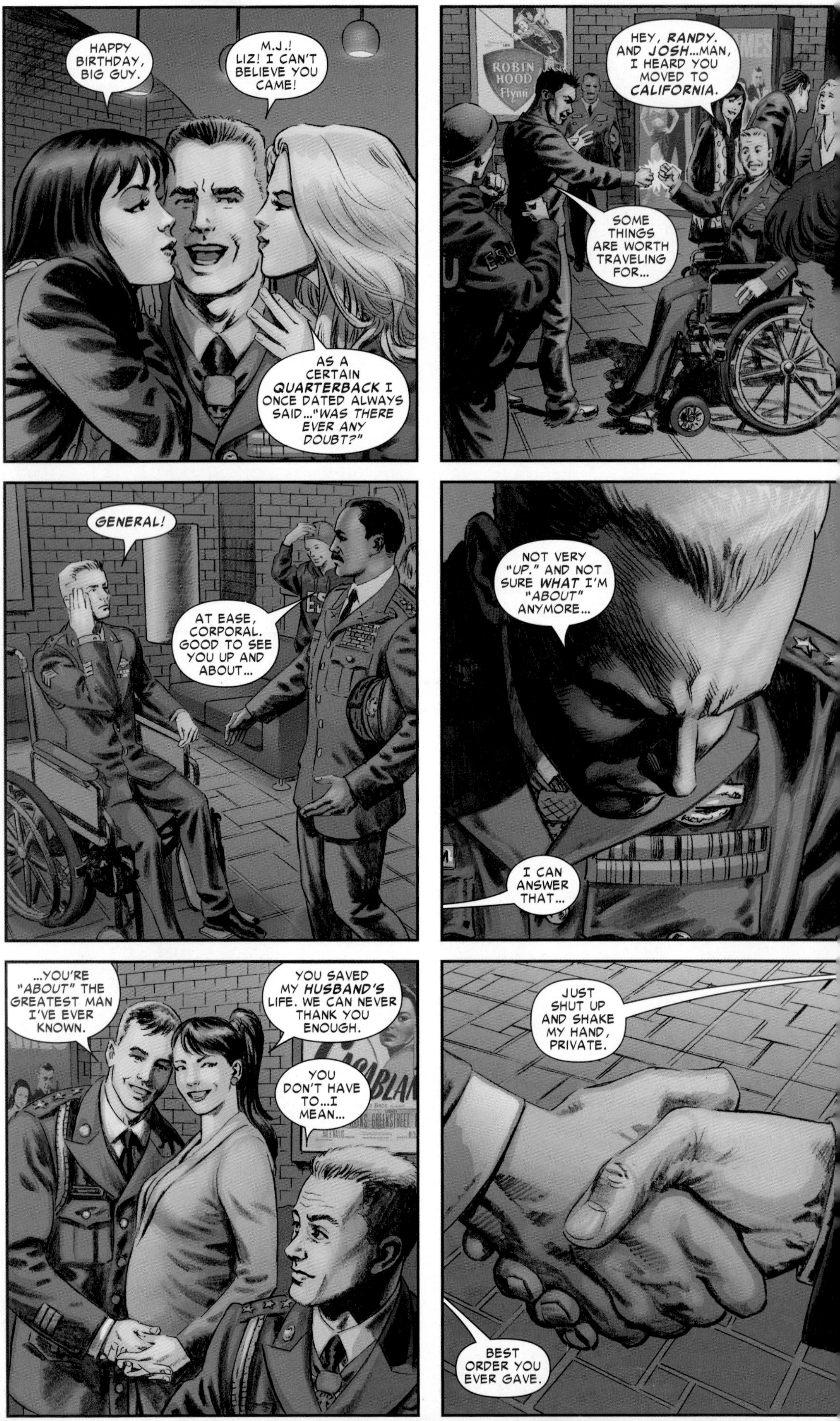
HAPPY BIRTHDAY, BIG GUY.
M.J.! LIZ! I CAN'T BELIEVE YOU CAME!
AS A CERTAIN QUARTERBACK I ONCE DATED ALWAYS SAID..."WAS THERE EVER ANY DOUBT?"
ROBIN HOOD Flynn
HEY, RANDY. AND JOSH...MAN, I HEARD YOU MOVED TO CALIFORNIA.
SOME THINGS ARE WORTH TRAVELING FOR...
GENERAL!
AT EASE, CORPORAL. GOOD TO SEE YOU UP AND ABOUT...
NOT VERY "UP." AND NOT SURE WHAT I'M "ABOUT" ANYMORE...
I CAN ANSWER THAT...
...YOU'RE "ABOUT" THE GREATEST MAN I'VE EVER KNOWN.
YOU SAVED MY HUSBAND'S LIFE. WE CAN NEVER THANK YOU ENOUGH.
YOU DON'T HAVE TO...I MEAN...
JUST SHUT UP AND SHAKE MY HAND, PRIVATE.
BEST ORDER YOU EVER GAVE.

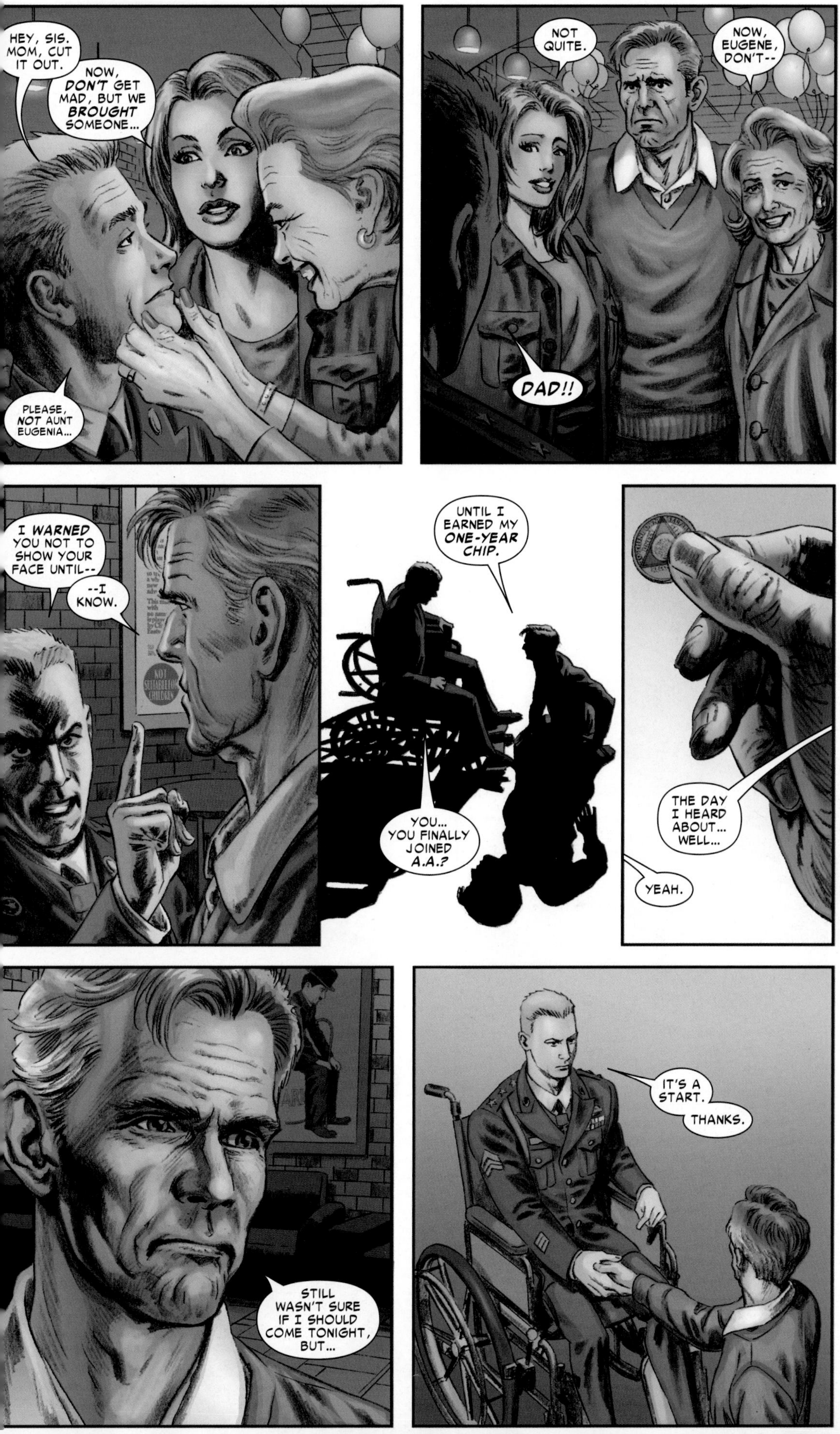
HEY, SIS. MOM, CUT IT OUT.
NOW, DON'T GET MAD, BUT WE BROUGHT SOMEONE...
PLEASE, NOT AUNT EUGENIA...
NOT QUITE.
NOW, EUGENE, DON'T--
DAD!!
I WARNED YOU NOT TO SHOW YOUR FACE UNTIL--
--I KNOW.
UNTIL I EARNED MY ONE-YEAR CHIP.
YOU... YOU FINALLY JOINED A.A.?
THE DAY I HEARD ABOUT... WELL...
YEAH.
STILL WASN'T SURE IF I SHOULD COME TONIGHT, BUT...
IT'S A START.
THANKS.

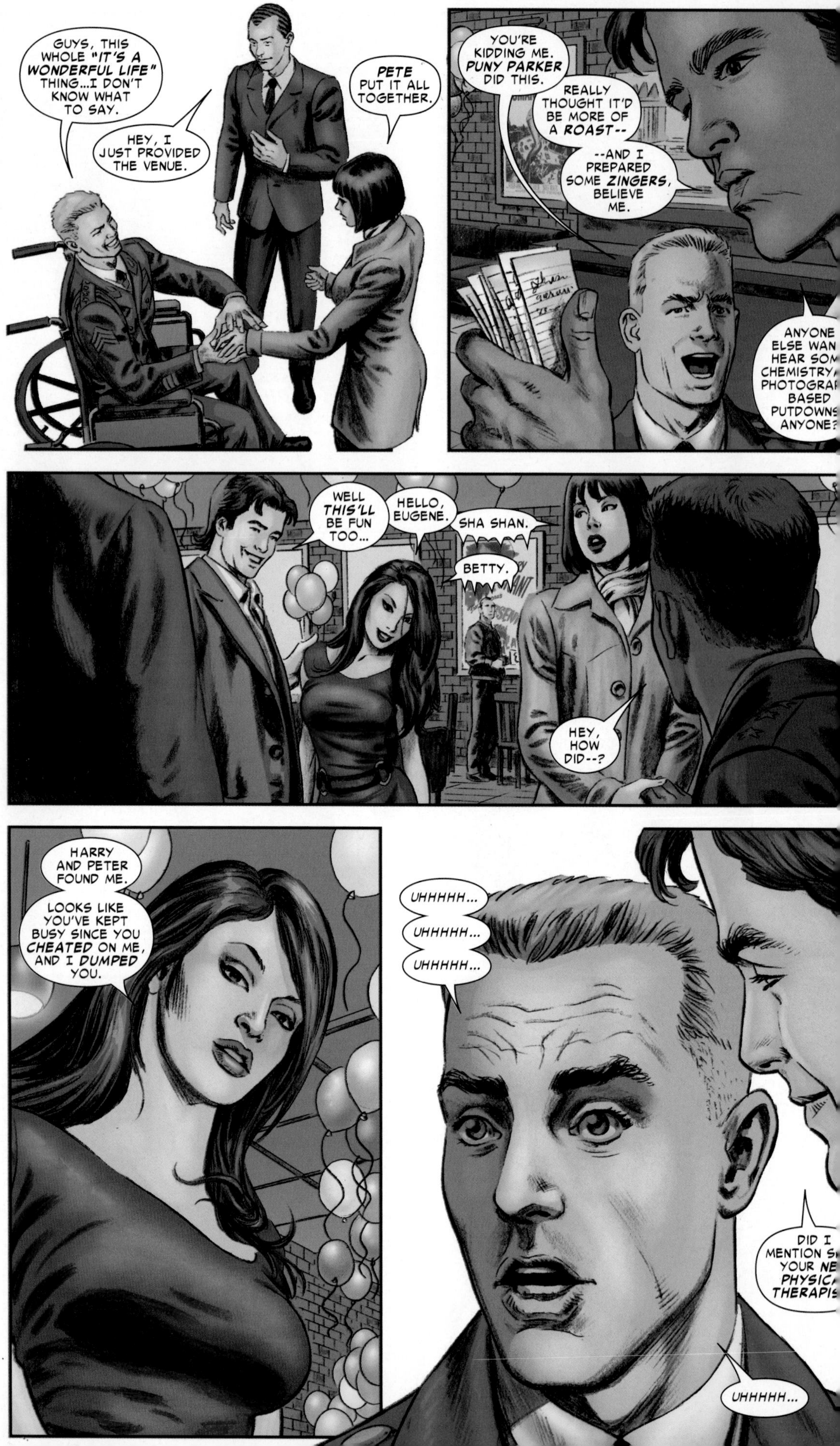
GUYS, THIS WHOLE "IT'S A WONDERFUL LIFE" THING...I DON'T KNOW WHAT TO SAY.
HEY, I JUST PROVIDED THE VENUE.
PETE PUT IT ALL TOGETHER.
YOU'RE KIDDING ME. PUNY PARKER DID THIS.
REALLY THOUGHT IT'D BE MORE OF A ROAST--
--AND I PREPARED SOME ZINGERS, BELIEVE ME.
ANYONE ELSE WAN HEAR SOM CHEMISTRY/ PHOTOGRAP BASED PUTDOWNS ANYONE?
WELL THIS'LL BE FUN TOO...
HELLO, EUGENE.
SHA SHAN.
BETTY.
HEY, HOW DID--?
HARRY AND PETER FOUND ME.
LOOKS LIKE YOU'VE KEPT BUSY SINCE YOU CHEATED ON ME, AND I DUMPED YOU.
UHHHHH...
UHHHHH...
UHHHHH...
DID I MENTION S YOUR NE PHYSIC THERAPIS
UHHHHH...

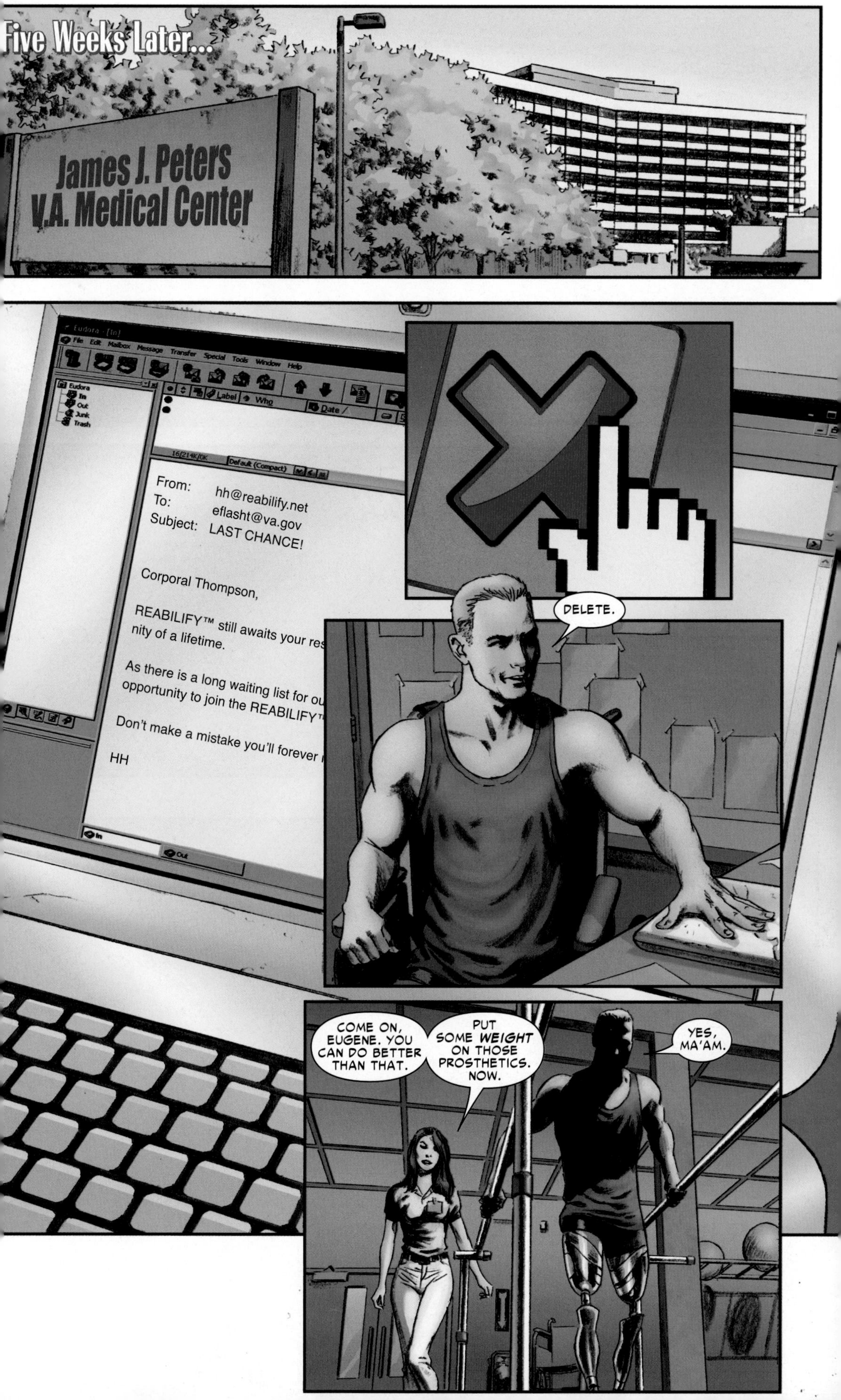
Five Weeks Later...
James J. Peters
V.A. Medical Center
From: hh@reabilify.net
To: eflasht@va.gov
Subject: LAST CHANCE!
Corporal Thompson,
REABILIFY™ still awaits your res
nity of a lifetime.
As there is a long waiting list for ou
opportunity to join the REABILIFY
Don't make a mistake you'll forever
HH
DELETE.
COME ON, EUGENE. YOU CAN DO BETTER THAN THAT.
PUT SOME *WEIGHT* ON THOSE PROSTHETICS. NOW.
YES, MA'AM.

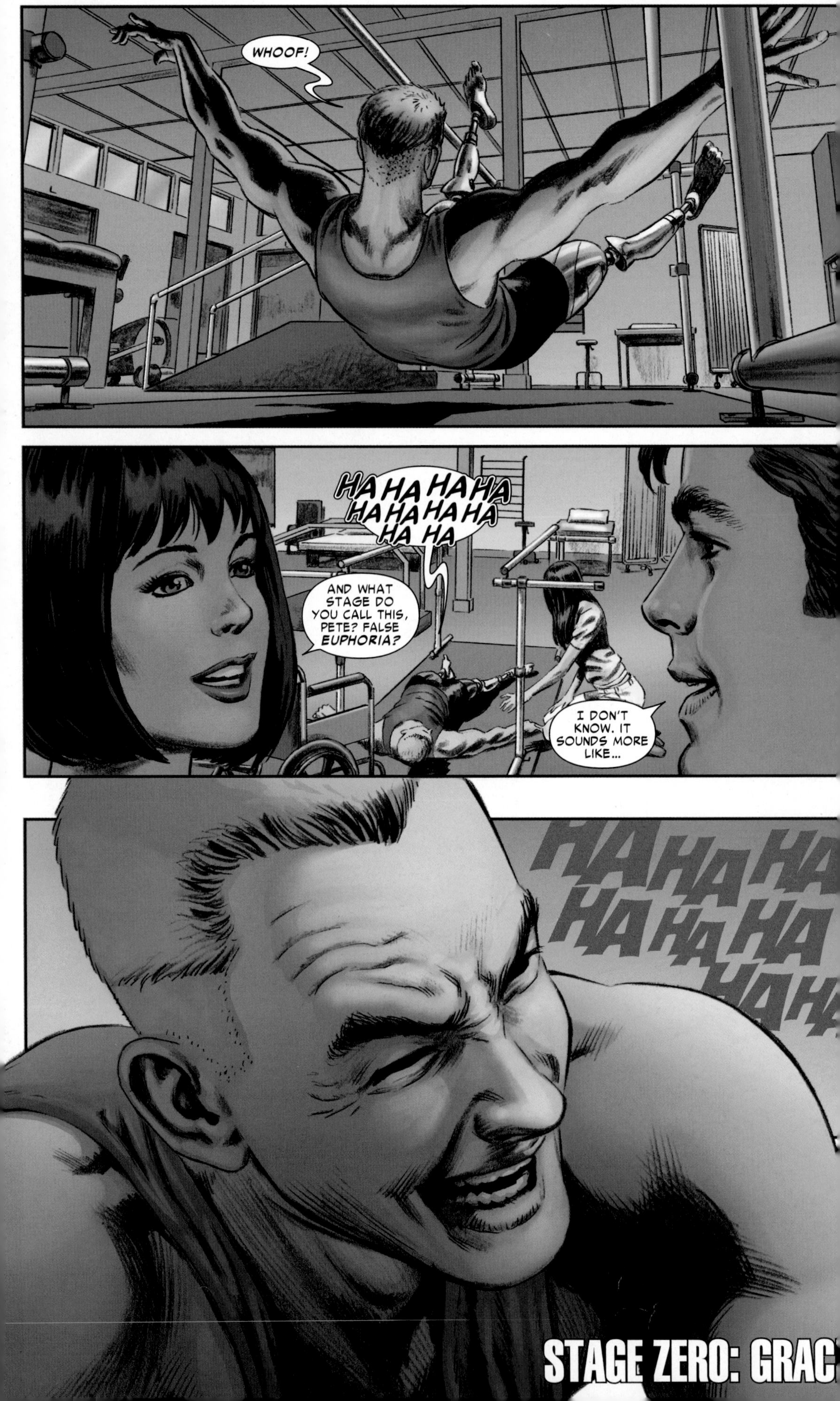
WHOOF!
HA HA HA HA HA HA HA HA HA HA HA HA
AND WHAT STAGE DO YOU CALL THIS, PETE? FALSE EUPHORIA?
I DON'T KNOW. IT SOUNDS MORE LIKE...
HA HA HA HA HA HA HA HA HA
STAGE ZERO: GRAC

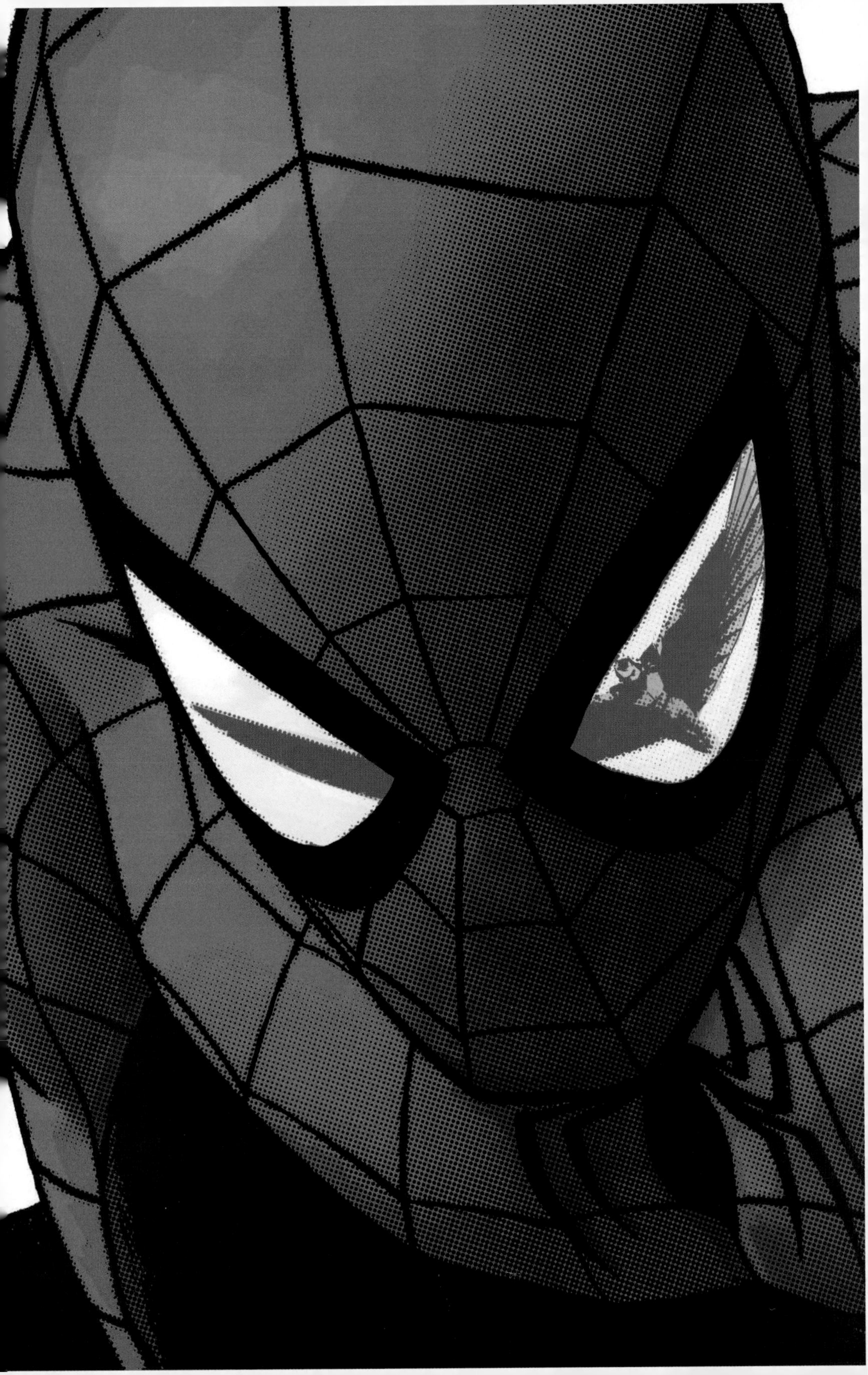

BUGLE GIRL

RSS | ARCHIVE | ABOUT | CONTACT | ADVERTIS

NEW USER? CREATE AN ACCOUNT!

FORGOT YOUR PASSWORD?

SEARCH GO

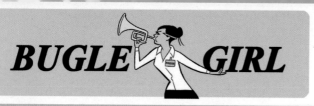

Mark Waid w/ Tom Peyer – Writers
Paul Azaceta – Art
Andres Mossa – Colors
VC's Joe Caramagna – Letters
Michael Lark & Jodi Wynne – Cover
Joe Quinones – Variant Cover
Joe Jusko – Variant Cover
Tom Brennan – Asst. Editor
Stephen Wacker – Editor
Tom Brevoort – Executive Editor
Joe Quesada – Editor in Chief
Dan Buckley – Publisher
Alan Fine – Executive Producer
Gale, Kelly, Slott, Van Lente, Waid & Wells – Web-Heads

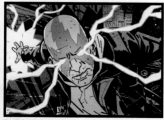

ELECTRO STILL AT LARGE! Maxwell Dillon, known to the public as Electro, has yet to be captured by authorities. Responsible for the destruction of The DB building, Electro is a fugitive... more...

09

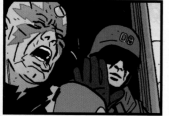

CORRUPTION IN PRISONS – An anonymous source has leaked information that suggests prison guards throughout the state could be on criminal payrolls. Are these "men on the inside" real...more...

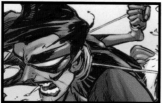

MATTIE FRANKLIN STILL MISSING – Friends and family of Mattie Franklin are urging anyone with any information on her whereabouts to please contact them...more...

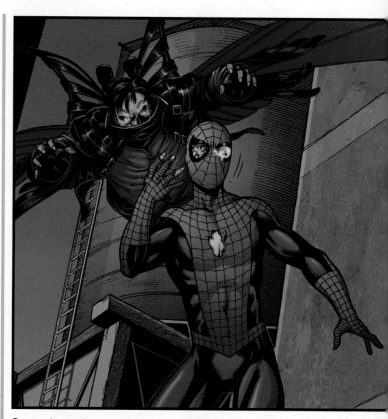

Several months ago, New York City's criminal underworld was rocke by the arrival of a new and deadly vigilante: the Vulture. Unlike hi predecessor, Adrian Toomes, this creature bears real wings, and host of other deadly abilities.

The new Vulture nearly proved to be a match for Spider-Man in the first encounter, but ol' Webhead was able to defeat the Vulture afte a battle in Yankee Stadium, in full view of his biggest critic, Mayor J Jonah Jameson.

Jameson, former publisher of the famed Daily Bugle newspaper, wa elected mayor of the city in a run-off election late last year. Jonah's running a tight ship, and employs former Bugle-lites Glory Grant a press secretary and Peter Parker as his staff photographer, but troubl always seems to follow Ol' Flat Top.

His term has been mired with financial meltdowns, super villain attack (Including one by Electro that resulted in the destruction of his forme newspaper) and Jonah's own mad-on for Spider-Man. Factor in lengthy public career, and it's only a matter of time before old enemie try to settle some scores...

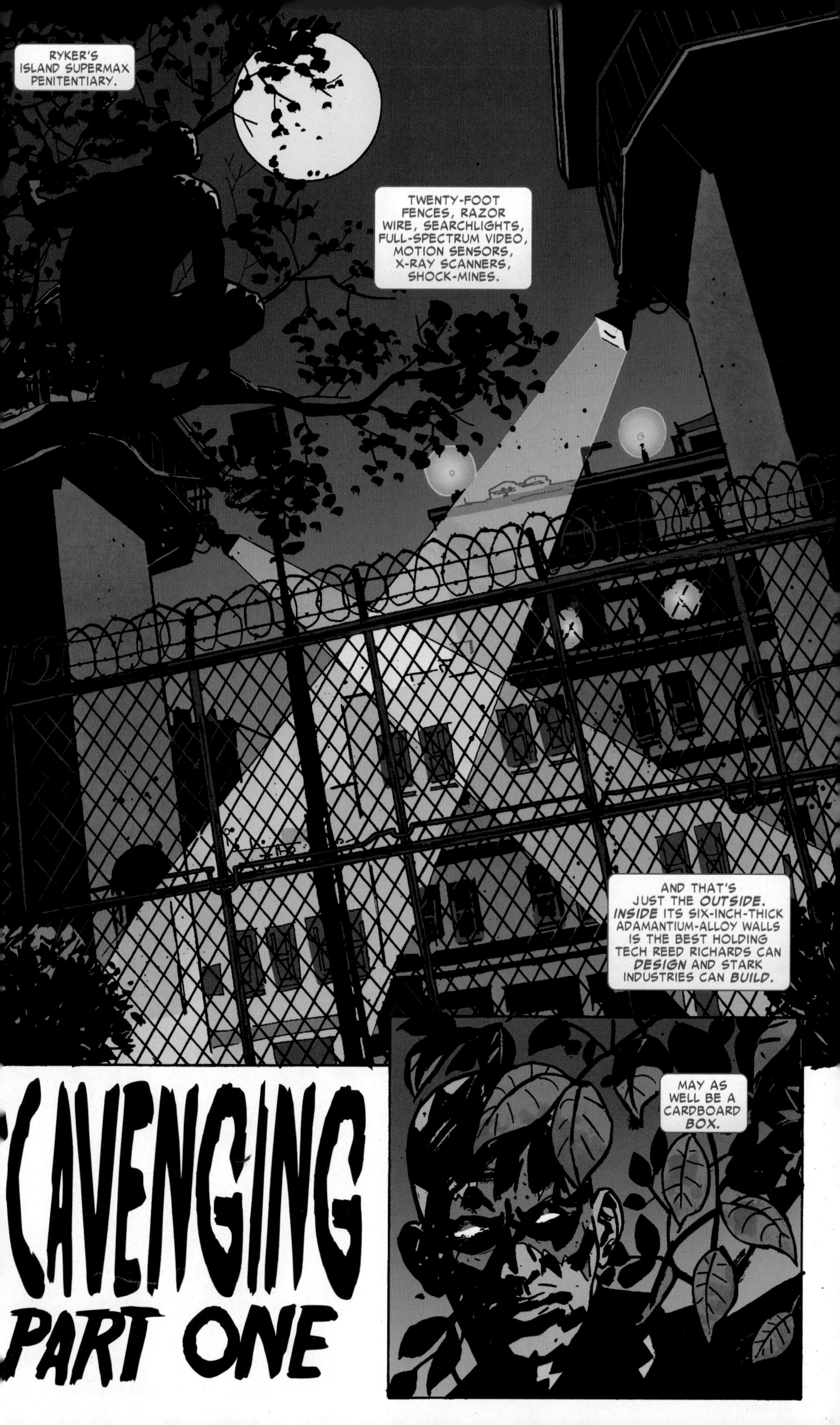

RYKER'S ISLAND SUPERMAX PENITENTIARY.
TWENTY-FOOT FENCES, RAZOR WIRE, SEARCHLIGHTS, FULL-SPECTRUM VIDEO, MOTION SENSORS, X-RAY SCANNERS, SHOCK-MINES.
AND THAT'S JUST THE *OUTSIDE*. *INSIDE* ITS SIX-INCH-THICK ADAMANTIUM-ALLOY WALLS IS THE BEST HOLDING TECH REED RICHARDS CAN *DESIGN* AND STARK INDUSTRIES CAN *BUILD*.
CAVENGING
PART ONE
MAY AS WELL BE A CARDBOARD *BOX*.

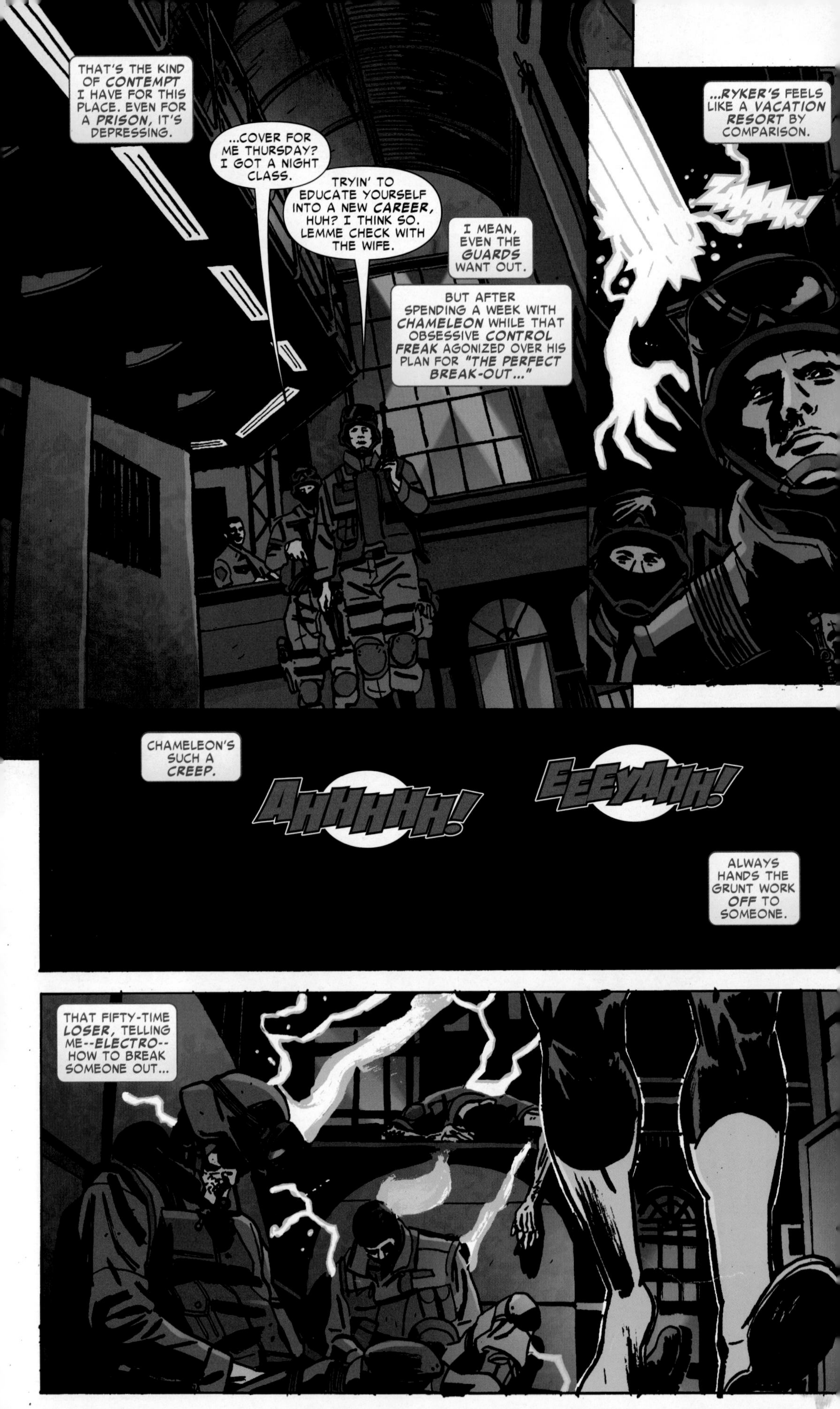
THAT'S THE KIND OF CONTEMPT I HAVE FOR THIS PLACE. EVEN FOR A PRISON, IT'S DEPRESSING.
...COVER FOR ME THURSDAY? I GOT A NIGHT CLASS.
TRYIN' TO EDUCATE YOURSELF INTO A NEW CAREER, HUH? I THINK SO. LEMME CHECK WITH THE WIFE.
I MEAN, EVEN THE GUARDS WANT OUT.
BUT AFTER SPENDING A WEEK WITH CHAMELEON WHILE THAT OBSESSIVE CONTROL FREAK AGONIZED OVER HIS PLAN FOR "THE PERFECT BREAK-OUT..."
...RYKER'S FEELS LIKE A VACATION RESORT BY COMPARISON.
ZAAAK!
CHAMELEON'S SUCH A CREEP.
AHHHHH!
EEEYAHH!
ALWAYS HANDS THE GRUNT WORK OFF TO SOMEONE.
THAT FIFTY-TIME LOSER, TELLING ME--ELECTRO--HOW TO BREAK SOMEONE OUT...

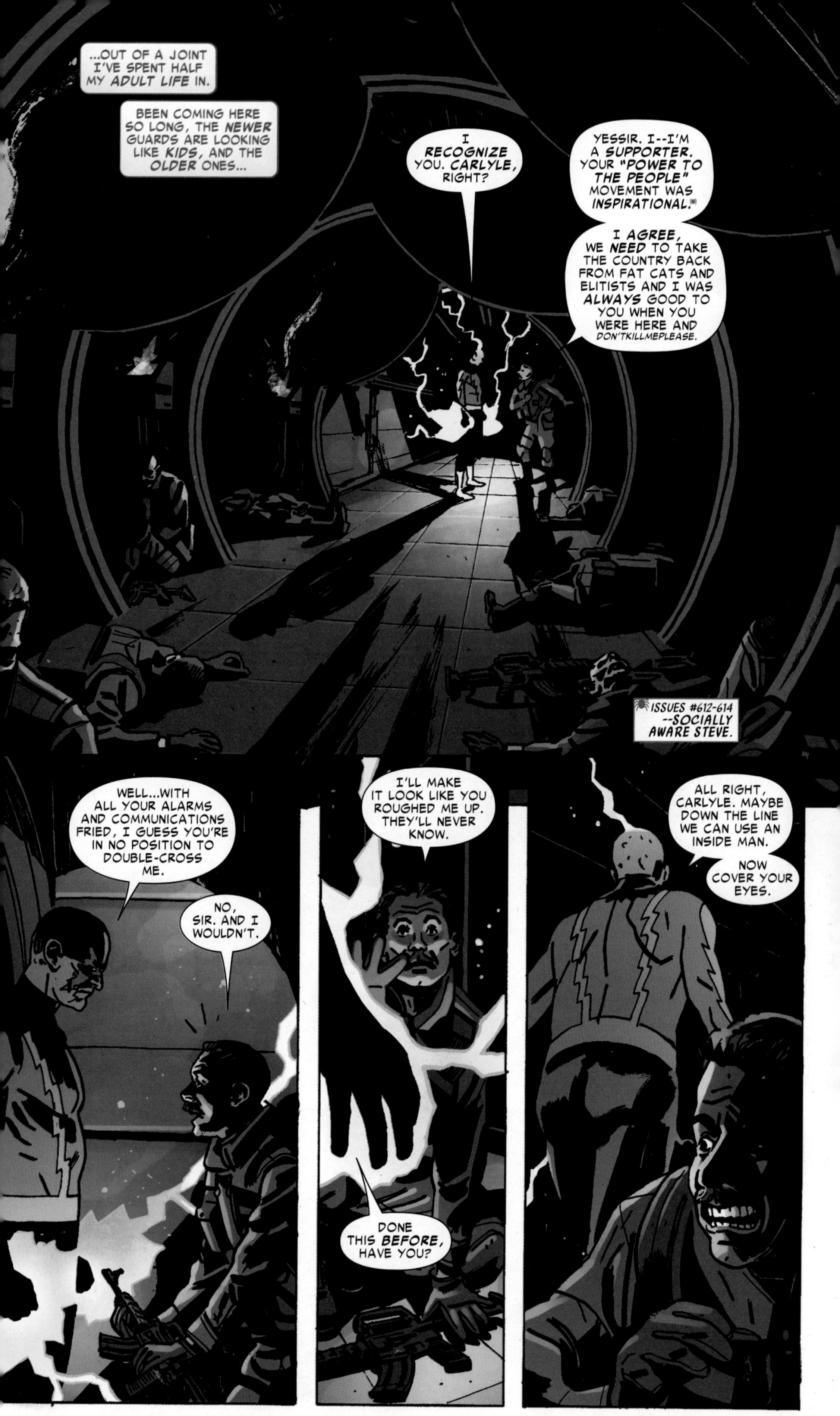
...OUT OF A JOINT I'VE SPENT HALF MY ADULT LIFE IN.
BEEN COMING HERE SO LONG, THE NEWER GUARDS ARE LOOKING LIKE KIDS, AND THE OLDER ONES...
I RECOGNIZE YOU. CARLYLE, RIGHT?
YESSIR. I--I'M A SUPPORTER. YOUR "POWER TO THE PEOPLE" MOVEMENT WAS INSPIRATIONAL.
I AGREE, WE NEED TO TAKE THE COUNTRY BACK FROM FAT CATS AND ELITISTS AND I WAS ALWAYS GOOD TO YOU WHEN YOU WERE HERE AND DON'TKILLMEPLEASE.
ISSUES #612-614 --SOCIALLY AWARE STEVE.
WELL...WITH ALL YOUR ALARMS AND COMMUNICATIONS FRIED, I GUESS YOU'RE IN NO POSITION TO DOUBLE-CROSS ME.
NO, SIR. AND I WOULDN'T.
I'LL MAKE IT LOOK LIKE YOU ROUGHED ME UP. THEY'LL NEVER KNOW.
DONE THIS BEFORE, HAVE YOU?
ALL RIGHT, CARLYLE. MAYBE DOWN THE LINE WE CAN USE AN INSIDE MAN.
NOW COVER YOUR EYES.

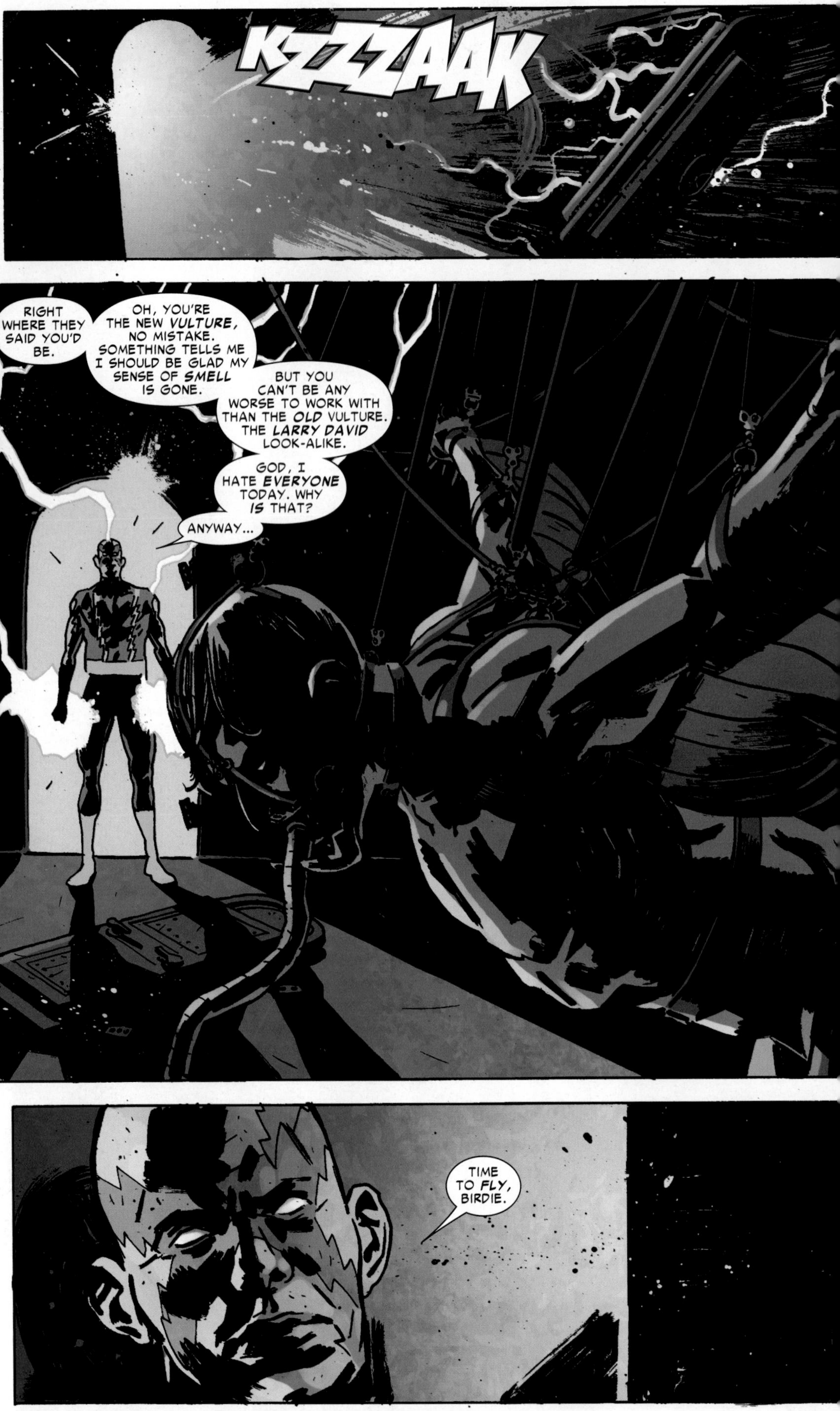
KZZZAAK
RIGHT WHERE THEY SAID YOU'D BE.
OH, YOU'RE THE NEW VULTURE, NO MISTAKE. SOMETHING TELLS ME I SHOULD BE GLAD MY SENSE OF SMELL IS GONE.
BUT YOU CAN'T BE ANY WORSE TO WORK WITH THAN THE OLD VULTURE. THE LARRY DAVID LOOK-ALIKE.
GOD, I HATE EVERYONE TODAY. WHY IS THAT?
ANYWAY...
TIME TO FLY, BIRDIE.

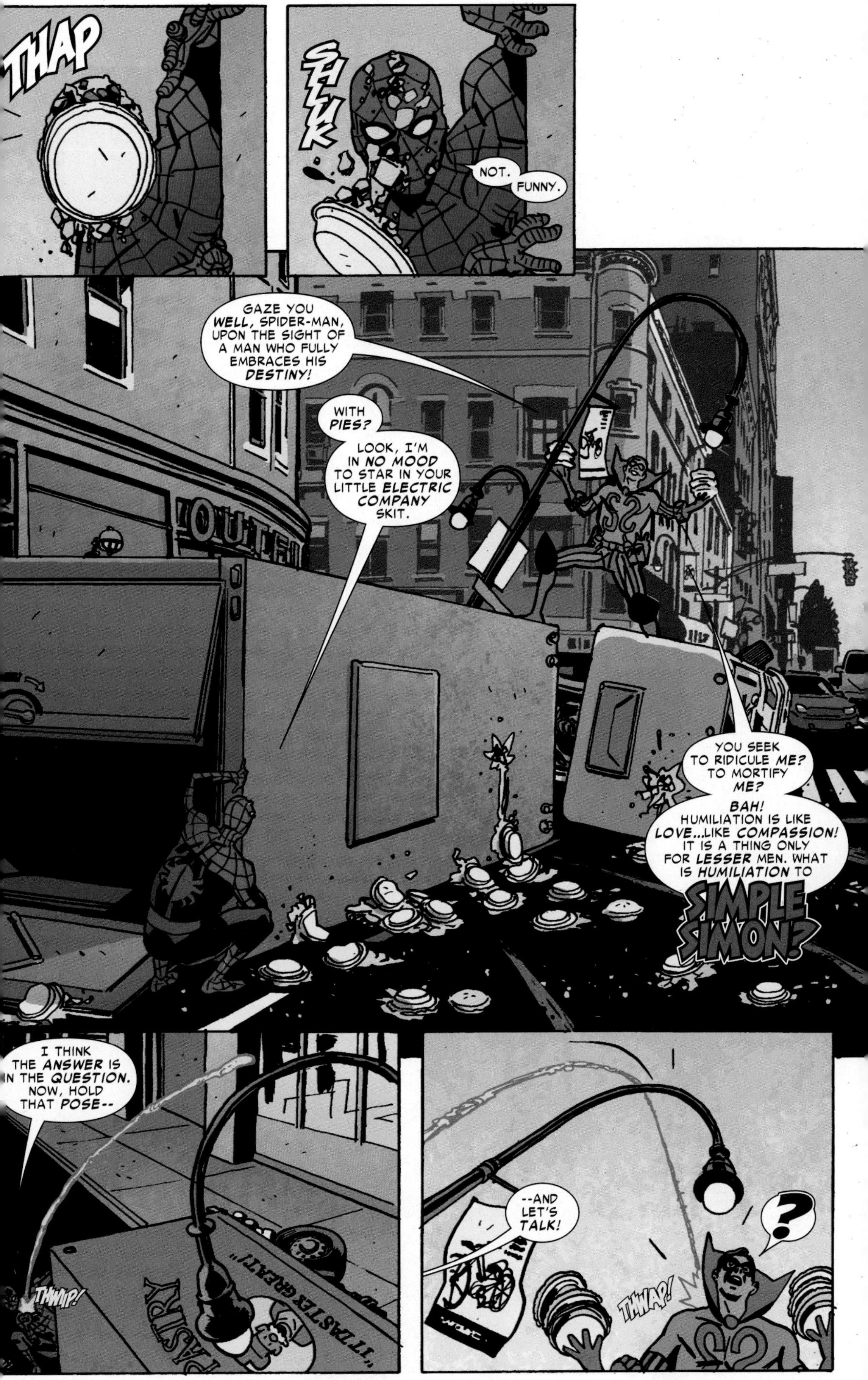
THAP
SHLUK
NOT.
FUNNY.
GAZE YOU *WELL*, SPIDER-MAN, UPON THE SIGHT OF A MAN WHO FULLY EMBRACES HIS *DESTINY!*
WITH *PIES?*
LOOK, I'M IN *NO MOOD* TO STAR IN YOUR LITTLE *ELECTRIC COMPANY* SKIT.
YOU SEEK TO RIDICULE *ME?* TO MORTIFY *ME?*
BAH! HUMILIATION IS LIKE *LOVE*...LIKE *COMPASSION!* IT IS A THING ONLY FOR *LESSER* MEN. WHAT IS *HUMILIATION* TO
SIMPLE SIMON?
I THINK THE *ANSWER* IS IN THE *QUESTION*. NOW, HOLD THAT *POSE*--
THWIP!
"IT TASTES GREAT!"
PASTRY
--AND LET'S *TALK!*
THWAP!
?

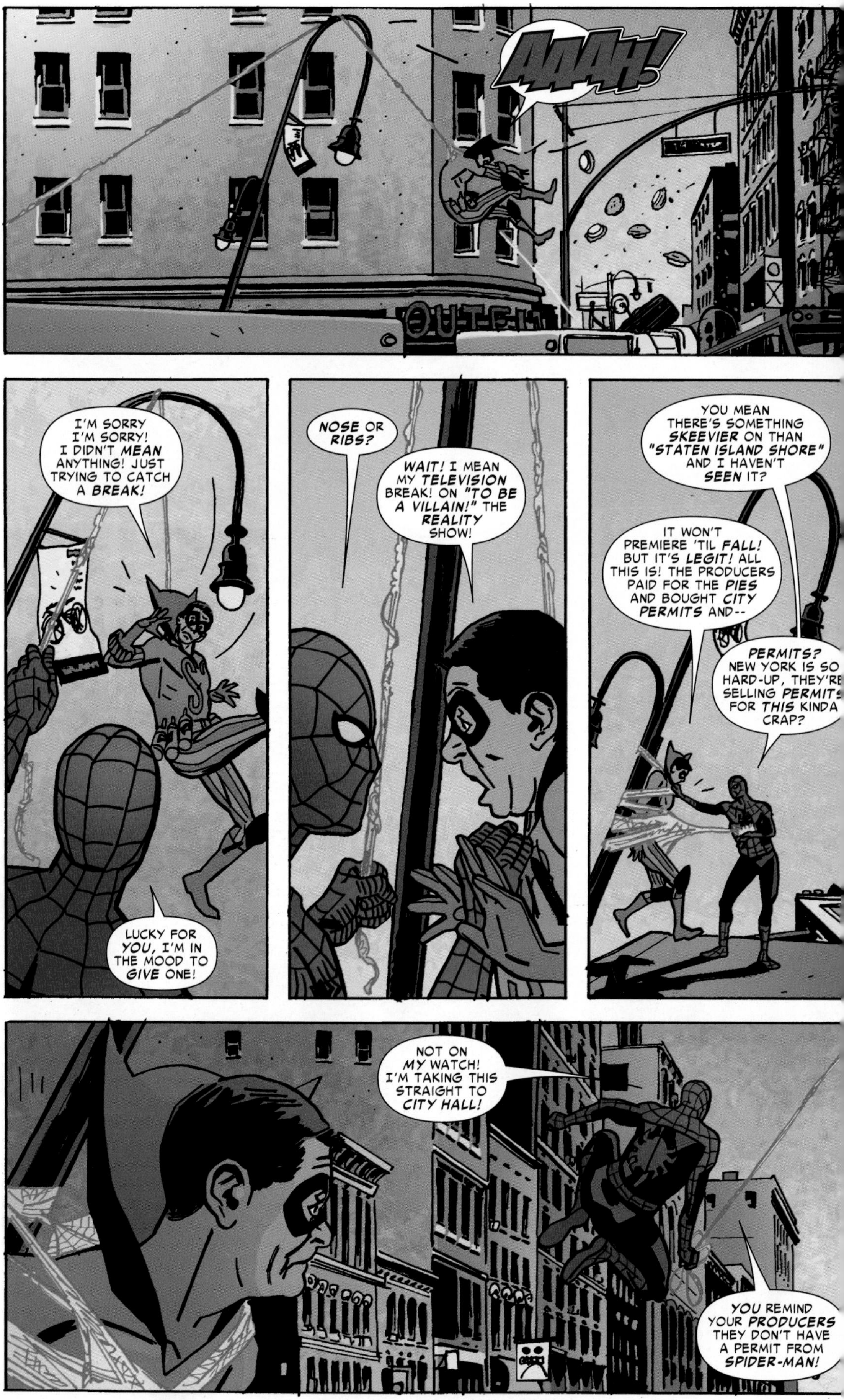
AAAH!
I'M SORRY I'M SORRY! I DIDN'T MEAN ANYTHING! JUST TRYING TO CATCH A BREAK!
LUCKY FOR YOU, I'M IN THE MOOD TO GIVE ONE!
NOSE OR RIBS?
WAIT! I MEAN MY TELEVISION BREAK! ON "TO BE A VILLAIN!" THE REALITY SHOW!
YOU MEAN THERE'S SOMETHING SKEEVIER ON THAN "STATEN ISLAND SHORE" AND I HAVEN'T SEEN IT?
IT WON'T PREMIERE 'TIL FALL! BUT IT'S LEGIT! ALL THIS IS! THE PRODUCERS PAID FOR THE PIES AND BOUGHT CITY PERMITS AND--
PERMITS? NEW YORK IS SO HARD-UP, THEY'RE SELLING PERMITS FOR THIS KINDA CRAP?
NOT ON MY WATCH! I'M TAKING THIS STRAIGHT TO CITY HALL!
YOU REMIND YOUR PRODUCERS THEY DON'T HAVE A PERMIT FROM SPIDER-MAN!

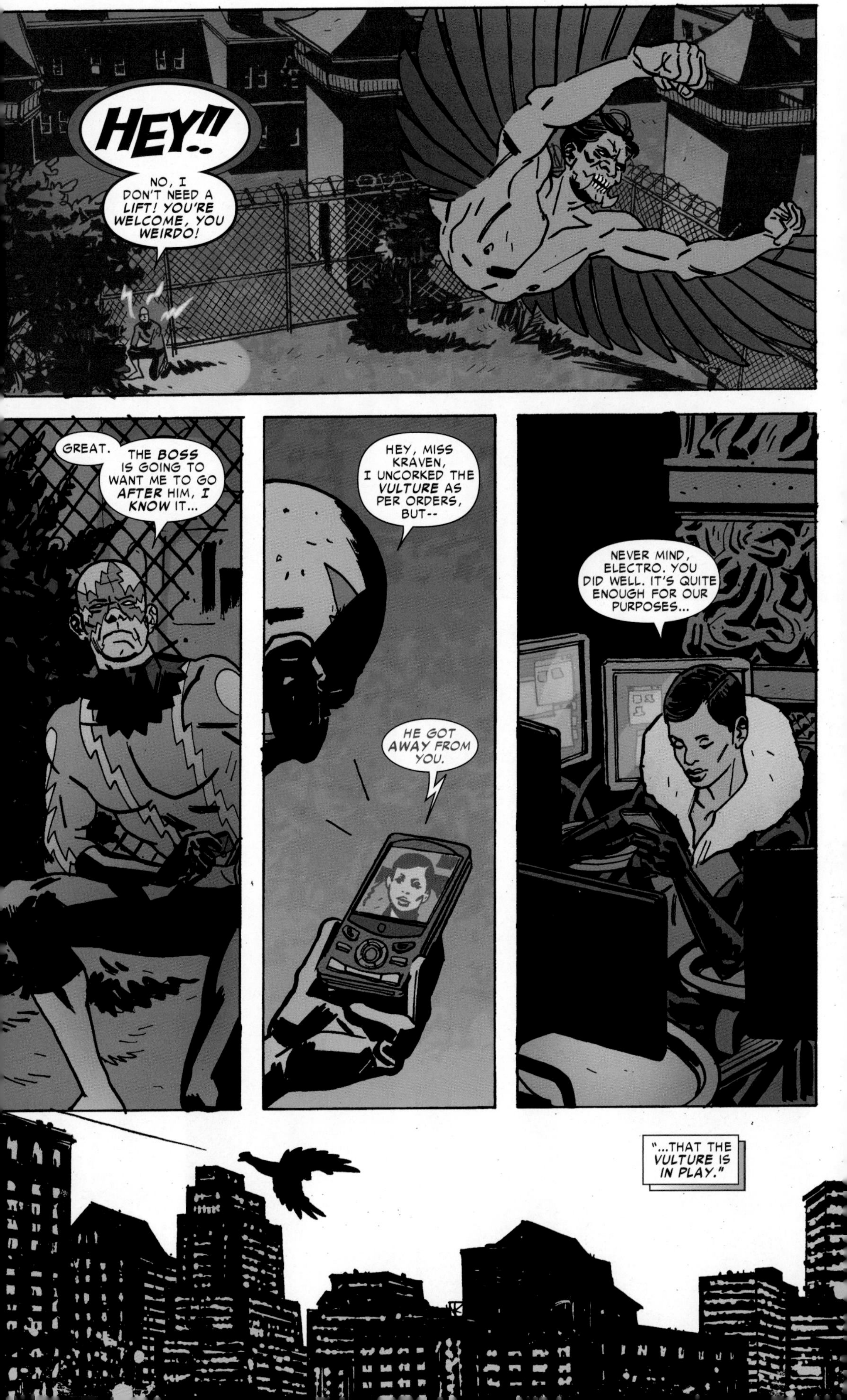
HEY!!
NO, I DON'T NEED A LIFT! YOU'RE WELCOME, YOU WEIRDO!
GREAT.
THE BOSS IS GOING TO WANT ME TO GO AFTER HIM, I KNOW IT...
HEY, MISS KRAVEN, I UNCORKED THE VULTURE AS PER ORDERS, BUT--
HE GOT AWAY FROM YOU.
NEVER MIND, ELECTRO. YOU DID WELL. IT'S QUITE ENOUGH FOR OUR PURPOSES...
"...THAT THE VULTURE IS IN PLAY."

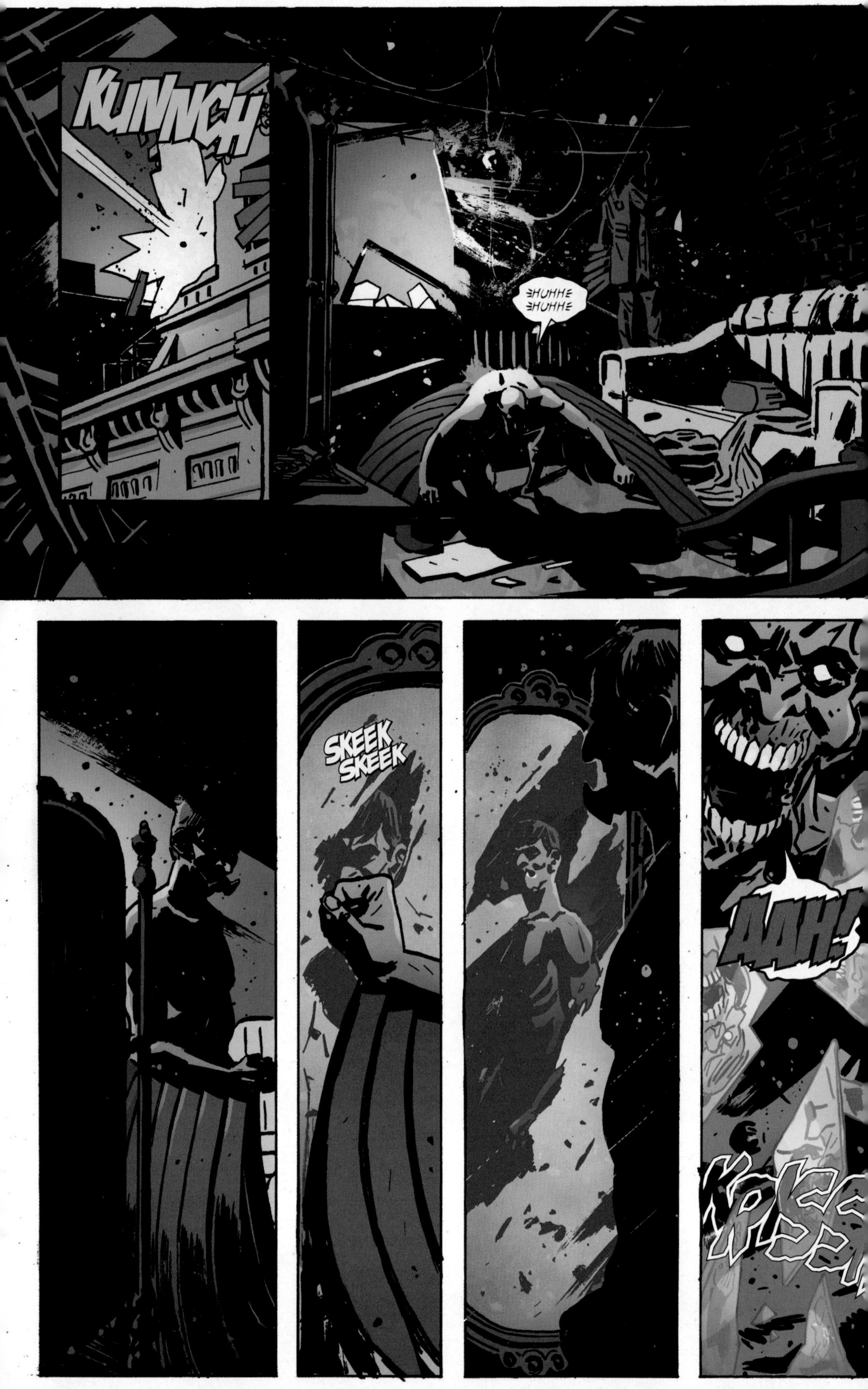
KUNNCH
HUHH HUHH
SKEEK SKEEK
AAH!

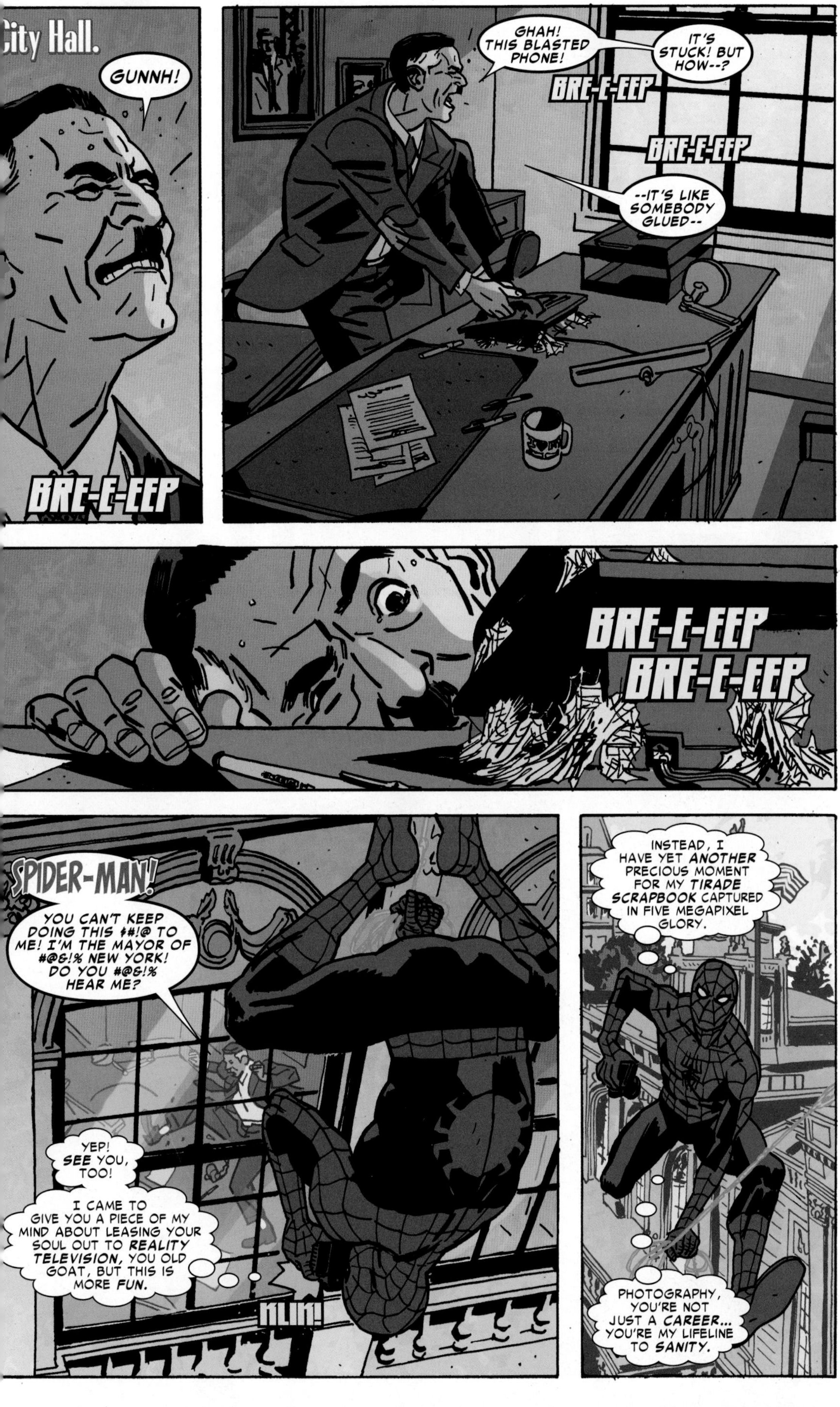
City Hall.
GUNNH!
BRE-E-EEP
GHAH! THIS BLASTED PHONE!
BRE-E-EEP
IT'S STUCK! BUT HOW--?
BRE-E-EEP
--IT'S LIKE SOMEBODY GLUED--
BRE-E-EEP
BRE-E-EEP
SPIDER-MAN!
YOU CAN'T KEEP DOING THIS $#!@ TO ME! I'M THE MAYOR OF #@&!% NEW YORK! DO YOU #@&!% HEAR ME?
YEP! SEE YOU, TOO!
I CAME TO GIVE YOU A PIECE OF MY MIND ABOUT LEASING YOUR SOUL OUT TO REALITY TELEVISION, YOU OLD GOAT, BUT THIS IS MORE FUN.
KLIK!
INSTEAD, I HAVE YET ANOTHER PRECIOUS MOMENT FOR MY TIRADE SCRAPBOOK CAPTURED IN FIVE MEGAPIXEL GLORY.
PHOTOGRAPHY, YOU'RE NOT JUST A CAREER... YOU'RE MY LIFELINE TO SANITY.

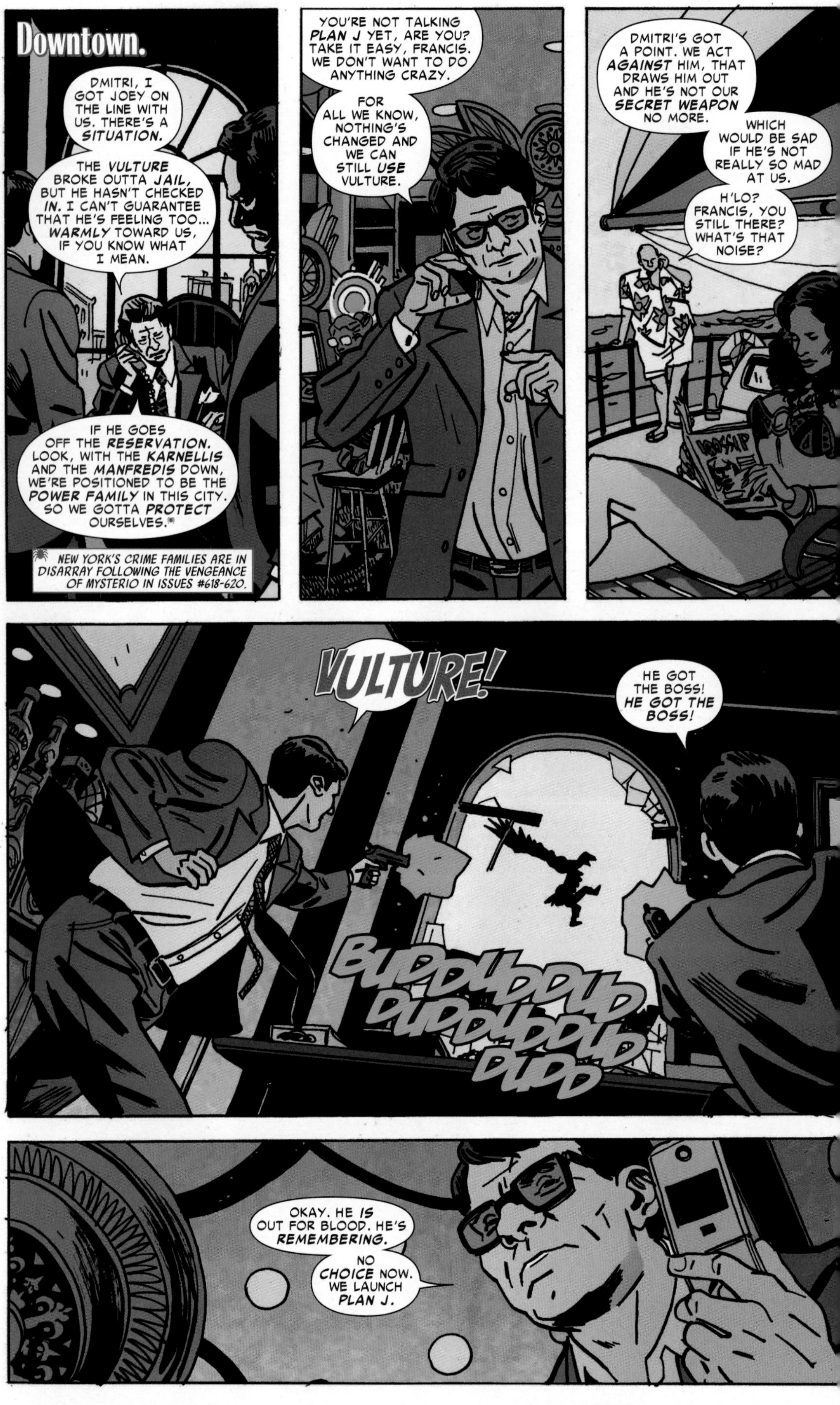
Downtown.
DMITRI, I GOT JOEY ON THE LINE WITH US. THERE'S A SITUATION.
THE VULTURE BROKE OUTTA JAIL, BUT HE HASN'T CHECKED IN. I CAN'T GUARANTEE THAT HE'S FEELING TOO... WARMLY TOWARD US, IF YOU KNOW WHAT I MEAN.
IF HE GOES OFF THE RESERVATION. LOOK, WITH THE KARNELLIS AND THE MANFREDIS DOWN, WE'RE POSITIONED TO BE THE POWER FAMILY IN THIS CITY. SO WE GOTTA PROTECT OURSELVES.
NEW YORK'S CRIME FAMILIES ARE IN DISARRAY FOLLOWING THE VENGEANCE OF MYSTERIO IN ISSUES #618-620.
YOU'RE NOT TALKING PLAN J YET, ARE YOU? TAKE IT EASY, FRANCIS. WE DON'T WANT TO DO ANYTHING CRAZY.
FOR ALL WE KNOW, NOTHING'S CHANGED AND WE CAN STILL USE VULTURE.
DMITRI'S GOT A POINT. WE ACT AGAINST HIM, THAT DRAWS HIM OUT AND HE'S NOT OUR SECRET WEAPON NO MORE.
WHICH WOULD BE SAD IF HE'S NOT REALLY SO MAD AT US.
H'LO? FRANCIS, YOU STILL THERE? WHAT'S THAT NOISE?
VULTURE!
HE GOT THE BOSS! HE GOT THE BOSS!
BUDDUDDUD DUDDUDDUD DUDD
OKAY. HE IS OUT FOR BLOOD. HE'S REMEMBERING.
NO CHOICE NOW. WE LAUNCH PLAN J.

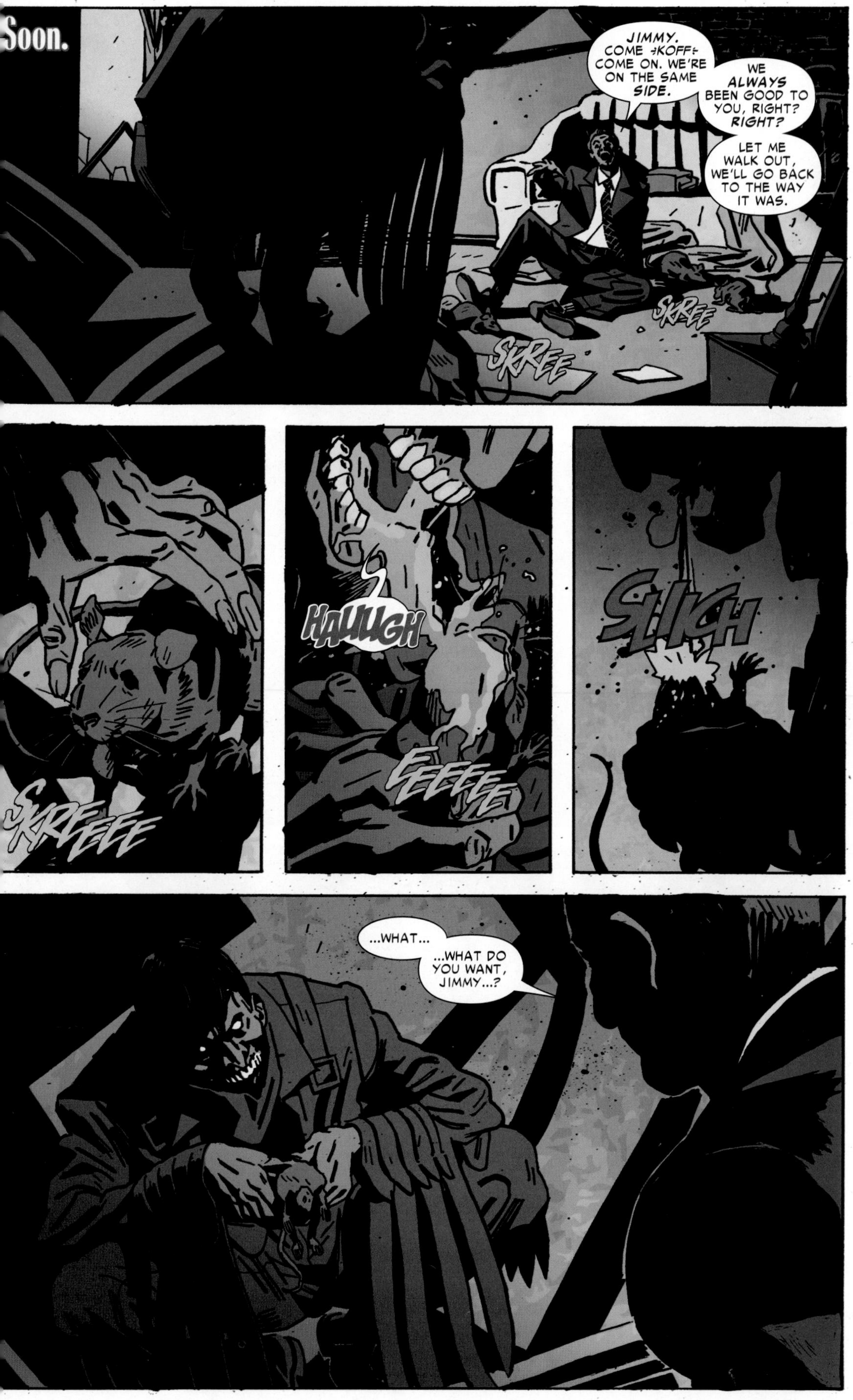
Soon.
JIMMY. COME ≠KOFF≠ COME ON. WE'RE ON THE SAME SIDE.
WE ALWAYS BEEN GOOD TO YOU, RIGHT? RIGHT?
LET ME WALK OUT, WE'LL GO BACK TO THE WAY IT WAS.
SKREE
SKREE
SKREEEEE
HAUUGH
EEEEEE
SLICH
...WHAT...
...WHAT DO YOU WANT, JIMMY...?

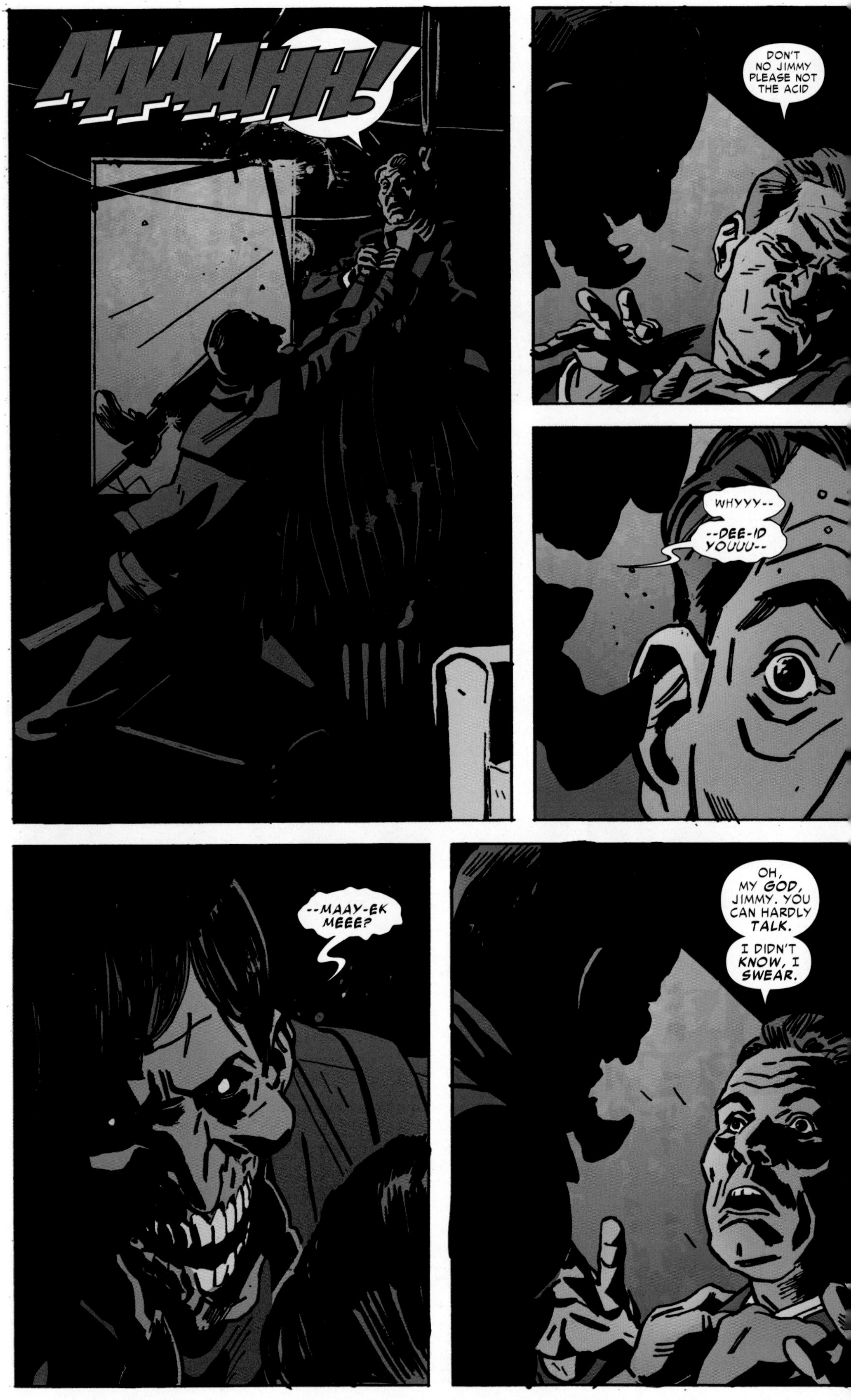
AAAAAHH!
DON'T NO JIMMY PLEASE NOT THE ACID
WHYYY--
--DEE-ID YOUUU--
--MAAY-EK MEEE?
OH, MY GOD, JIMMY. YOU CAN HARDLY TALK.
I DIDN'T KNOW, I SWEAR.

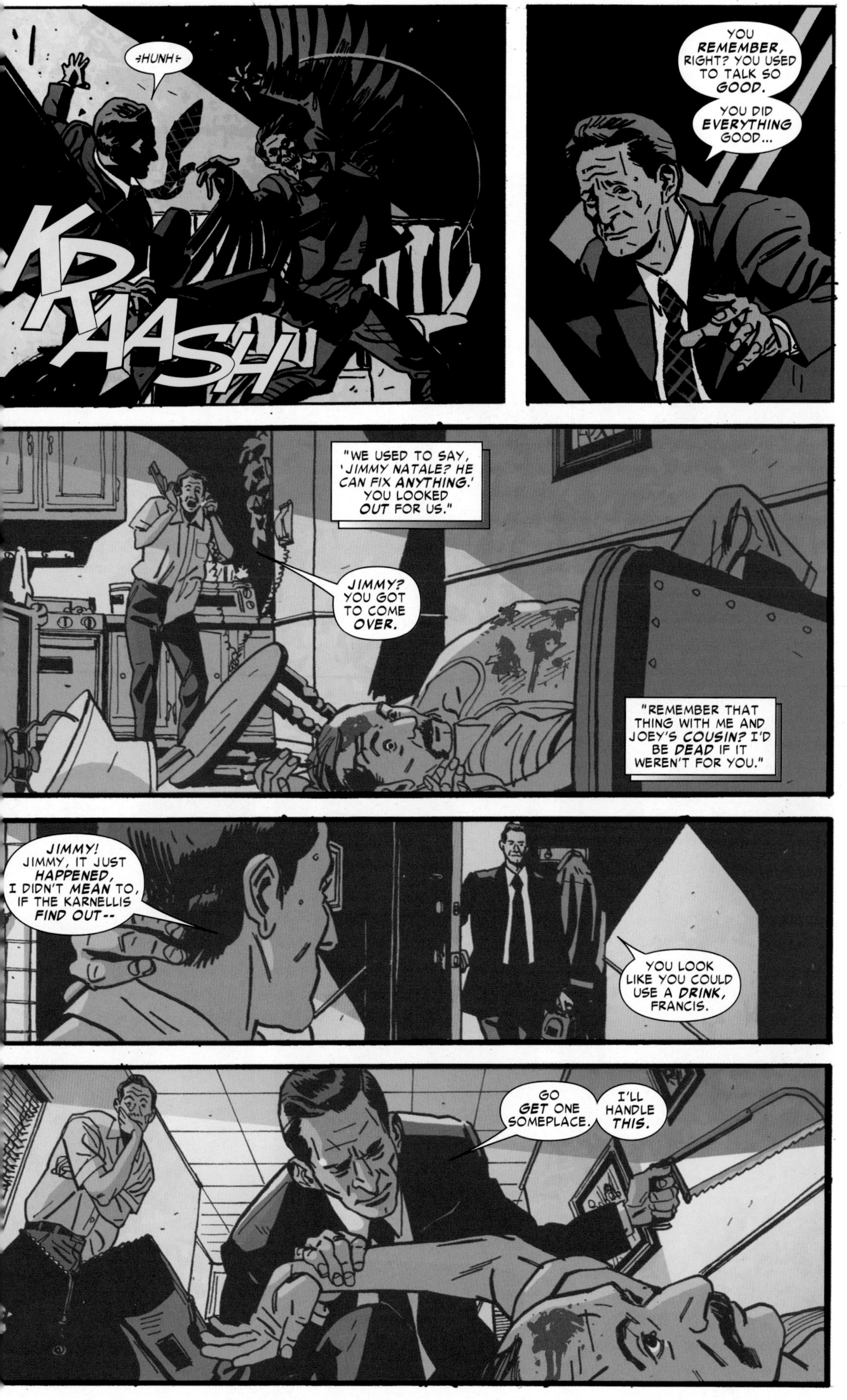

KRAASH
HUNH
YOU REMEMBER, RIGHT? YOU USED TO TALK SO GOOD.
YOU DID EVERYTHING GOOD...
"WE USED TO SAY, 'JIMMY NATALE? HE CAN FIX ANYTHING.' YOU LOOKED OUT FOR US."
JIMMY? YOU GOT TO COME OVER.
"REMEMBER THAT THING WITH ME AND JOEY'S COUSIN? I'D BE DEAD IF IT WEREN'T FOR YOU."
JIMMY! JIMMY, IT JUST HAPPENED, I DIDN'T MEAN TO, IF THE KARNELLIS FIND OUT--
YOU LOOK LIKE YOU COULD USE A DRINK, FRANCIS.
GO GET ONE SOMEPLACE.
I'LL HANDLE THIS.

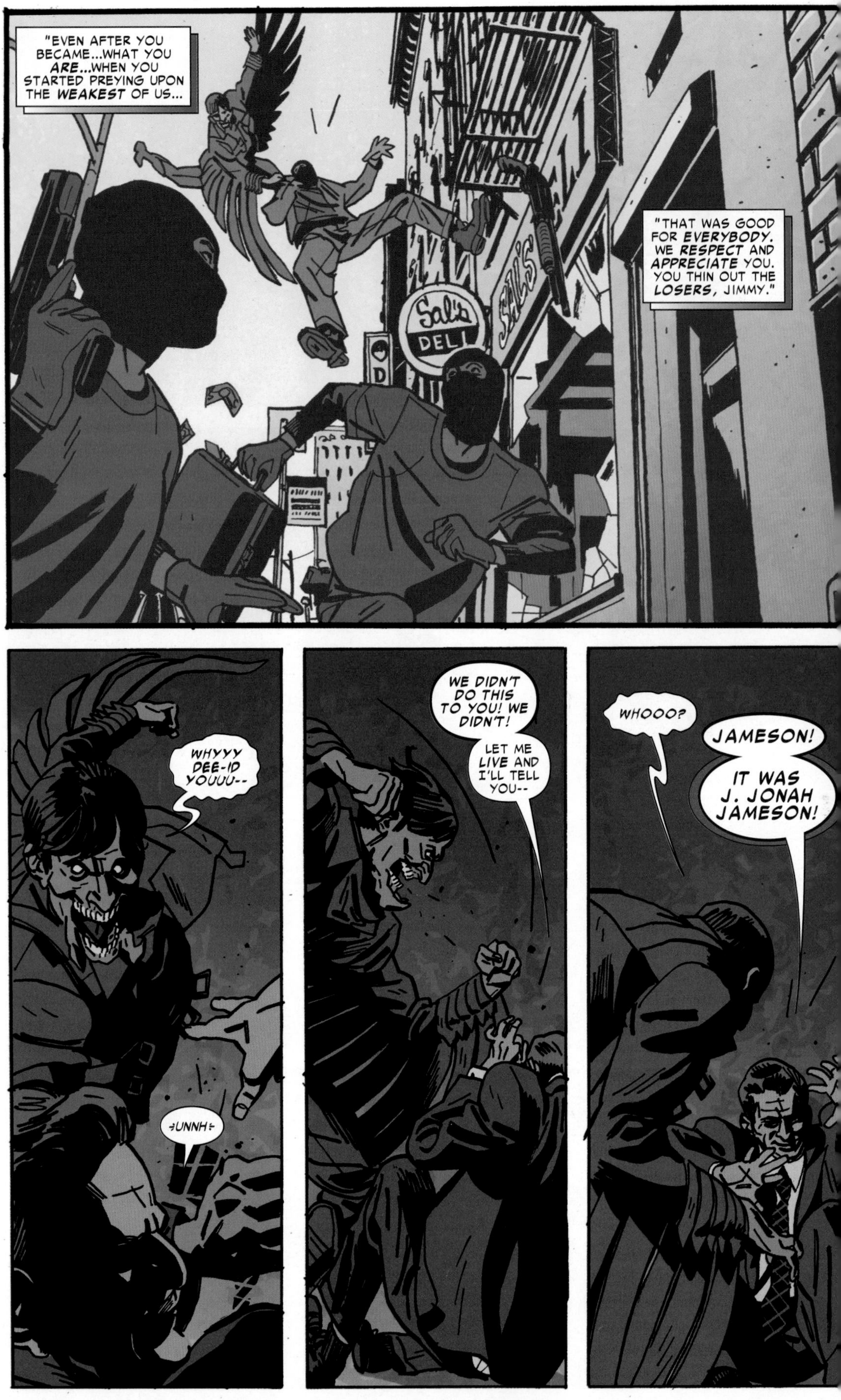
"EVEN AFTER YOU BECAME...WHAT YOU ARE...WHEN YOU STARTED PREYING UPON THE WEAKEST OF US...
"THAT WAS GOOD FOR EVERYBODY. WE RESPECT AND APPRECIATE YOU. YOU THIN OUT THE LOSERS, JIMMY."
Sal's DELI
SAL'S
WHYYY DEE-ID YOUUU--
UNNH
WE DIDN'T DO THIS TO YOU! WE DIDN'T!
LET ME LIVE AND I'LL TELL YOU--
WHOOO?
JAMESON!
IT WAS J. JONAH JAMESON!

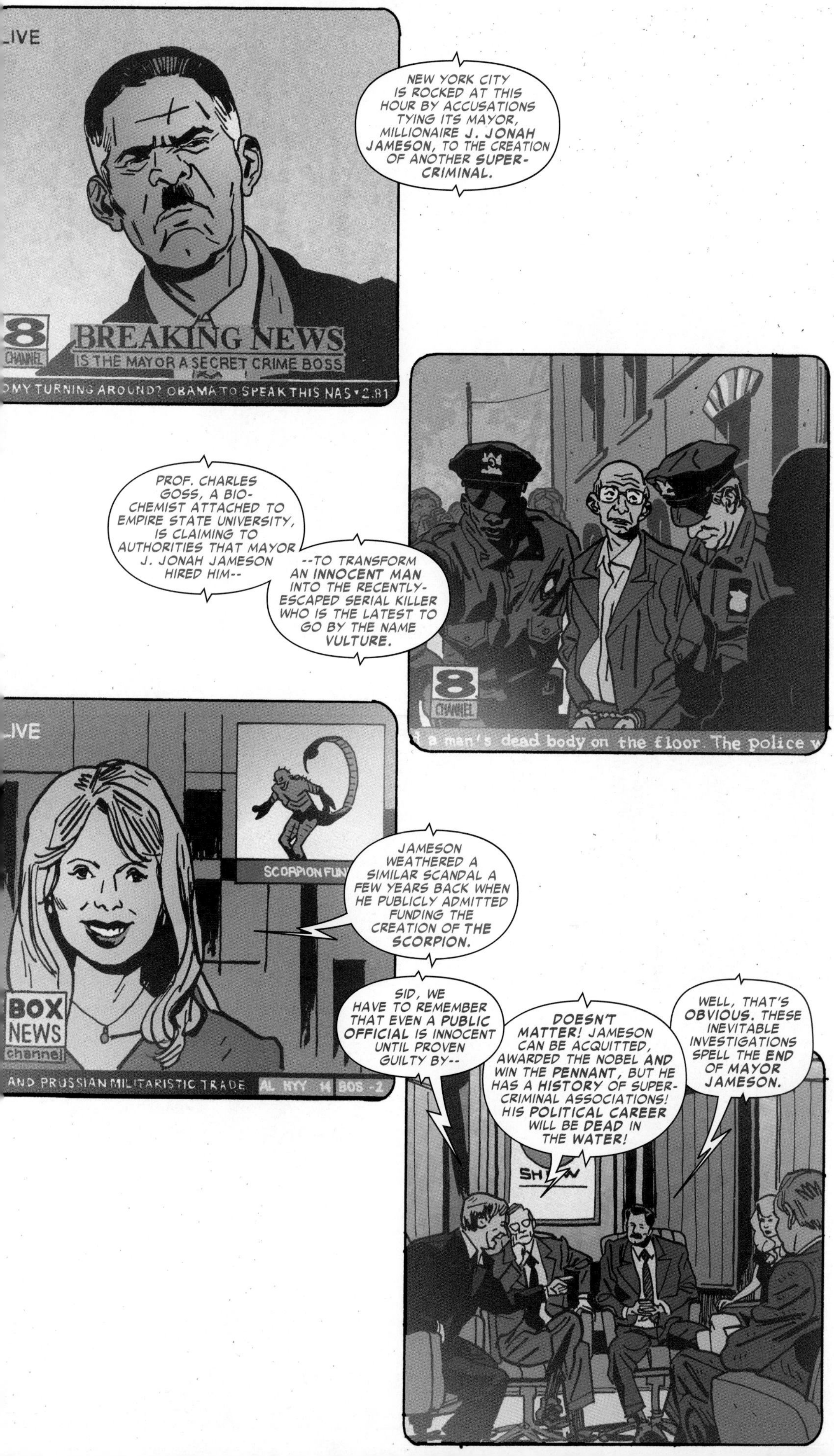
LIVE
NEW YORK CITY IS ROCKED AT THIS HOUR BY ACCUSATIONS TYING ITS MAYOR, MILLIONAIRE J. JONAH JAMESON, TO THE CREATION OF ANOTHER SUPER-CRIMINAL.
8 CHANNEL
BREAKING NEWS
IS THE MAYOR A SECRET CRIME BOSS
OMY TURNING AROUND? OBAMA TO SPEAK THIS NAS • 2.81
PROF. CHARLES GOSS, A BIO-CHEMIST ATTACHED TO EMPIRE STATE UNIVERSITY, IS CLAIMING TO AUTHORITIES THAT MAYOR J. JONAH JAMESON HIRED HIM--
--TO TRANSFORM AN INNOCENT MAN INTO THE RECENTLY-ESCAPED SERIAL KILLER WHO IS THE LATEST TO GO BY THE NAME VULTURE.
8 CHANNEL
d a man's dead body on the floor. The police w
LIVE
SCORPION FUN
JAMESON WEATHERED A SIMILAR SCANDAL A FEW YEARS BACK WHEN HE PUBLICLY ADMITTED FUNDING THE CREATION OF THE SCORPION.
BOX NEWS channel
AND PRUSSIAN MILITARISTIC TRADE AL NYY 14 BOS -2
SID, WE HAVE TO REMEMBER THAT EVEN A PUBLIC OFFICIAL IS INNOCENT UNTIL PROVEN GUILTY BY--
DOESN'T MATTER! JAMESON CAN BE ACQUITTED, AWARDED THE NOBEL AND WIN THE PENNANT, BUT HE HAS A HISTORY OF SUPER-CRIMINAL ASSOCIATIONS! HIS POLITICAL CAREER WILL BE DEAD IN THE WATER!
WELL, THAT'S OBVIOUS. THESE INEVITABLE INVESTIGATIONS SPELL THE END OF MAYOR JAMESON.

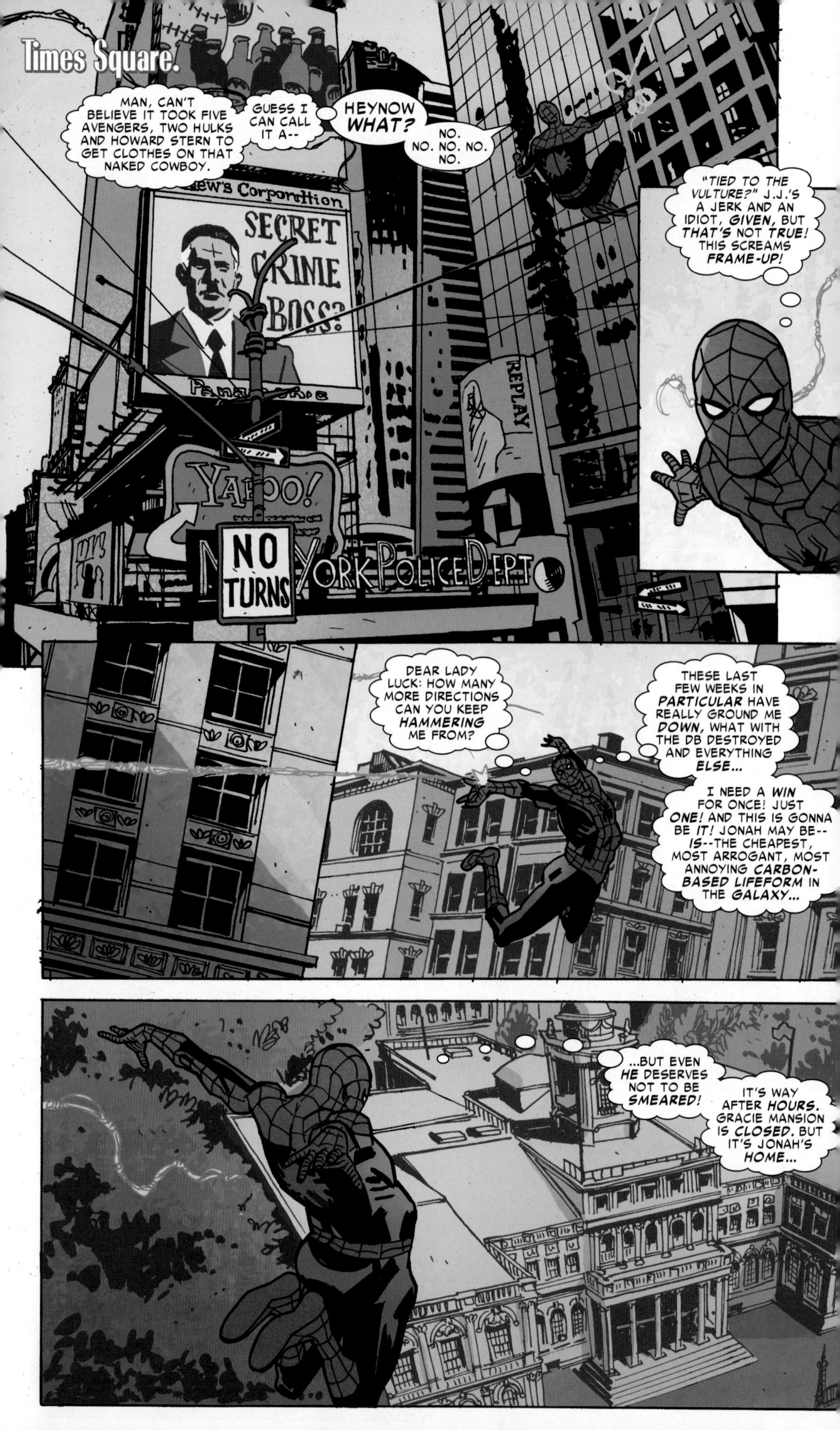
Times Square.
MAN, CAN'T BELIEVE IT TOOK FIVE AVENGERS, TWO HULKS AND HOWARD STERN TO GET CLOTHES ON THAT NAKED COWBOY.
GUESS I CAN CALL IT A--
HEYNOW WHAT?
NO. NO. NO. NO. NO.
SECRET CRIME BOSS?
YAHOO!
NO TURNS
YORK POLICE DEPT
REPLAY
"TIED TO THE VULTURE?" J.J.'S A JERK AND AN IDIOT, GIVEN, BUT THAT'S NOT TRUE! THIS SCREAMS FRAME-UP!
DEAR LADY LUCK: HOW MANY MORE DIRECTIONS CAN YOU KEEP HAMMERING ME FROM?
THESE LAST FEW WEEKS IN PARTICULAR HAVE REALLY GROUND ME DOWN, WHAT WITH THE DB DESTROYED AND EVERYTHING ELSE...
I NEED A WIN FOR ONCE! JUST ONE! AND THIS IS GONNA BE IT! JONAH MAY BE-- IS--THE CHEAPEST, MOST ARROGANT, MOST ANNOYING CARBON-BASED LIFEFORM IN THE GALAXY...
...BUT EVEN HE DESERVES NOT TO BE SMEARED!
IT'S WAY AFTER HOURS. GRACIE MANSION IS CLOSED. BUT IT'S JONAH'S HOME...

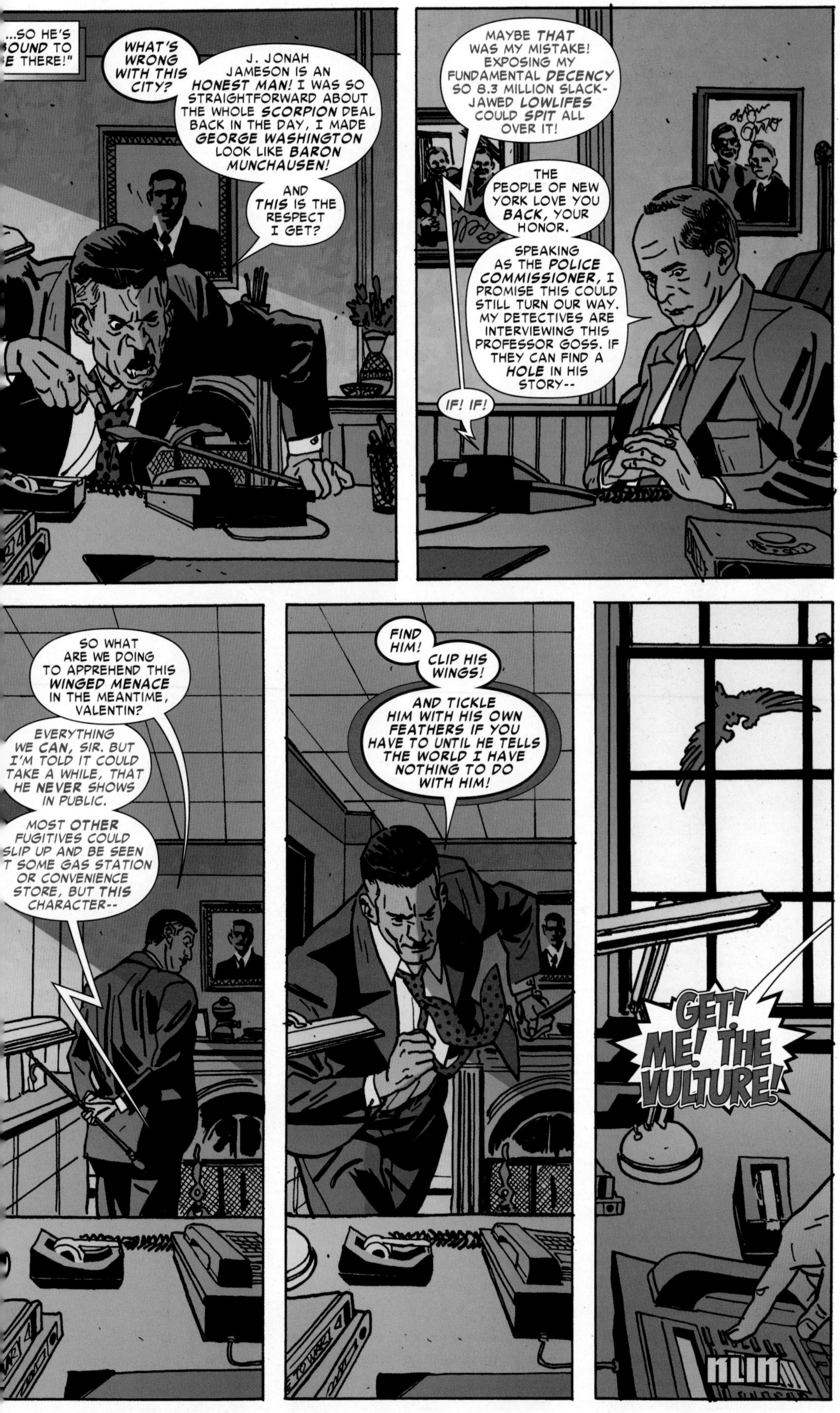
...SO HE'S BOUND TO BE THERE!"
WHAT'S WRONG WITH THIS CITY?
J. JONAH JAMESON IS AN HONEST MAN! I WAS SO STRAIGHTFORWARD ABOUT THE WHOLE SCORPION DEAL BACK IN THE DAY, I MADE GEORGE WASHINGTON LOOK LIKE BARON MUNCHAUSEN!
AND THIS IS THE RESPECT I GET?
MAYBE THAT WAS MY MISTAKE! EXPOSING MY FUNDAMENTAL DECENCY SO 8.3 MILLION SLACK-JAWED LOWLIFES COULD SPIT ALL OVER IT!
THE PEOPLE OF NEW YORK LOVE YOU BACK, YOUR HONOR.
SPEAKING AS THE POLICE COMMISSIONER, I PROMISE THIS COULD STILL TURN OUR WAY. MY DETECTIVES ARE INTERVIEWING THIS PROFESSOR GOSS. IF THEY CAN FIND A HOLE IN HIS STORY--
IF! IF!
SO WHAT ARE WE DOING TO APPREHEND THIS WINGED MENACE IN THE MEANTIME, VALENTIN?
EVERYTHING WE CAN, SIR. BUT I'M TOLD IT COULD TAKE A WHILE, THAT HE NEVER SHOWS IN PUBLIC.
MOST OTHER FUGITIVES COULD SLIP UP AND BE SEEN AT SOME GAS STATION OR CONVENIENCE STORE, BUT THIS CHARACTER--
FIND HIM!
CLIP HIS WINGS!
AND TICKLE HIM WITH HIS OWN FEATHERS IF YOU HAVE TO UNTIL HE TELLS THE WORLD I HAVE NOTHING TO DO WITH HIM!
GET! ME! THE VULTURE!
NLIN

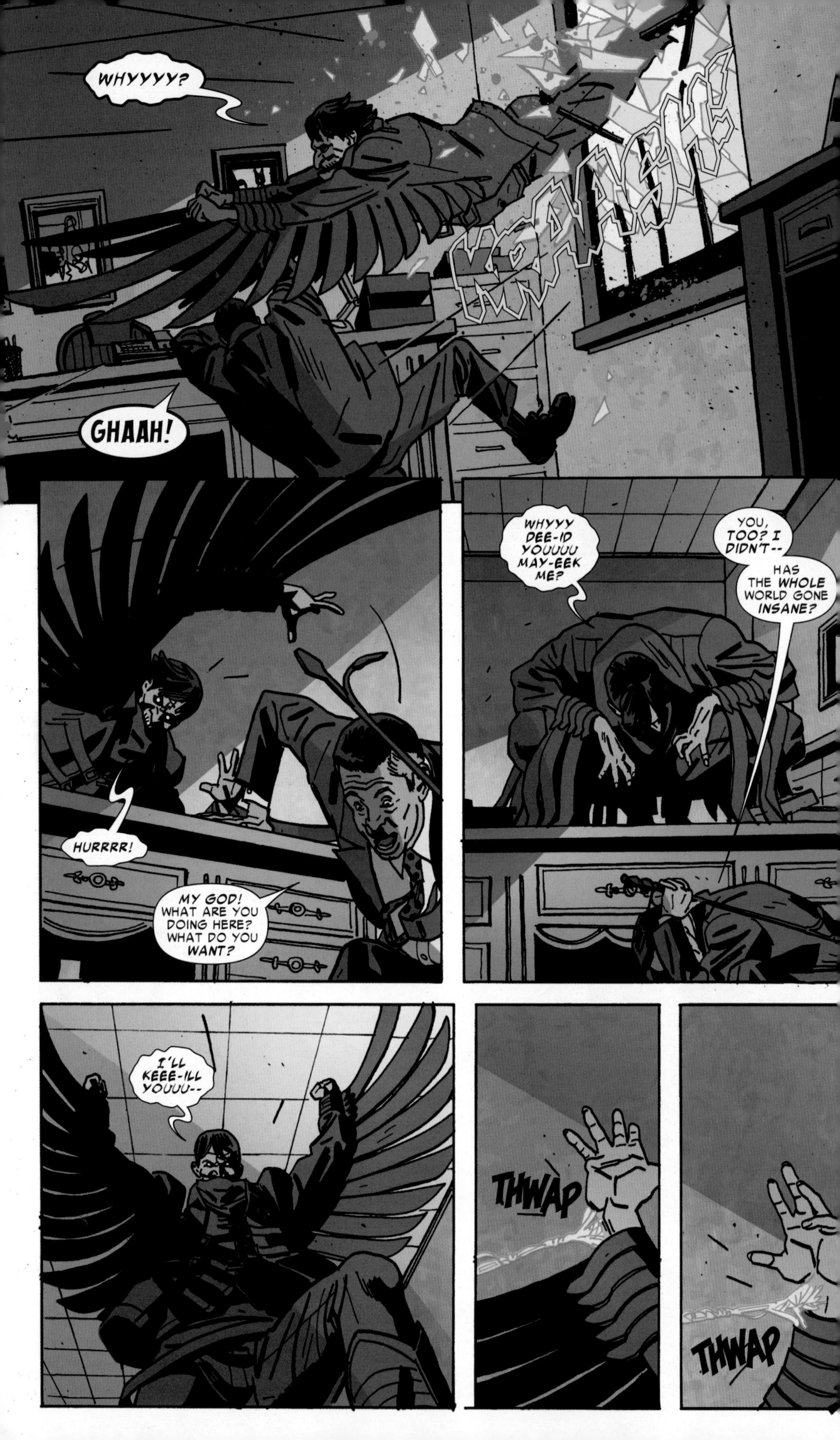
WHYYYY?
KRAASH
GHAAH!
HURRRR!
MY GOD! WHAT ARE YOU DOING HERE? WHAT DO YOU WANT?
WHYYY DEE-ID YOUUUU MAY-EEK ME?
YOU, TOO? I DIDN'T--
HAS THE WHOLE WORLD GONE INSANE?
I'LL KEEE-ILL YOUUU--
THWAP
THWAP

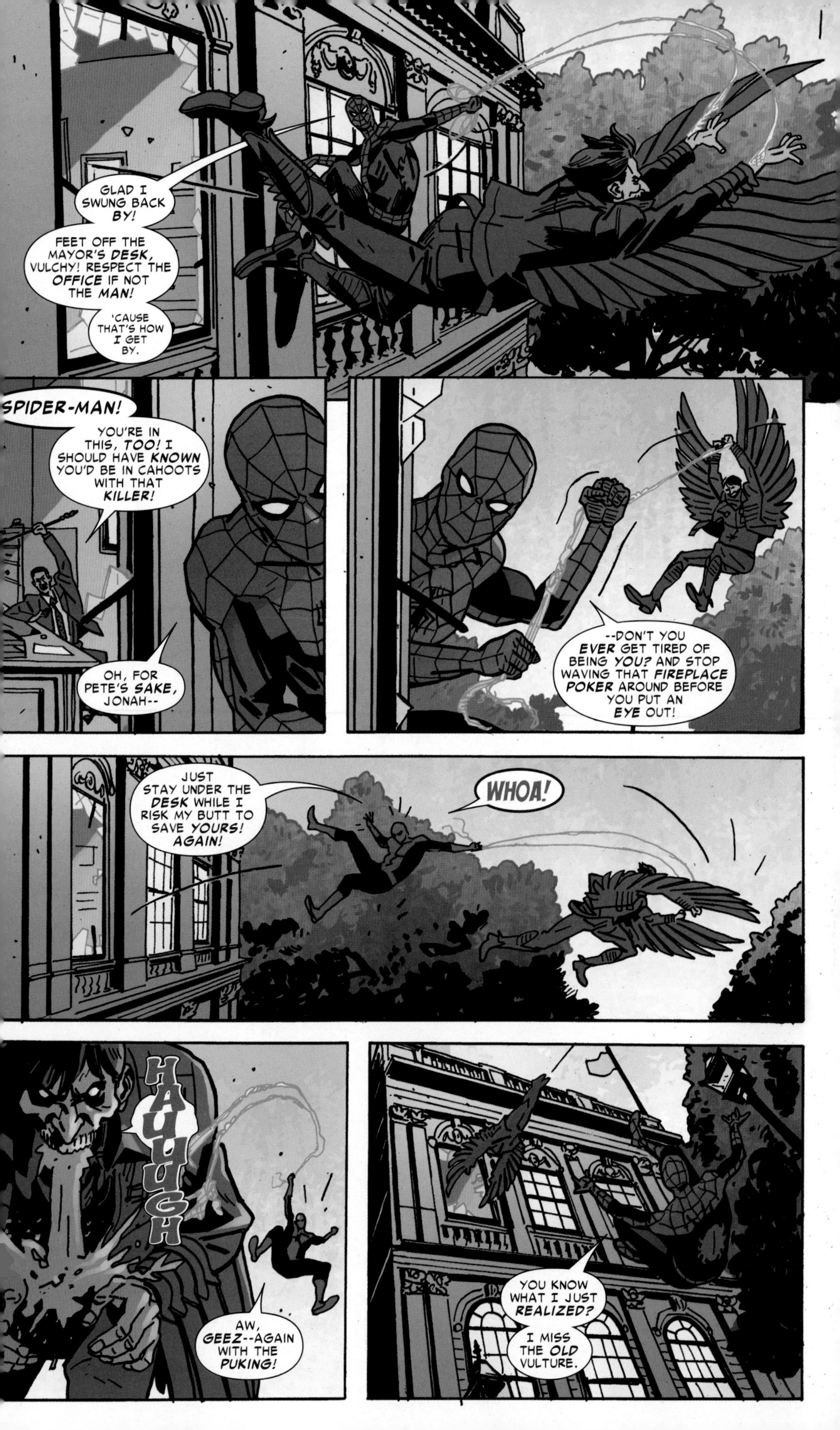
GLAD I SWUNG BACK BY!
FEET OFF THE MAYOR'S DESK, VULCHY! RESPECT THE OFFICE IF NOT THE MAN!
'CAUSE THAT'S HOW I GET BY.
SPIDER-MAN!
YOU'RE IN THIS, TOO! I SHOULD HAVE KNOWN YOU'D BE IN CAHOOTS WITH THAT KILLER!
OH, FOR PETE'S SAKE, JONAH--
--DON'T YOU EVER GET TIRED OF BEING YOU? AND STOP WAVING THAT FIREPLACE POKER AROUND BEFORE YOU PUT AN EYE OUT!
JUST STAY UNDER THE DESK WHILE I RISK MY BUTT TO SAVE YOURS! AGAIN!
WHOA!
HAUUGH
AW, GEEZ--AGAIN WITH THE PUKING!
YOU KNOW WHAT I JUST REALIZED?
I MISS THE OLD VULTURE.

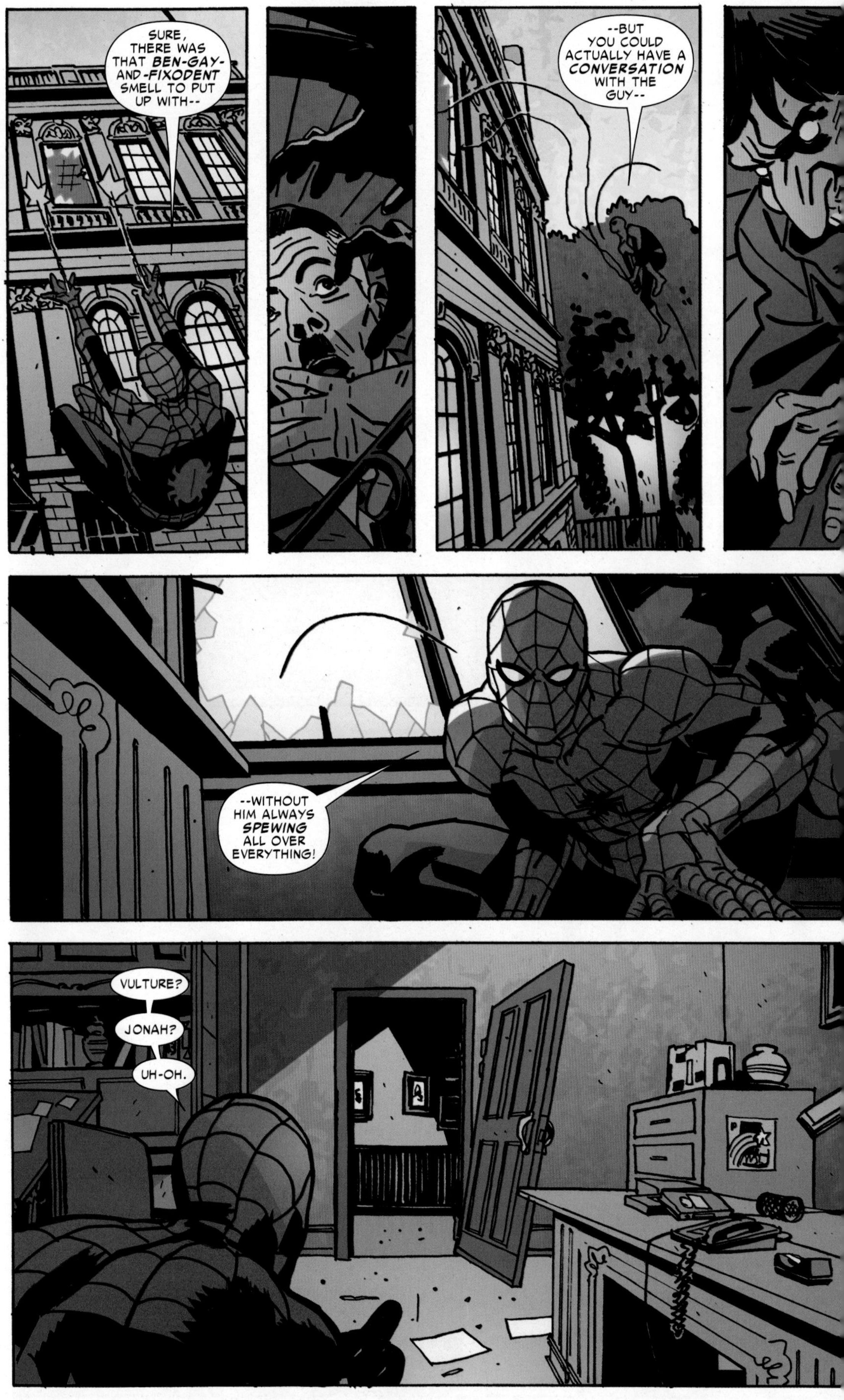
SURE, THERE WAS THAT BEN-GAY-AND-FIXODENT SMELL TO PUT UP WITH--
--BUT YOU COULD ACTUALLY HAVE A CONVERSATION WITH THE GUY--
--WITHOUT HIM ALWAYS SPEWING ALL OVER EVERYTHING!
VULTURE?
JONAH?
UH-OH.

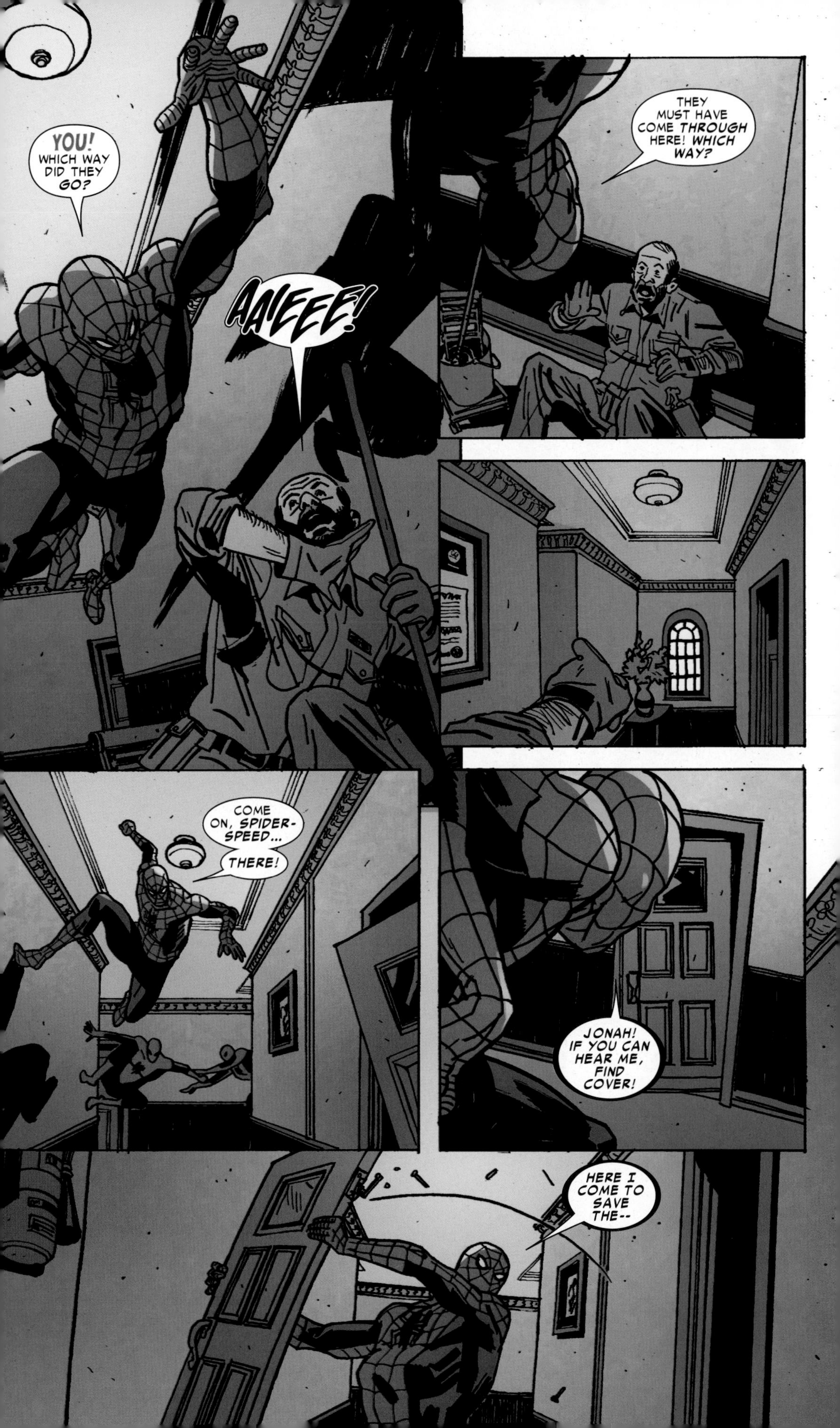
YOU! WHICH WAY DID THEY GO?
AAIEEE!
THEY MUST HAVE COME THROUGH HERE! WHICH WAY?
COME ON, SPIDER-SPEED...
THERE!
JONAH! IF YOU CAN HEAR ME, FIND COVER!
HERE I COME TO SAVE THE--

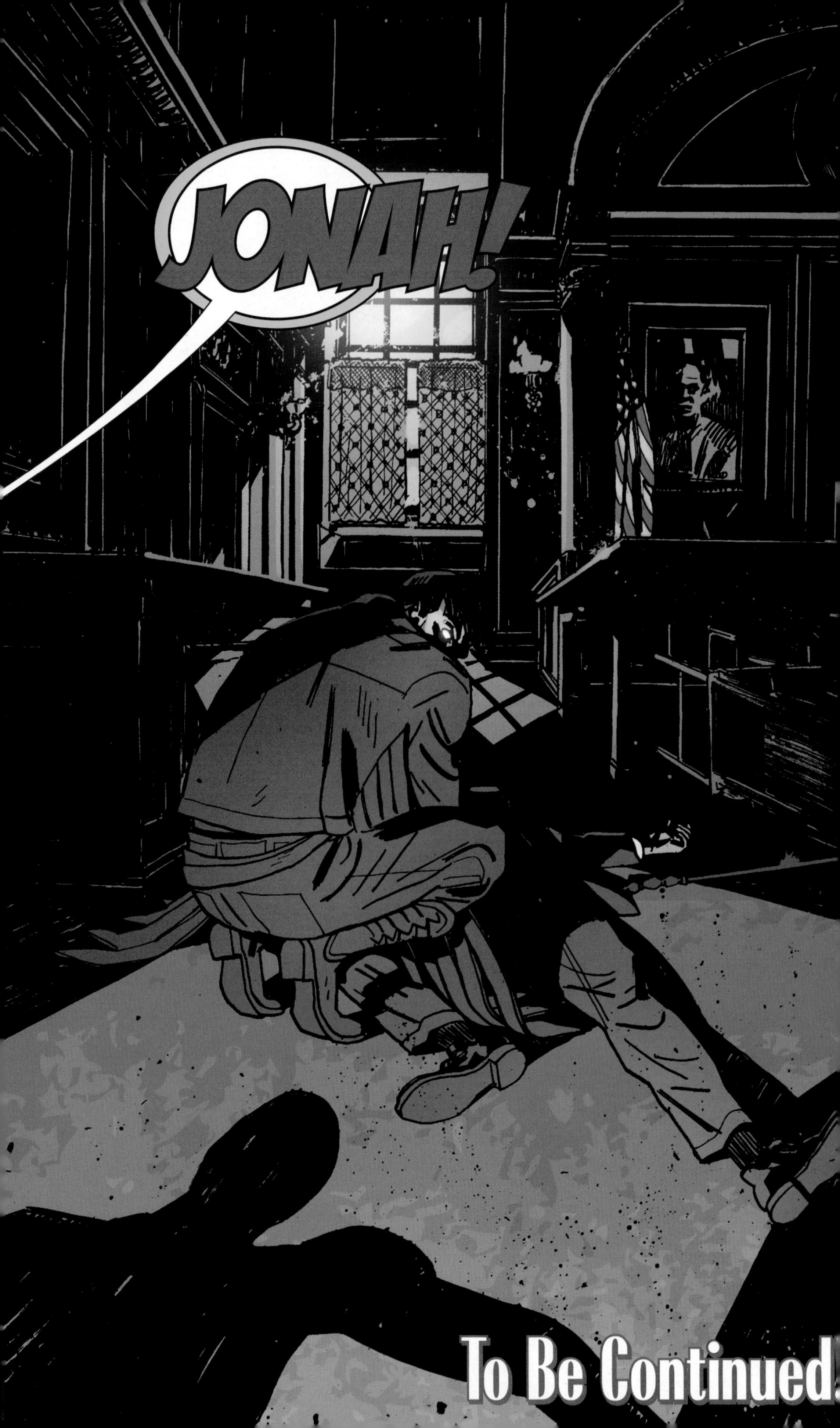
JONAH!
To Be Continued!

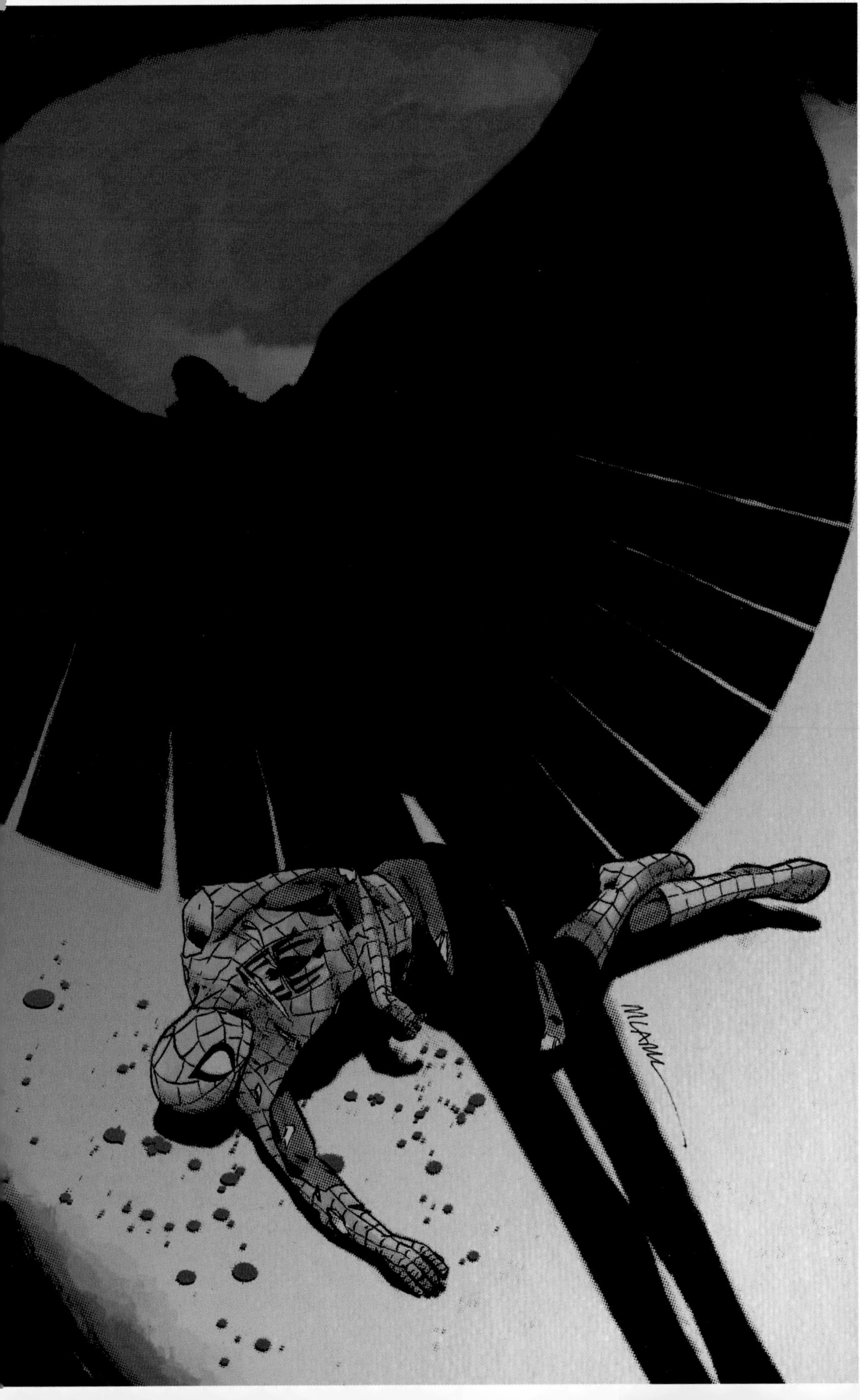

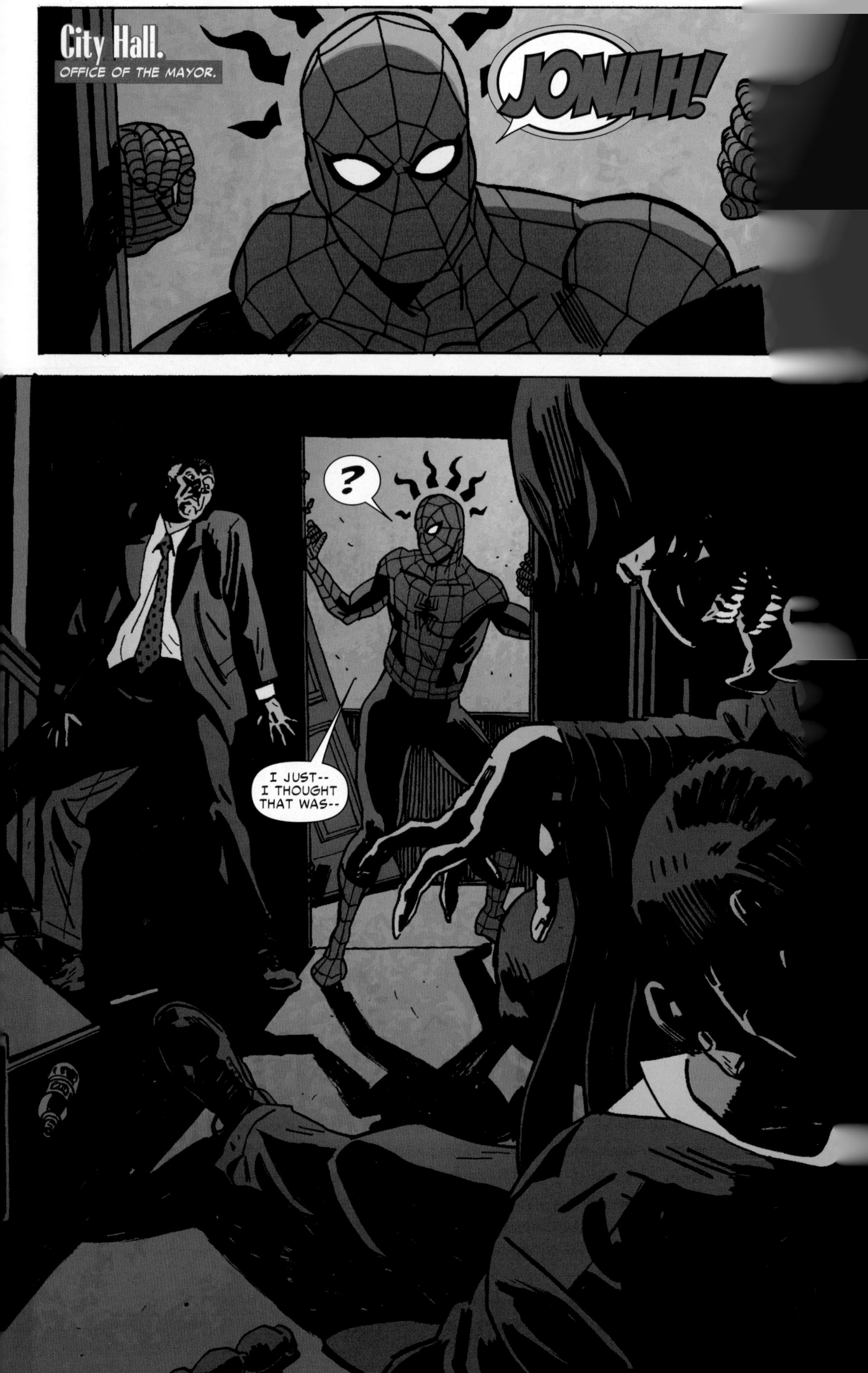
City Hall.
OFFICE OF THE MAYOR.
JONAH!
?
I JUST-- I THOUGHT THAT WAS--

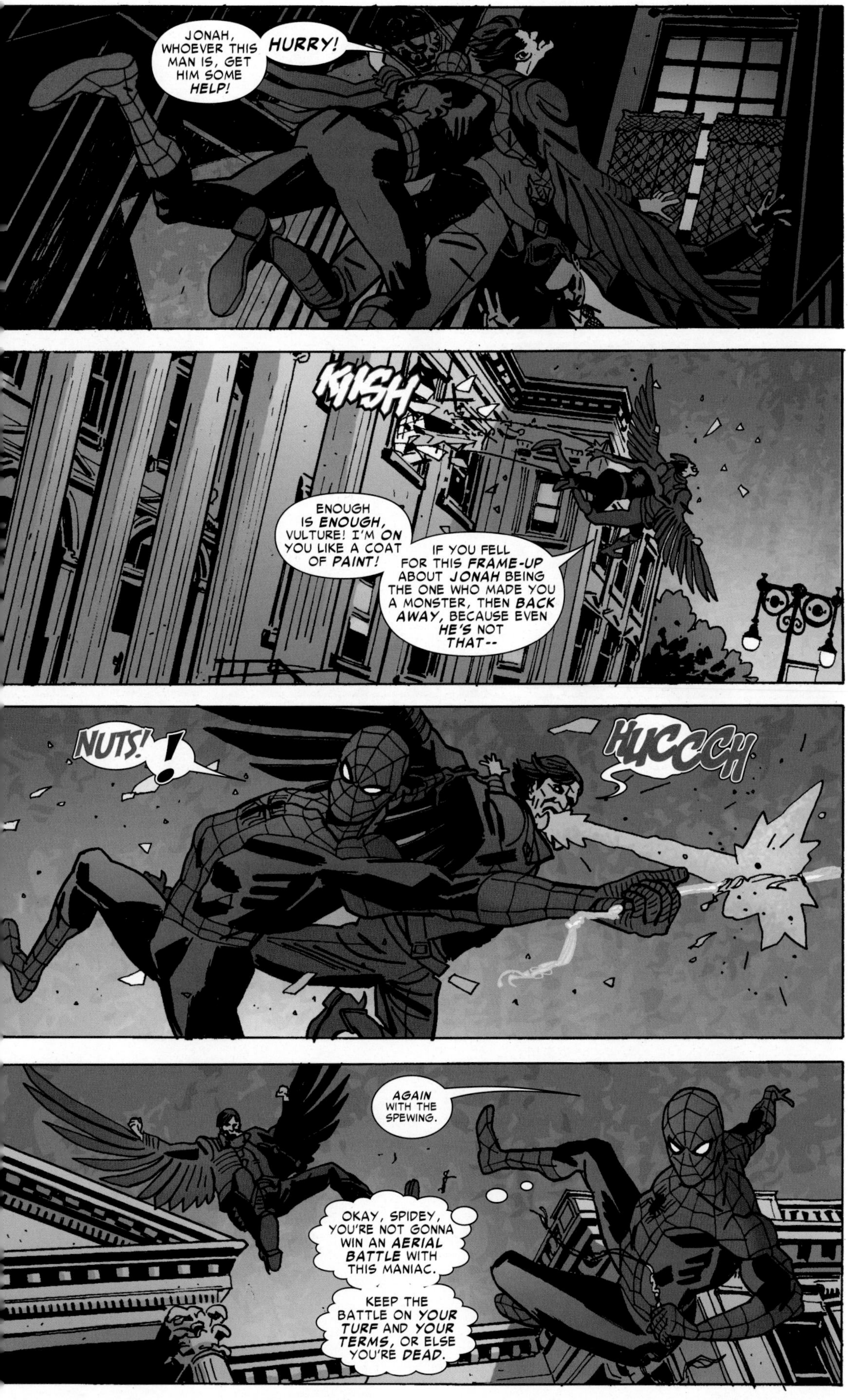
JONAH, WHOEVER THIS MAN IS, GET HIM SOME HELP!
HURRY!
KRISH
ENOUGH IS ENOUGH, VULTURE! I'M ON YOU LIKE A COAT OF PAINT!
IF YOU FELL FOR THIS FRAME-UP ABOUT JONAH BEING THE ONE WHO MADE YOU A MONSTER, THEN BACK AWAY, BECAUSE EVEN HE'S NOT THAT--
NUTS!
!
HUCCCH
AGAIN WITH THE SPEWING.
OKAY, SPIDEY, YOU'RE NOT GONNA WIN AN AERIAL BATTLE WITH THIS MANIAC.
KEEP THE BATTLE ON YOUR TURF AND YOUR TERMS, OR ELSE YOU'RE DEAD.

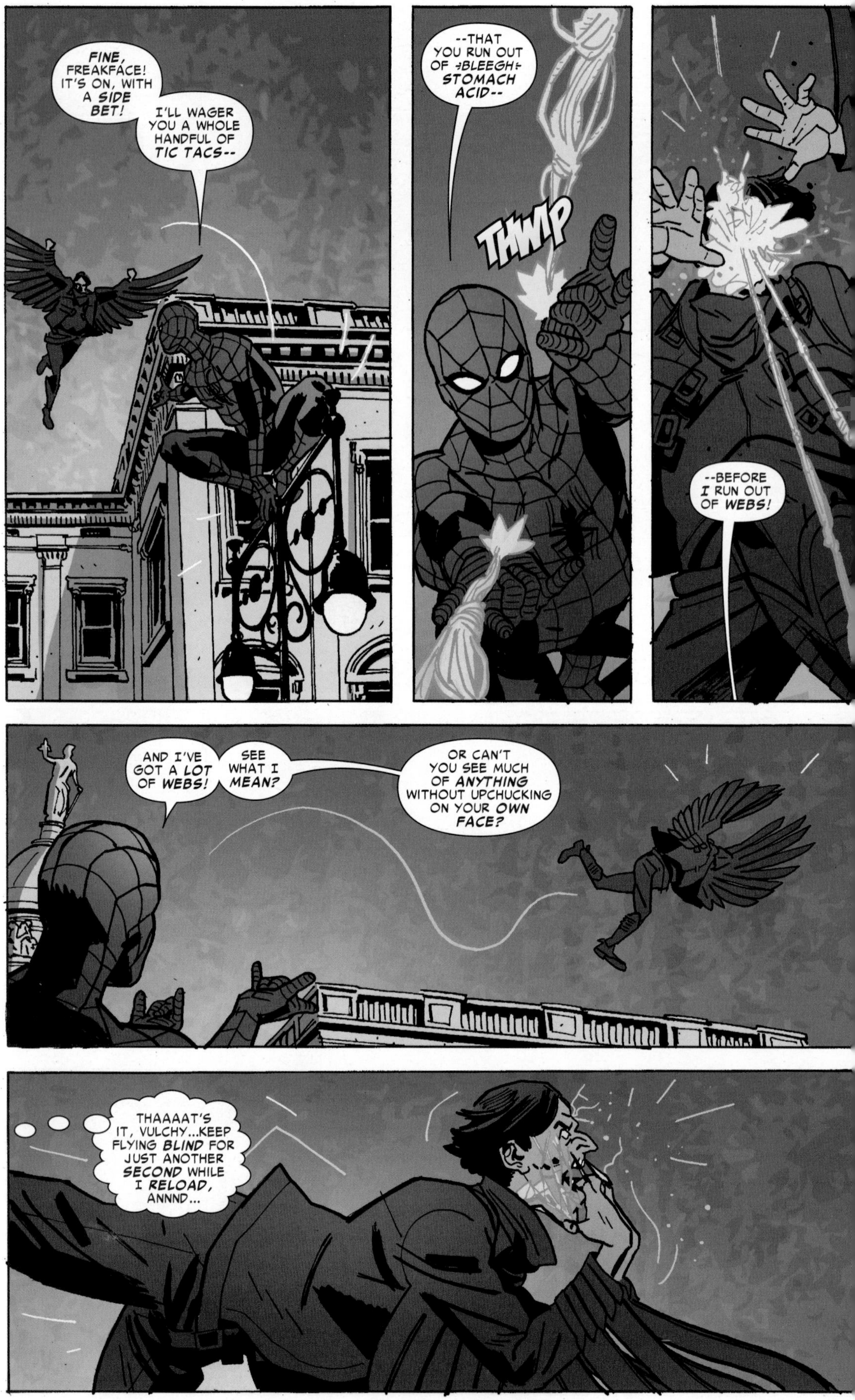
FINE, FREAKFACE! IT'S ON, WITH A SIDE BET!
I'LL WAGER YOU A WHOLE HANDFUL OF TIC TACS--
--THAT YOU RUN OUT OF ⇛BLEEGH⇚ STOMACH ACID--
THWIP
--BEFORE I RUN OUT OF WEBS!
AND I'VE GOT A LOT OF WEBS!
SEE WHAT I MEAN?
OR CAN'T YOU SEE MUCH OF ANYTHING WITHOUT UPCHUCKING ON YOUR OWN FACE?
THAAAAT'S IT, VULCHY...KEEP FLYING BLIND FOR JUST ANOTHER SECOND WHILE I RELOAD, ANNND...

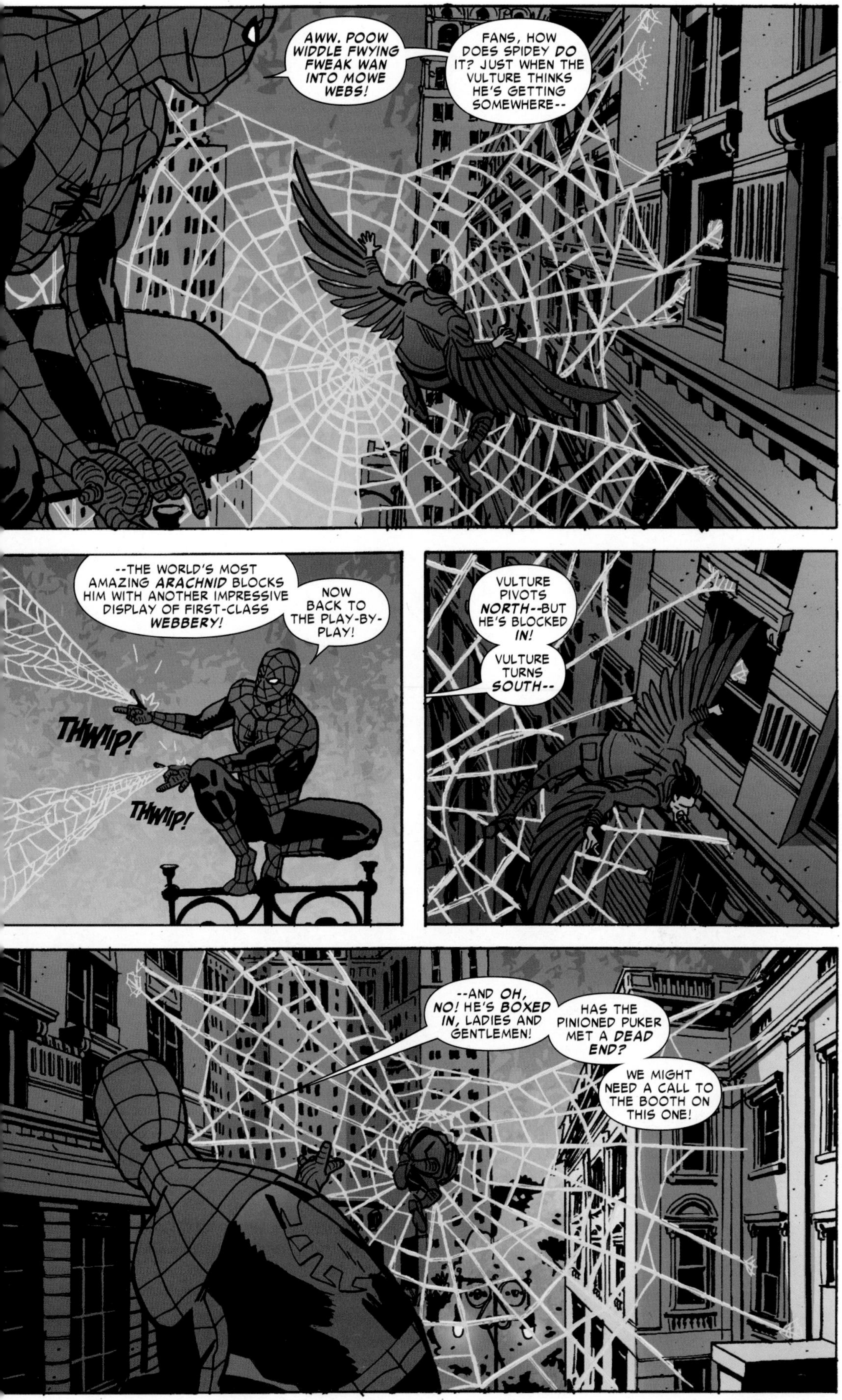
AWW. POOW WIDDLE FWYING FWEAK WAN INTO MOWE WEBS!
FANS, HOW DOES SPIDEY DO IT? JUST WHEN THE VULTURE THINKS HE'S GETTING SOMEWHERE--
--THE WORLD'S MOST AMAZING ARACHNID BLOCKS HIM WITH ANOTHER IMPRESSIVE DISPLAY OF FIRST-CLASS WEBBERY!
NOW BACK TO THE PLAY-BY-PLAY!
THWIP!
THWIP!
VULTURE PIVOTS NORTH--BUT HE'S BLOCKED IN!
VULTURE TURNS SOUTH--
--AND OH, NO! HE'S BOXED IN, LADIES AND GENTLEMEN!
HAS THE PINIONED PUKER MET A DEAD END?
WE MIGHT NEED A CALL TO THE BOOTH ON THIS ONE!

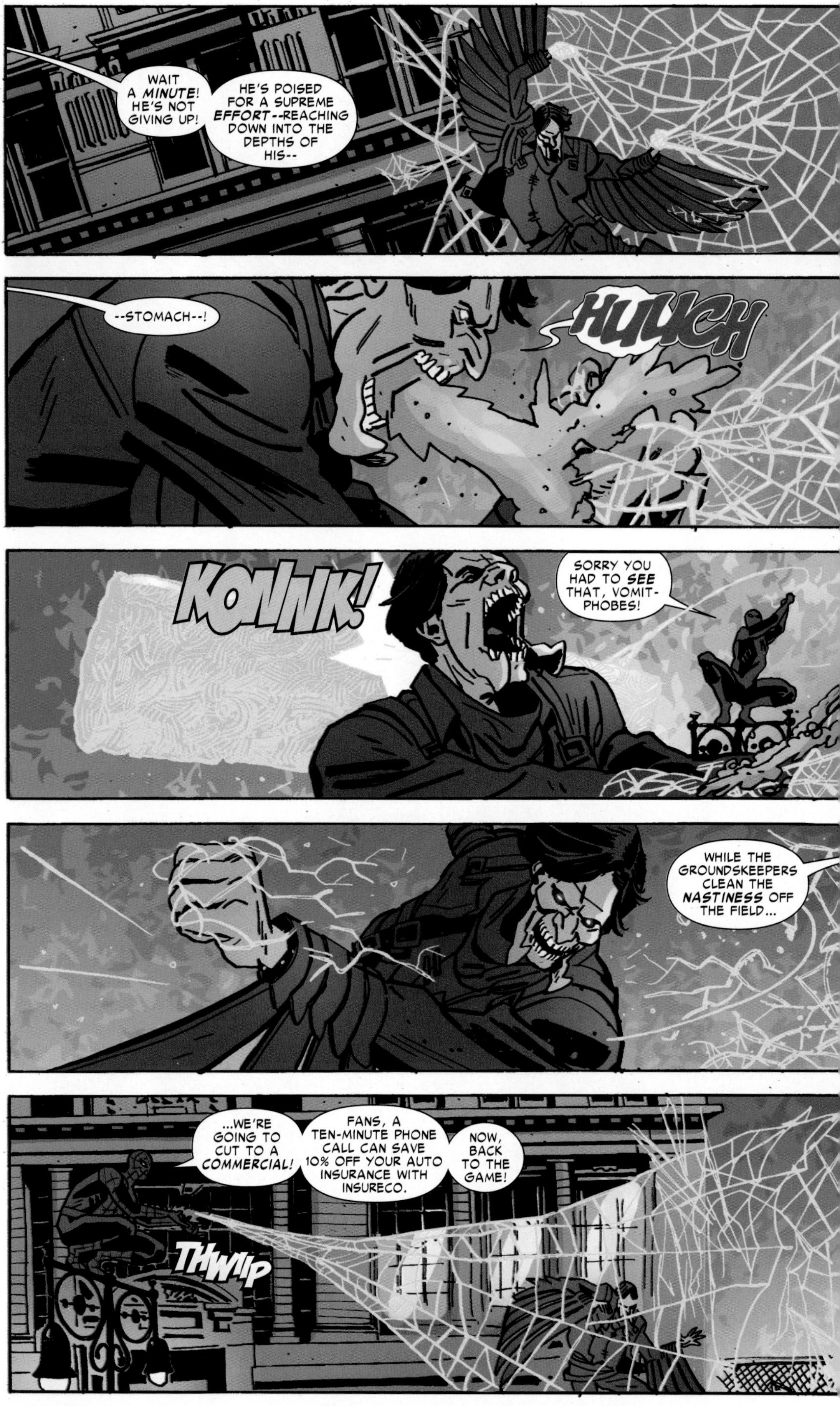
WAIT A MINUTE! HE'S NOT GIVING UP!
HE'S POISED FOR A SUPREME EFFORT--REACHING DOWN INTO THE DEPTHS OF HIS--
--STOMACH--!
HUUCH
KONNK!
SORRY YOU HAD TO SEE THAT, VOMIT-PHOBES!
WHILE THE GROUNDSKEEPERS CLEAN THE NASTINESS OFF THE FIELD...
...WE'RE GOING TO CUT TO A COMMERCIAL!
FANS, A TEN-MINUTE PHONE CALL CAN SAVE 10% OFF YOUR AUTO INSURANCE WITH INSURECO.
NOW, BACK TO THE GAME!
THWIIP

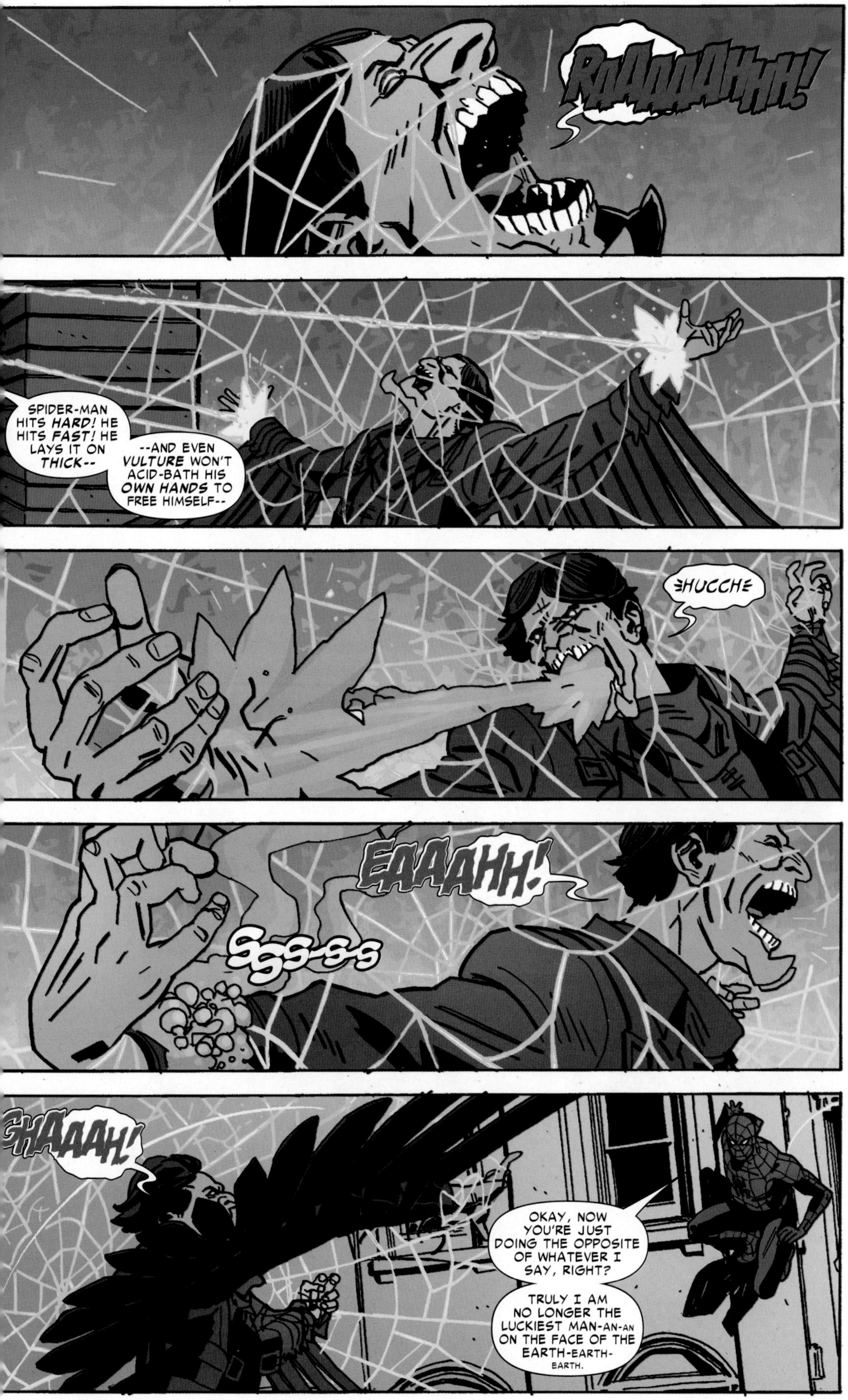
RAAAAAHHH!
SPIDER-MAN HITS HARD! HE HITS FAST! HE LAYS IT ON THICK--
--AND EVEN VULTURE WON'T ACID-BATH HIS OWN HANDS TO FREE HIMSELF--
HUCCH
EAAAHH!
SSS-S-S
GHAAAH!
OKAY, NOW YOU'RE JUST DOING THE OPPOSITE OF WHATEVER I SAY, RIGHT?
TRULY I AM NO LONGER THE LUCKIEST MAN-AN-AN ON THE FACE OF THE EARTH-EARTH-EARTH.

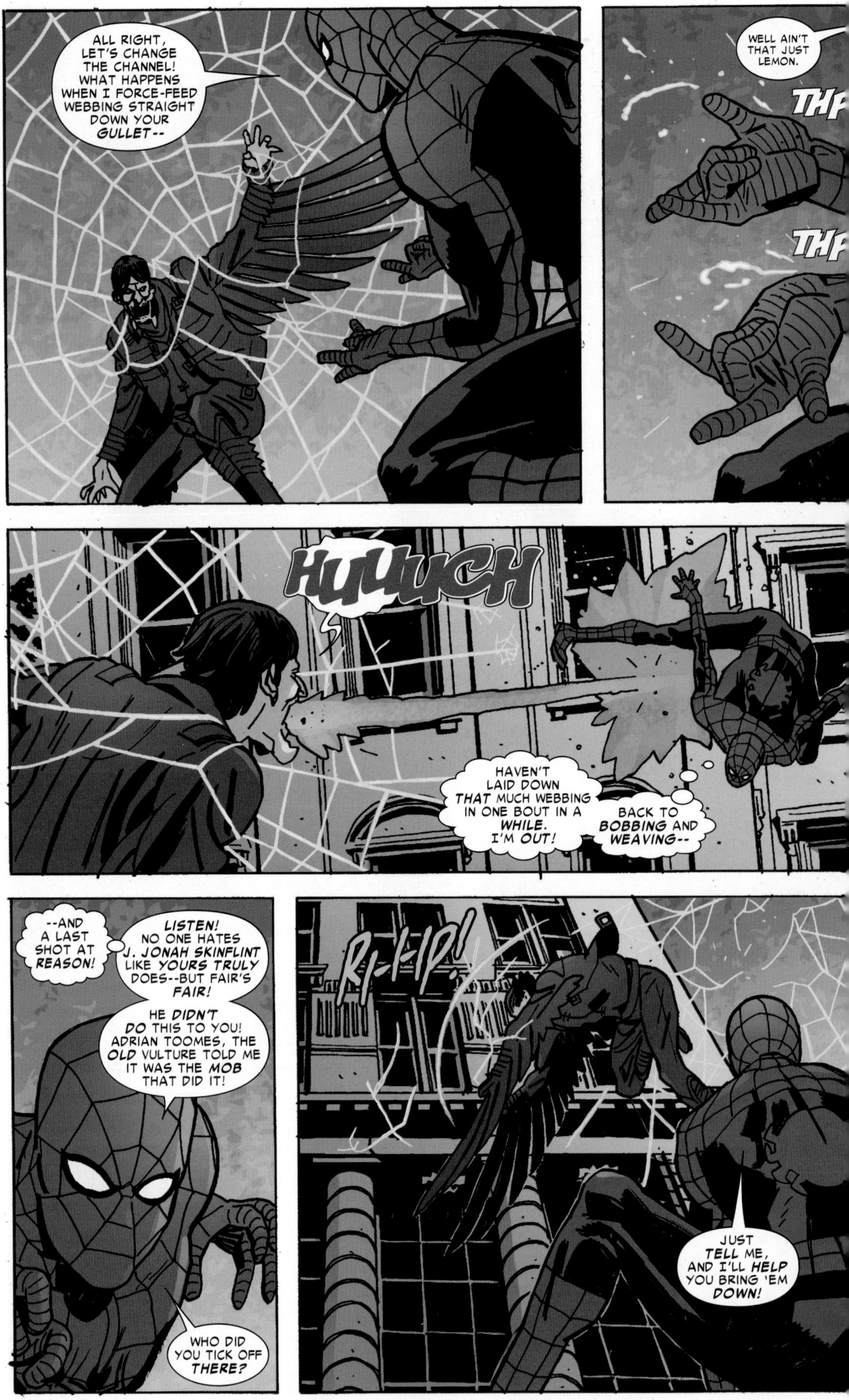
ALL RIGHT, LET'S CHANGE THE CHANNEL! WHAT HAPPENS WHEN I FORCE-FEED WEBBING STRAIGHT DOWN YOUR GULLET--
WELL AIN'T THAT JUST LEMON.
HUUUCH
HAVEN'T LAID DOWN THAT MUCH WEBBING IN ONE BOUT IN A WHILE. I'M OUT!
BACK TO BOBBING AND WEAVING--
--AND A LAST SHOT AT REASON!
LISTEN! NO ONE HATES J. JONAH SKINFLINT LIKE YOURS TRULY DOES--BUT FAIR'S FAIR!
HE DIDN'T DO THIS TO YOU! ADRIAN TOOMES, THE OLD VULTURE TOLD ME IT WAS THE MOB THAT DID IT!
WHO DID YOU TICK OFF THERE?
RI-I-IP!
JUST TELL ME, AND I'LL HELP YOU BRING 'EM DOWN!

OR NOT.

HOLD UP--!

D'AAAAH.

ME AND MY BIG *MOUTH.* NOW VULCHY'S OFF TO FACE *MOBSTERS!* PROBABLY! MAYBE!

I KNOW THEY'RE NOT THE *SWEETEST* BUNCH IN THE WORLD--

--BUT NO MATTER *WHO* HIS INTENDED VICTIM, I CAN'T JUST LET A MURDERER *GO.*

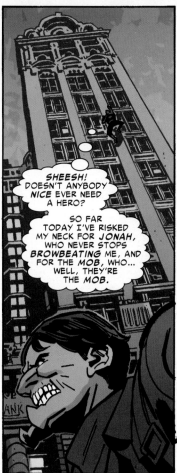

SHEESH! DOESN'T ANYBODY *NICE* EVER NEED A HERO?

SO FAR TODAY I'VE RISKED MY NECK FOR *JONAH,* WHO NEVER STOPS *BROWBEATING* ME, AND FOR THE *MOB,* WHO... WELL, THEY'RE THE MOB.

I WONDER IF THE *RED SKULL* NEEDS CHEERING UP?

OR MAYBE I CAN MOW DOCTOR DOOM'S *LAWN.*

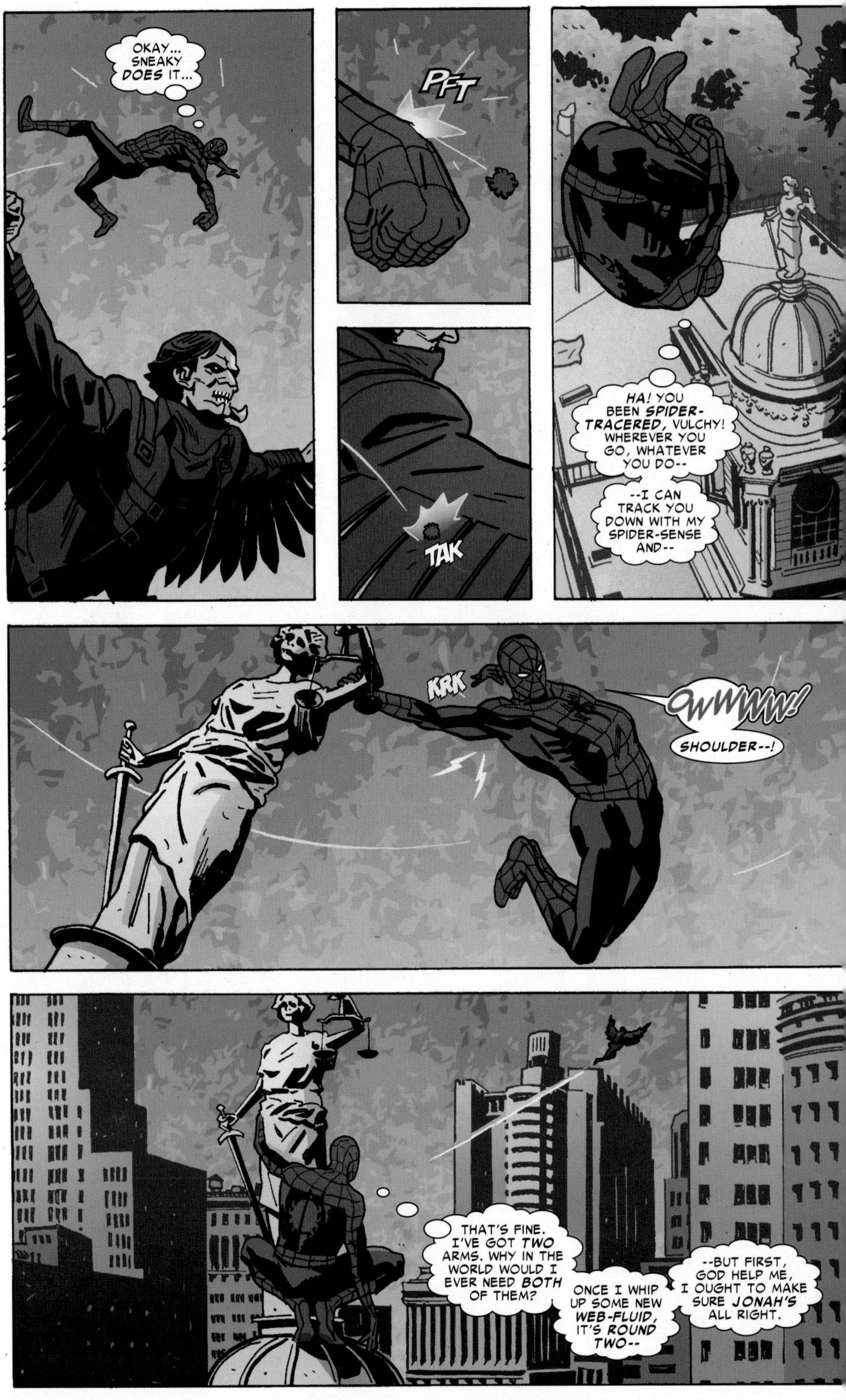
OKAY... SNEAKY DOES IT...
PFFT
TAK
HA! YOU BEEN SPIDER-TRACERED, VULCHY! WHEREVER YOU GO, WHATEVER YOU DO--
--I CAN TRACK YOU DOWN WITH MY SPIDER-SENSE AND--
KRK
OWWWW!
SHOULDER--!
THAT'S FINE. I'VE GOT TWO ARMS. WHY IN THE WORLD WOULD I EVER NEED BOTH OF THEM?
ONCE I WHIP UP SOME NEW WEB-FLUID, IT'S ROUND TWO--
--BUT FIRST, GOD HELP ME, I OUGHT TO MAKE SURE JONAH'S ALL RIGHT.

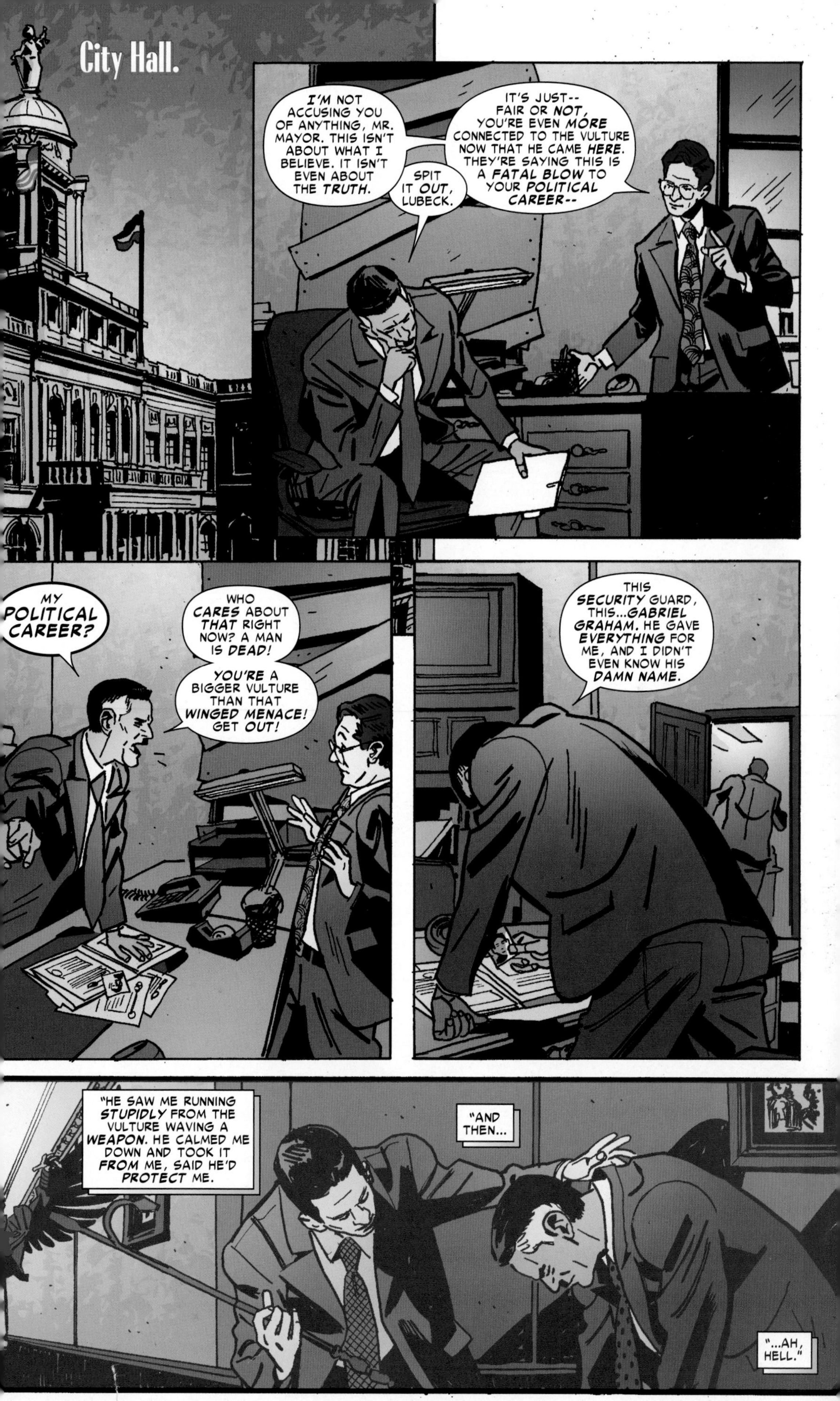
City Hall.
I'M NOT ACCUSING YOU OF ANYTHING, MR. MAYOR. THIS ISN'T ABOUT WHAT I BELIEVE. IT ISN'T EVEN ABOUT THE TRUTH.
IT'S JUST-- FAIR OR NOT, YOU'RE EVEN MORE CONNECTED TO THE VULTURE NOW THAT HE CAME HERE. THEY'RE SAYING THIS IS A FATAL BLOW TO YOUR POLITICAL CAREER--
SPIT IT OUT, LUBECK.
MY POLITICAL CAREER?
WHO CARES ABOUT THAT RIGHT NOW? A MAN IS DEAD!
YOU'RE A BIGGER VULTURE THAN THAT WINGED MENACE! GET OUT!
THIS SECURITY GUARD, THIS...GABRIEL GRAHAM. HE GAVE EVERYTHING FOR ME, AND I DIDN'T EVEN KNOW HIS DAMN NAME.
"HE SAW ME RUNNING STUPIDLY FROM THE VULTURE WAVING A WEAPON. HE CALMED ME DOWN AND TOOK IT FROM ME, SAID HE'D PROTECT ME.
"AND THEN...
"...AH, HELL."

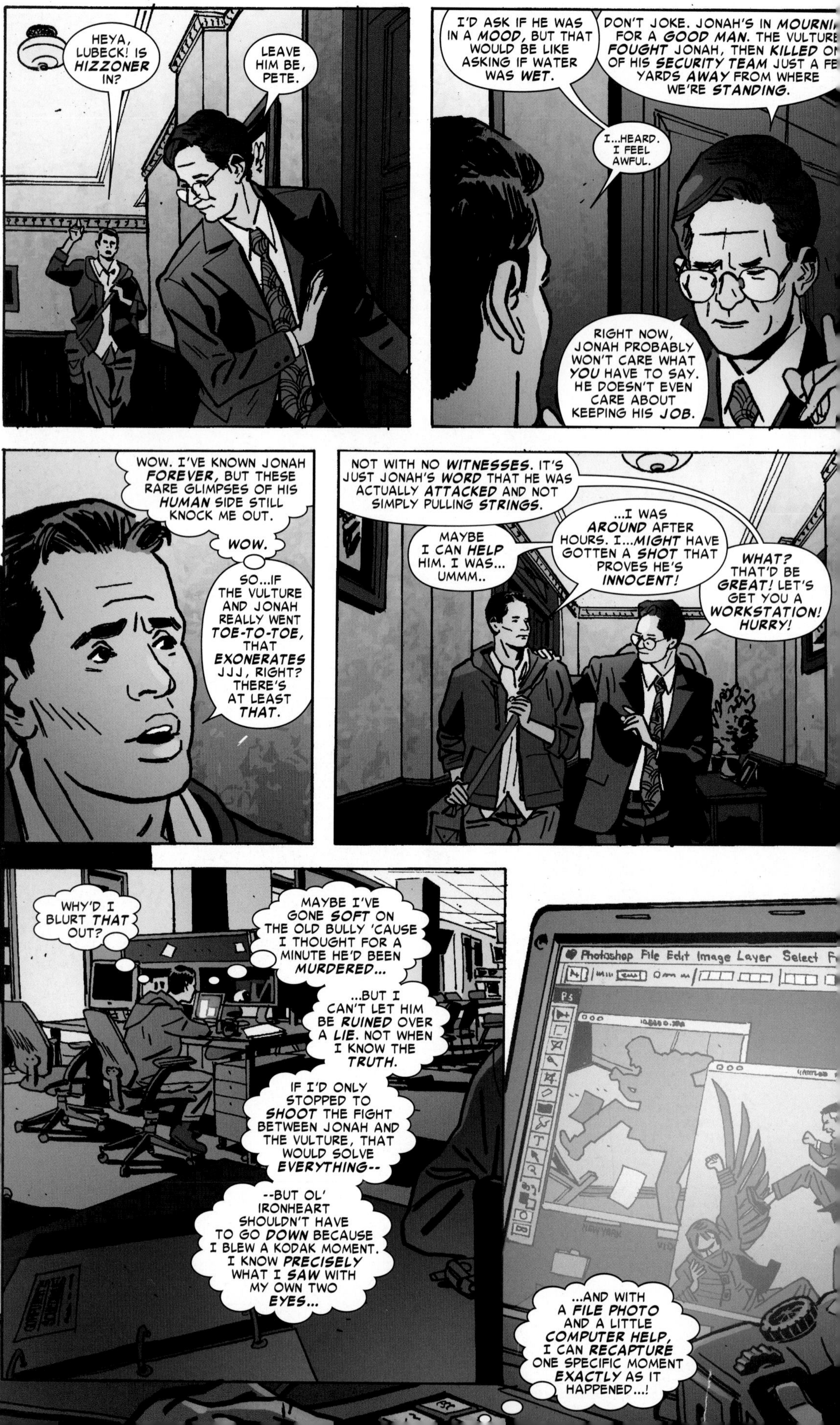
HEYA, LUBECK! IS HIZZONER IN?
LEAVE HIM BE, PETE.
I'D ASK IF HE WAS IN A MOOD, BUT THAT WOULD BE LIKE ASKING IF WATER WAS WET.
DON'T JOKE. JONAH'S IN MOURNI FOR A GOOD MAN. THE VULTURE FOUGHT JONAH, THEN KILLED O OF HIS SECURITY TEAM JUST A FE YARDS AWAY FROM WHERE WE'RE STANDING.
I...HEARD. I FEEL AWFUL.
RIGHT NOW, JONAH PROBABLY WON'T CARE WHAT YOU HAVE TO SAY. HE DOESN'T EVEN CARE ABOUT KEEPING HIS JOB.
WOW. I'VE KNOWN JONAH FOREVER, BUT THESE RARE GLIMPSES OF HIS HUMAN SIDE STILL KNOCK ME OUT.
WOW.
SO...IF THE VULTURE AND JONAH REALLY WENT TOE-TO-TOE, THAT EXONERATES JJJ, RIGHT? THERE'S AT LEAST THAT.
NOT WITH NO WITNESSES. IT'S JUST JONAH'S WORD THAT HE WAS ACTUALLY ATTACKED AND NOT SIMPLY PULLING STRINGS.
MAYBE I CAN HELP HIM. I WAS... UMMM..
...I WAS AROUND AFTER HOURS. I...MIGHT HAVE GOTTEN A SHOT THAT PROVES HE'S INNOCENT!
WHAT? THAT'D BE GREAT! LET'S GET YOU A WORKSTATION! HURRY!
WHY'D I BLURT THAT OUT?
MAYBE I'VE GONE SOFT ON THE OLD BULLY 'CAUSE I THOUGHT FOR A MINUTE HE'D BEEN MURDERED...
...BUT I CAN'T LET HIM BE RUINED OVER A LIE. NOT WHEN I KNOW THE TRUTH.
IF I'D ONLY STOPPED TO SHOOT THE FIGHT BETWEEN JONAH AND THE VULTURE, THAT WOULD SOLVE EVERYTHING--
--BUT OL' IRONHEART SHOULDN'T HAVE TO GO DOWN BECAUSE I BLEW A KODAK MOMENT. I KNOW PRECISELY WHAT I SAW WITH MY OWN TWO EYES...
Photoshop File Edit Image Layer Select
...AND WITH A FILE PHOTO AND A LITTLE COMPUTER HELP, I CAN RECAPTURE ONE SPECIFIC MOMENT EXACTLY AS IT HAPPENED...!

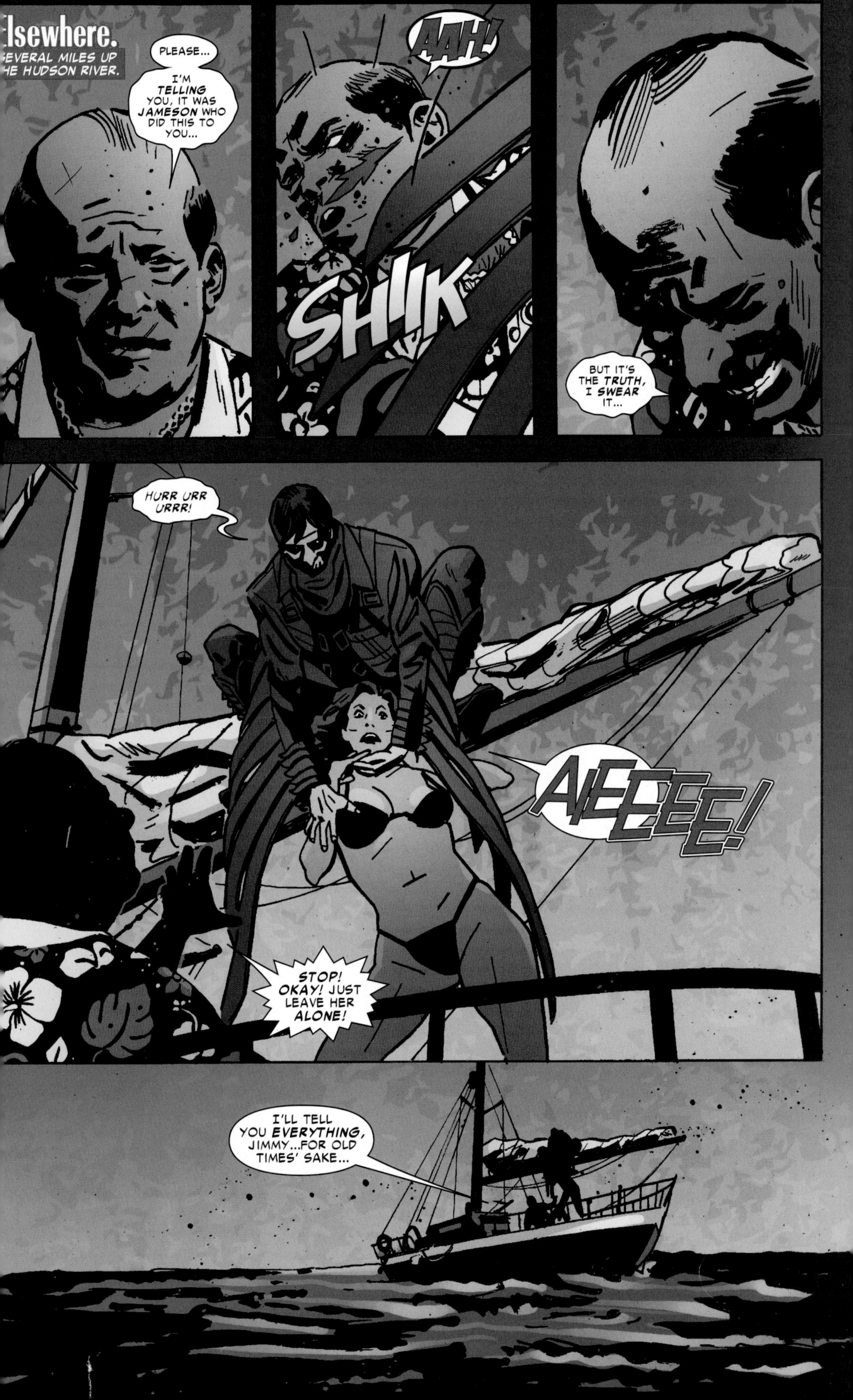
lsewhere.
EVERAL MILES UP
HE HUDSON RIVER.
PLEASE...
I'M TELLING YOU, IT WAS JAMESON WHO DID THIS TO YOU...
AAH!
SHIIK
BUT IT'S THE TRUTH, I SWEAR IT...
HURR URR URRR!
AIEEEEE!
STOP! OKAY! JUST LEAVE HER ALONE!
I'LL TELL YOU EVERYTHING, JIMMY...FOR OLD TIMES' SAKE...

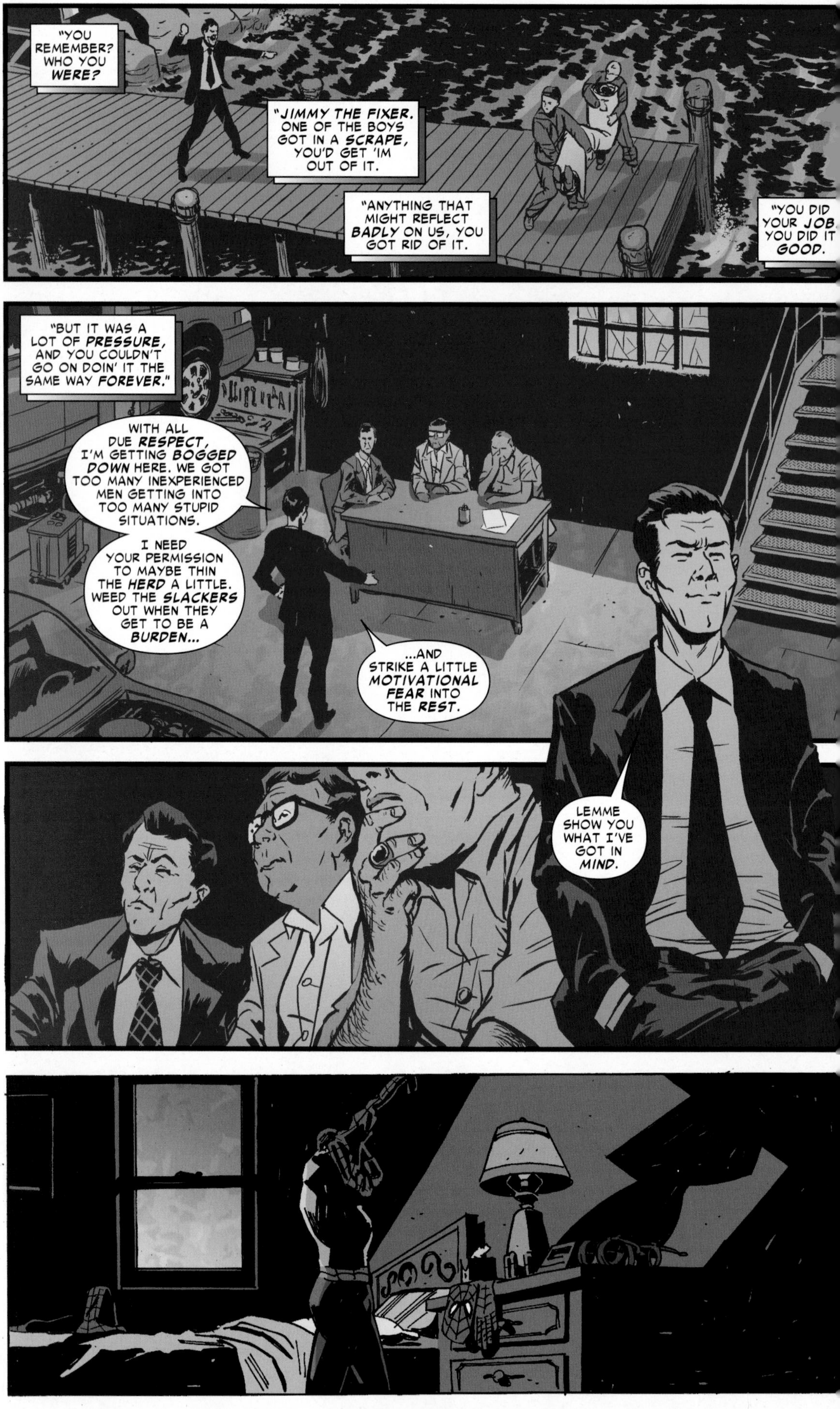
"YOU REMEMBER? WHO YOU WERE?
"JIMMY THE FIXER. ONE OF THE BOYS GOT IN A SCRAPE, YOU'D GET 'IM OUT OF IT.
"ANYTHING THAT MIGHT REFLECT BADLY ON US, YOU GOT RID OF IT.
"YOU DID YOUR JOB. YOU DID IT GOOD.
"BUT IT WAS A LOT OF PRESSURE, AND YOU COULDN'T GO ON DOIN' IT THE SAME WAY FOREVER."
WITH ALL DUE RESPECT, I'M GETTING BOGGED DOWN HERE. WE GOT TOO MANY INEXPERIENCED MEN GETTING INTO TOO MANY STUPID SITUATIONS.
I NEED YOUR PERMISSION TO MAYBE THIN THE HERD A LITTLE. WEED THE SLACKERS OUT WHEN THEY GET TO BE A BURDEN...
...AND STRIKE A LITTLE MOTIVATIONAL FEAR INTO THE REST.
LEMME SHOW YOU WHAT I'VE GOT IN MIND.

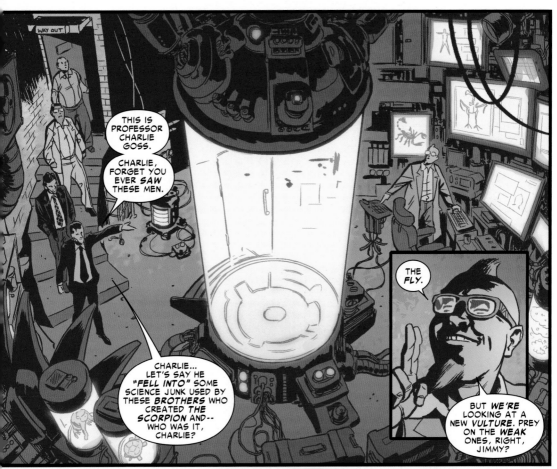

THIS IS PROFESSOR CHARLIE GOSS.

CHARLIE, FORGET YOU EVER *SAW* THESE MEN.

THE *FLY.*

CHARLIE... LET'S SAY HE *"FELL INTO"* SOME SCIENCE JUNK USED BY THESE *BROTHERS* WHO CREATED *THE SCORPION* AND-- WHO WAS IT, CHARLIE?

BUT *WE'RE* LOOKING AT A NEW *VULTURE.* PREY ON THE *WEAK* ONES, RIGHT, JIMMY?

RIGHT. AS I SEE IT, OUR VULTURE'S GOT TO BE QUICK, ATHLETIC AND MAYBE ON THE *RUTHLESS* SIDE.

ALL *YOU* FELLAS NEED TO DO IS *FUND* THIS AND BRING GOSS THE RIGHT *CANDIDATE.* I'LL SEE TO THE *REST.*

DON'T BOTHER, JIMMY.

AAAAAH!

BAM!

WE ALREADY *GOT* THE PERFECT MAN FOR THE JOB.

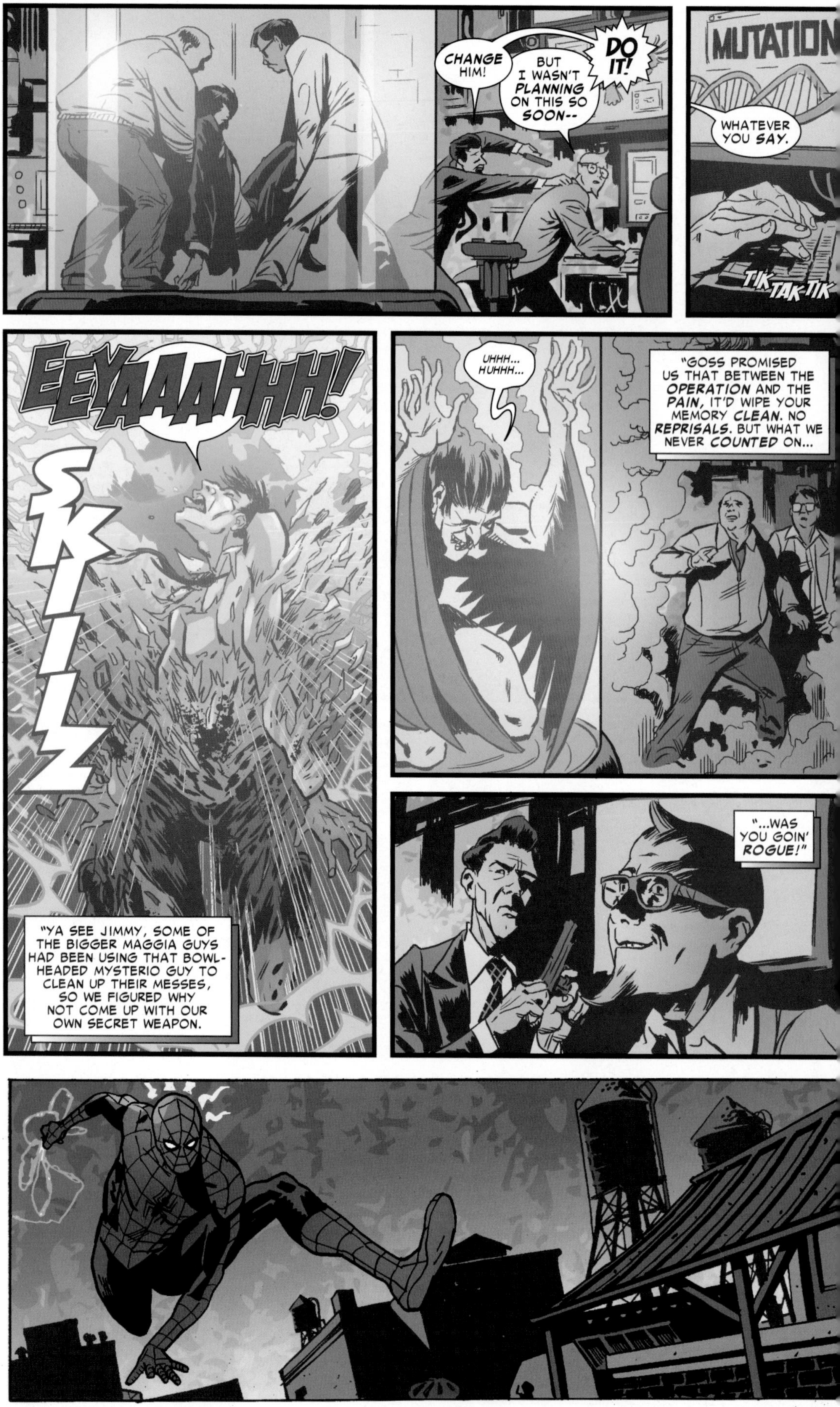

CHANGE HIM!
BUT I WASN'T PLANNING ON THIS SO SOON--
DO IT!
MUTATION
WHATEVER YOU SAY.
TIK TAK TIK
EEYAAAHHH!
SKIZZ
"YA SEE JIMMY, SOME OF THE BIGGER MAGGIA GUYS HAD BEEN USING THAT BOWL-HEADED MYSTERIO GUY TO CLEAN UP THEIR MESSES, SO WE FIGURED WHY NOT COME UP WITH OUR OWN SECRET WEAPON.
UHHH... HUHHH...
"GOSS PROMISED US THAT BETWEEN THE OPERATION AND THE PAIN, IT'D WIPE YOUR MEMORY CLEAN. NO REPRISALS. BUT WHAT WE NEVER COUNTED ON...
"...WAS YOU GOIN' ROGUE!"

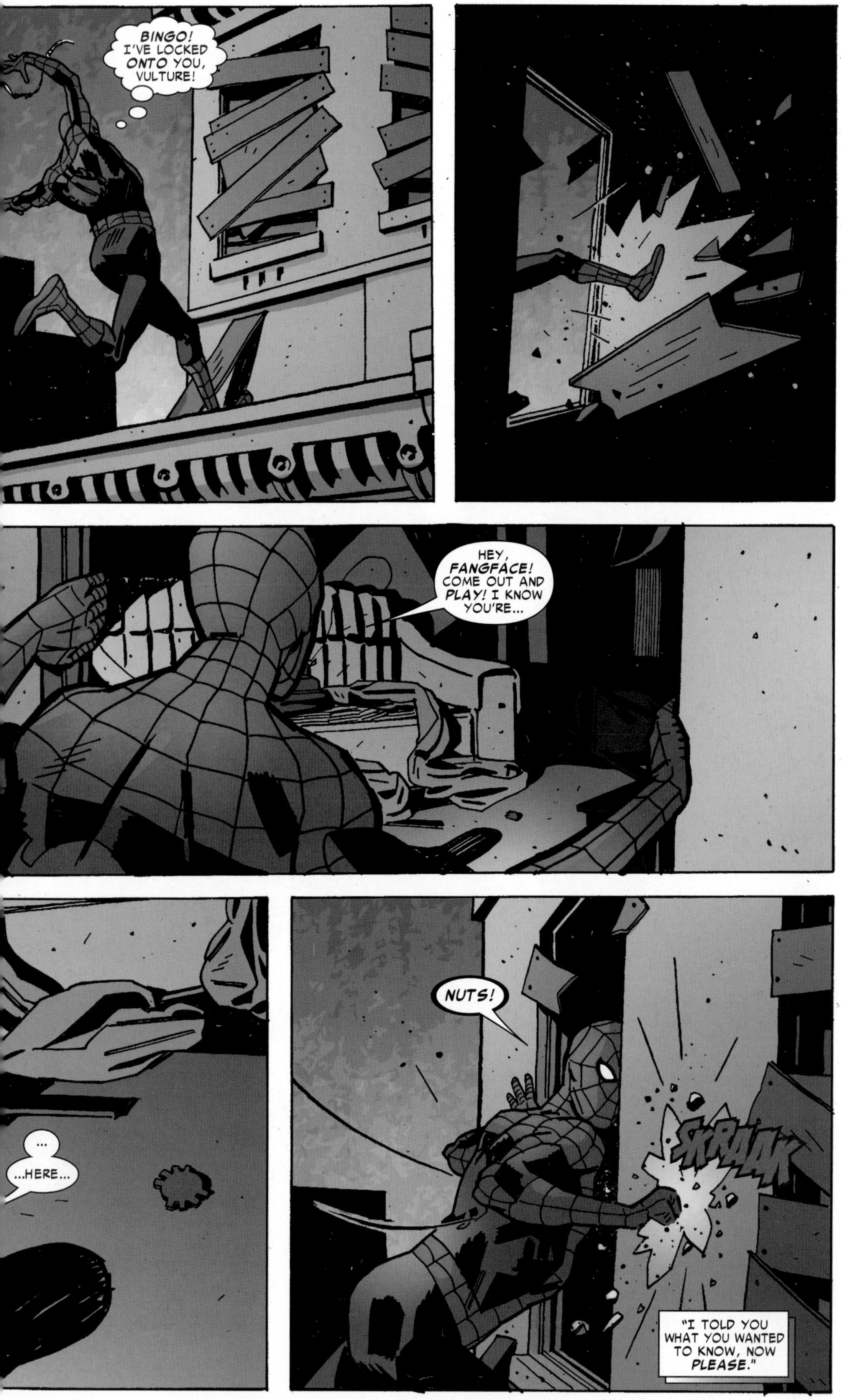
BINGO! I'VE LOCKED ONTO YOU, VULTURE!
HEY, FANGFACE! COME OUT AND PLAY! I KNOW YOU'RE...
...
...HERE...
NUTS!
SKRAAK
"I TOLD YOU WHAT YOU WANTED TO KNOW, NOW PLEASE."

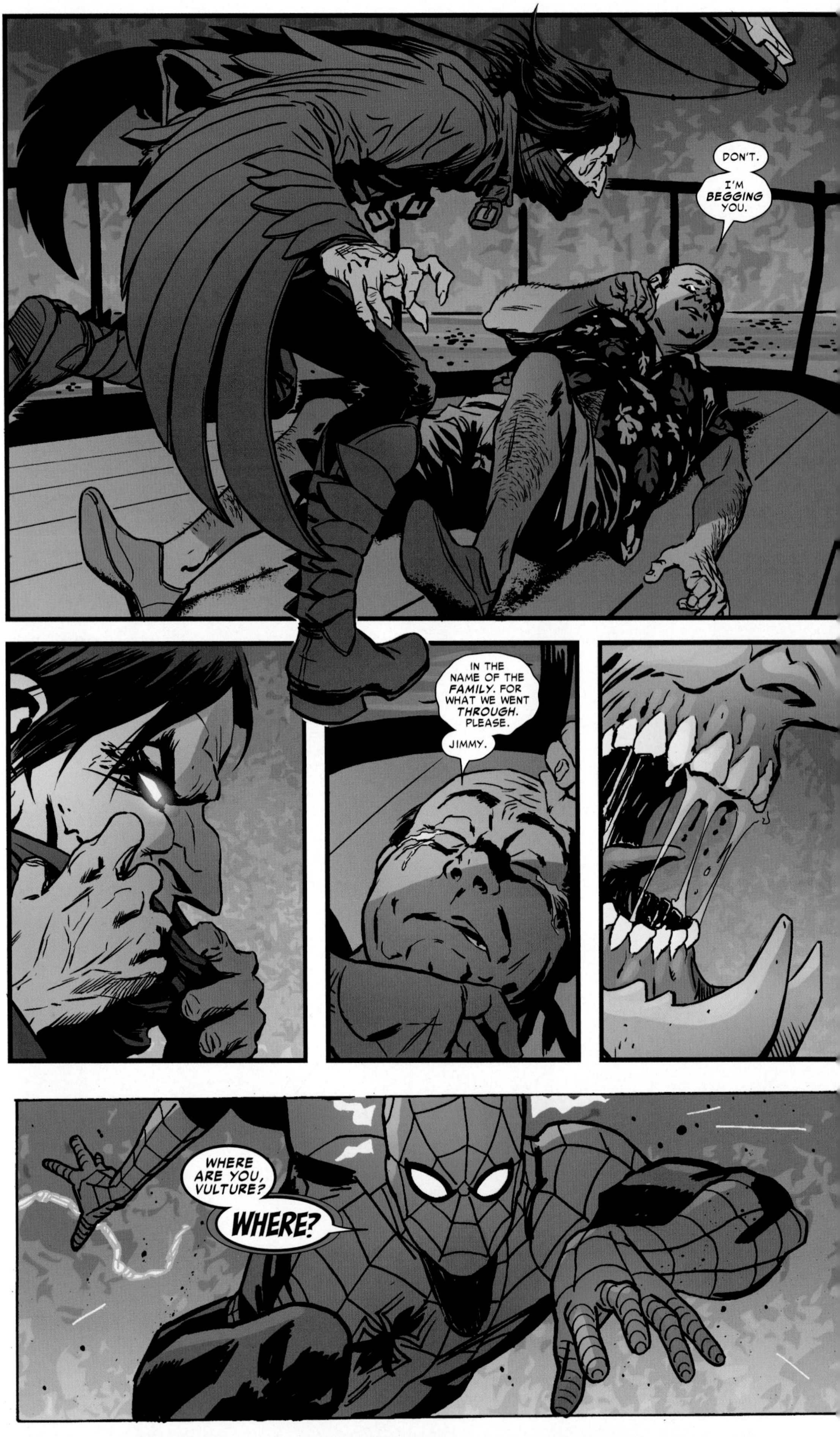
DON'T.
I'M BEGGING YOU.
IN THE NAME OF THE FAMILY. FOR WHAT WE WENT THROUGH. PLEASE.
JIMMY.
WHERE ARE YOU, VULTURE?
WHERE?

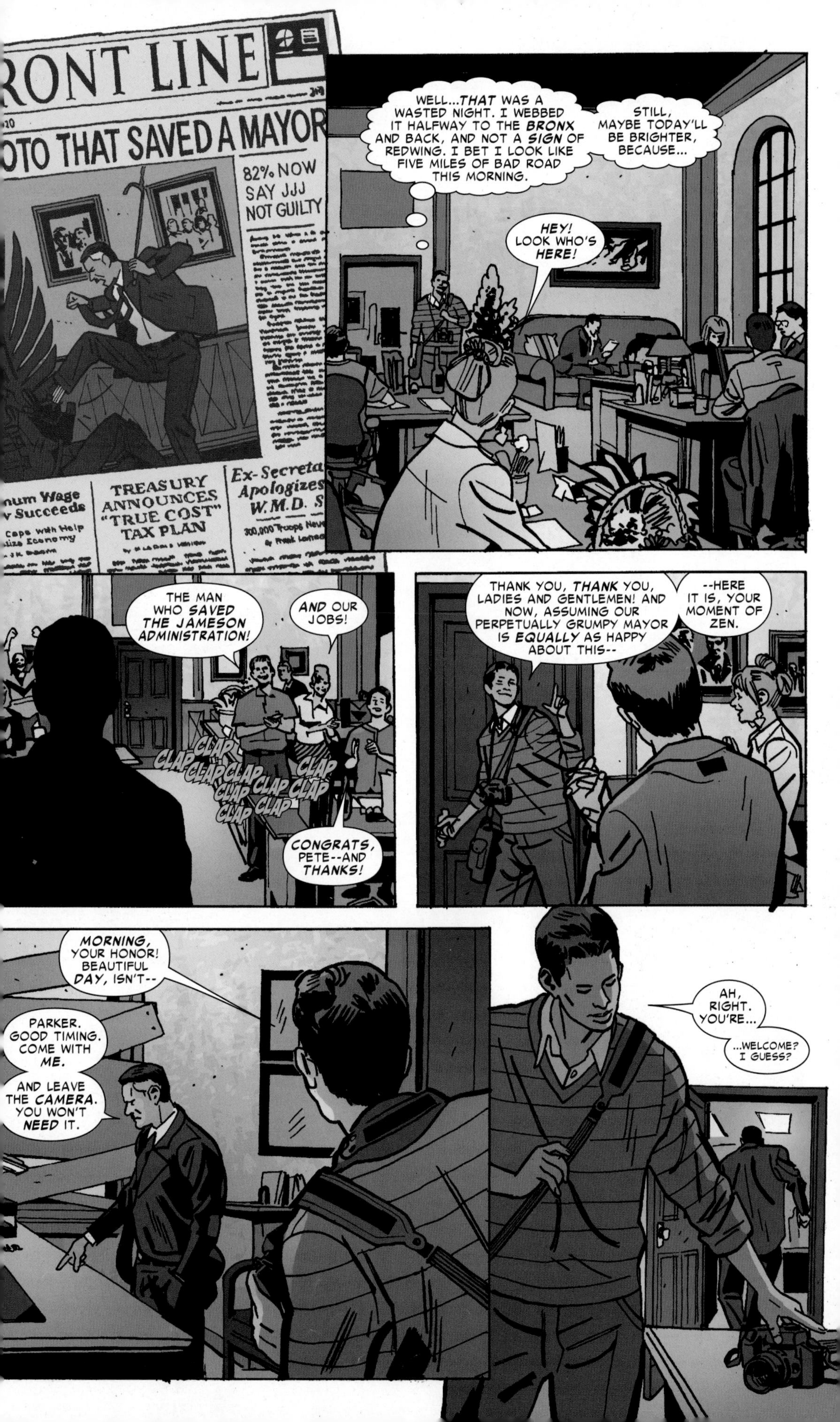

RONT LINE
OTO THAT SAVED A MAYOR
82% NOW SAY JJJ NOT GUILTY
num Wage y Succeeds
TREASURY ANNOUNCES "TRUE COST" TAX PLAN
Ex-Secreta Apologizes W.M.D. S
WELL...THAT WAS A WASTED NIGHT. I WEBBED IT HALFWAY TO THE BRONX AND BACK, AND NOT A SIGN OF REDWING. I BET I LOOK LIKE FIVE MILES OF BAD ROAD THIS MORNING.
STILL, MAYBE TODAY'LL BE BRIGHTER, BECAUSE...
HEY! LOOK WHO'S HERE!
THE MAN WHO SAVED THE JAMESON ADMINISTRATION!
AND OUR JOBS!
CLAP CLAP CLAP CLAP CLAP CLAP CLAP CLAP CLAP CLAP CLAP
CONGRATS, PETE--AND THANKS!
THANK YOU, THANK YOU, LADIES AND GENTLEMEN! AND NOW, ASSUMING OUR PERPETUALLY GRUMPY MAYOR IS EQUALLY AS HAPPY ABOUT THIS--
--HERE IT IS, YOUR MOMENT OF ZEN.
MORNING, YOUR HONOR! BEAUTIFUL DAY, ISN'T--
PARKER. GOOD TIMING. COME WITH ME.
AND LEAVE THE CAMERA. YOU WON'T NEED IT.
AH, RIGHT. YOU'RE...
...WELCOME? I GUESS?

PRESS CONFERENCE? WHAT ARE WE *DOING* HERE? LOOK, JONAH, I DON'T NEED A *PUBLIC* THANK YOU...JUST RENAMING A STREET AFTER ME WILL SUFFICE.

I *KNOW* THIS ISN'T A DREAM, BECAUSE I'M WEARING *PANTS.*

SIT DOWN, PARKER.

SIT DOWN, PARKER.

MEMBERS OF THE PRESS, I WANT TO *BEGIN* BY REAFFIRMING MY *INNOCENCE* IN THIS *VULTURE* MATTER.

YOU ALL *KNOW PETER PARKER.* HIS PHOTOGRAPH OF A *KEY MOMENT* MADE ALL THE DIFFERENCE IN GETTING THE PUBLIC TO *LISTEN* TO MY PROTESTS--

--AND AS A *RESULT, ADDITIONAL* EVIDENCE AND WITNESSES HAVE COME FORTH TO FULLY CLEAR ME.

BUT BACK TO *PARKER.* I'VE WORKED WITH HIM SINCE HE WAS A *KID* IN *SCHOOL.* I MADE HIM MY *STAFF PHOTOGRAPHER* HERE. I *BELIEVED* IN HIM.

WHICH MAKES IT ALL THE MORE *HEARTBREAKING* FOR ME TO HAVE TO *TELL* YOU--

--HIS *PICTURE* IS PHONY. A MOCK-UP.

WHAT?

MR. MAYOR--!

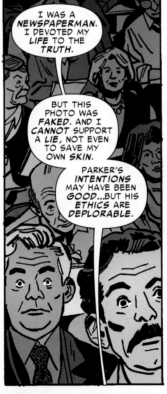

I WAS A *NEWSPAPERMAN.* I DEVOTED MY *LIFE* TO THE *TRUTH.*

BUT THIS PHOTO WAS *FAKED.* AND I *CANNOT* SUPPORT A LIE, NOT EVEN TO SAVE MY OWN *SKIN.*

PARKER'S *INTENTIONS* MAY HAVE BEEN *GOOD*...BUT HIS *ETHICS* ARE *DEPLORABLE.*

AND THAT IS WHY, EFFECTIVE *IMMEDIATELY,* I AM *FIRING* PETER PARKER FROM MY PAYROLL...

...AND *STRONGLY* ADVISING *EVERY* HONEST ORGANIZATION NEWS OR *OTHERWISE* TO STAY *WELL AWAY* FROM HIM.

THIS MAN HAS VIOLATED A *BASIC TRUST* OF THE *PUBLIC*...AND HIS CAREER IS *FINISHED.*

B-BUT... BUT...

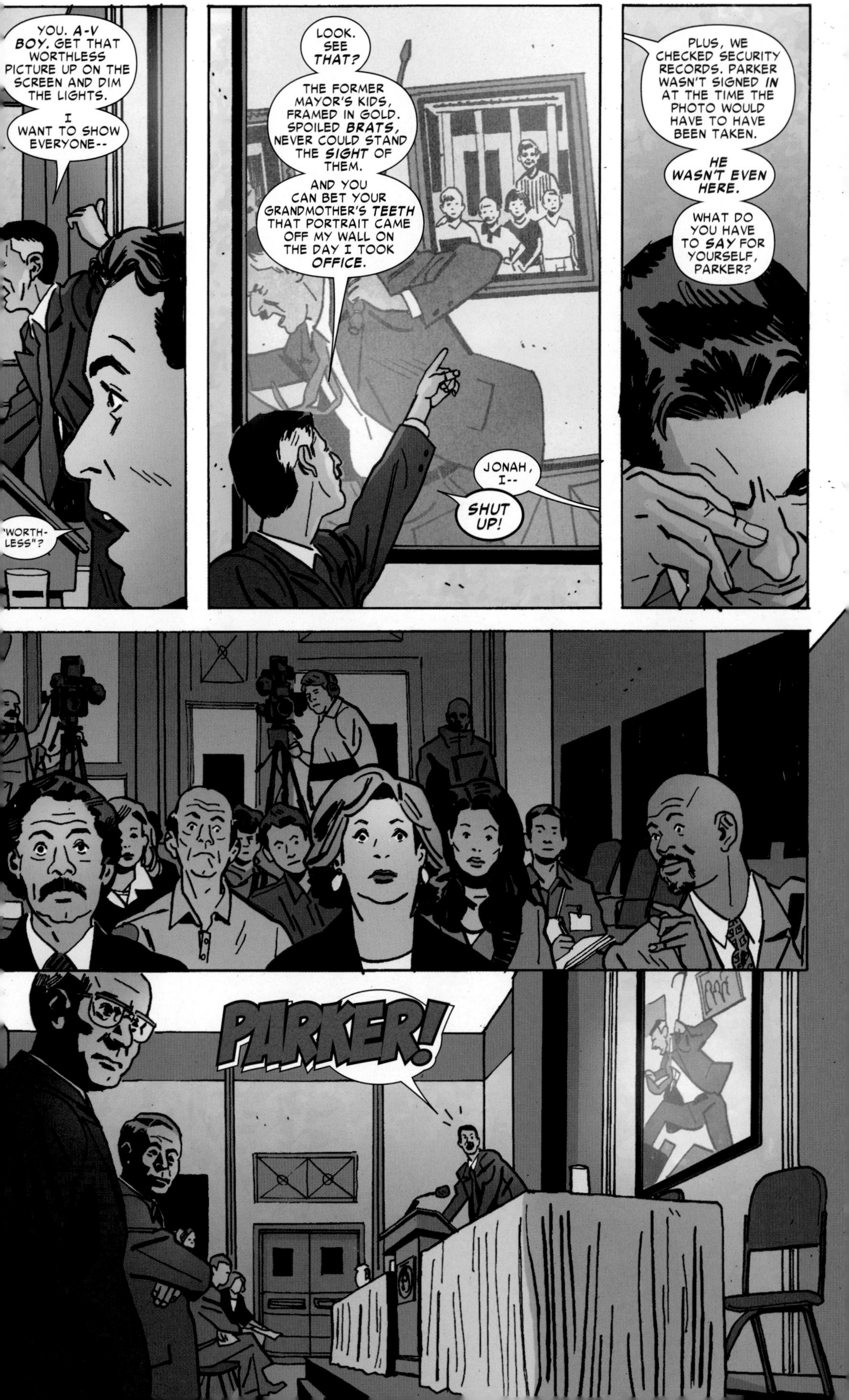
YOU. A-V BOY. GET THAT WORTHLESS PICTURE UP ON THE SCREEN AND DIM THE LIGHTS.
I WANT TO SHOW EVERYONE--
"WORTH-LESS"?
LOOK. SEE THAT?
THE FORMER MAYOR'S KIDS, FRAMED IN GOLD. SPOILED BRATS, NEVER COULD STAND THE SIGHT OF THEM.
AND YOU CAN BET YOUR GRANDMOTHER'S TEETH THAT PORTRAIT CAME OFF MY WALL ON THE DAY I TOOK OFFICE.
JONAH, I--
SHUT UP!
PLUS, WE CHECKED SECURITY RECORDS. PARKER WASN'T SIGNED IN AT THE TIME THE PHOTO WOULD HAVE TO HAVE BEEN TAKEN.
HE WASN'T EVEN HERE.
WHAT DO YOU HAVE TO SAY FOR YOURSELF, PARKER?
PARKER!

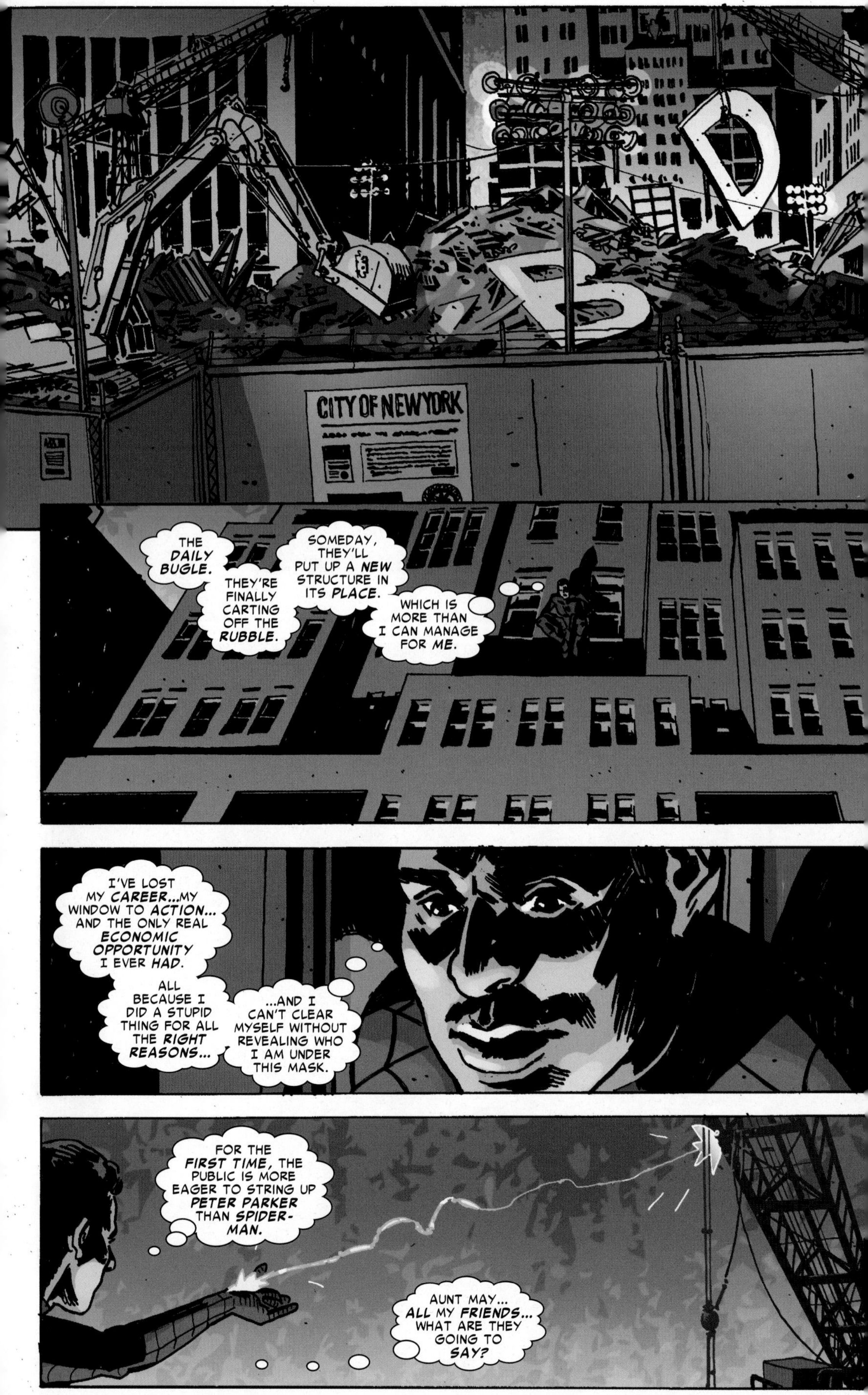
CITY OF NEW YORK
THE DAILY BUGLE.
THEY'RE FINALLY CARTING OFF THE RUBBLE.
SOMEDAY, THEY'LL PUT UP A NEW STRUCTURE IN ITS PLACE.
WHICH IS MORE THAN I CAN MANAGE FOR ME.
I'VE LOST MY CAREER...MY WINDOW TO ACTION... AND THE ONLY REAL ECONOMIC OPPORTUNITY I EVER HAD.
ALL BECAUSE I DID A STUPID THING FOR ALL THE RIGHT REASONS...
...AND I CAN'T CLEAR MYSELF WITHOUT REVEALING WHO I AM UNDER THIS MASK.
FOR THE FIRST TIME, THE PUBLIC IS MORE EAGER TO STRING UP PETER PARKER THAN SPIDER-MAN.
AUNT MAY... ALL MY FRIENDS... WHAT ARE THEY GOING TO SAY?

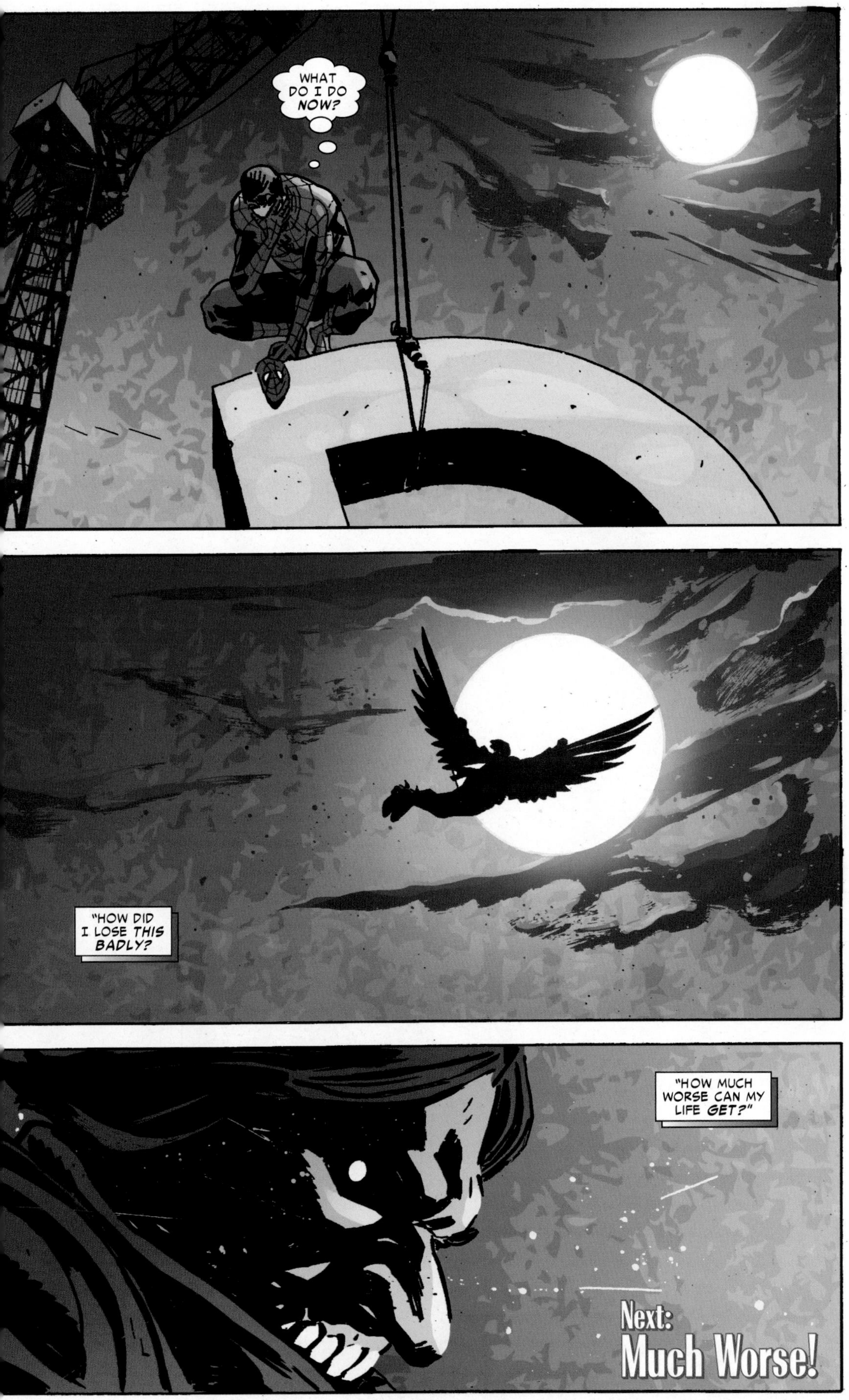
WHAT DO I DO NOW?
"HOW DID I LOSE THIS BADLY?
"HOW MUCH WORSE CAN MY LIFE GET?"
Next: Much Worse!

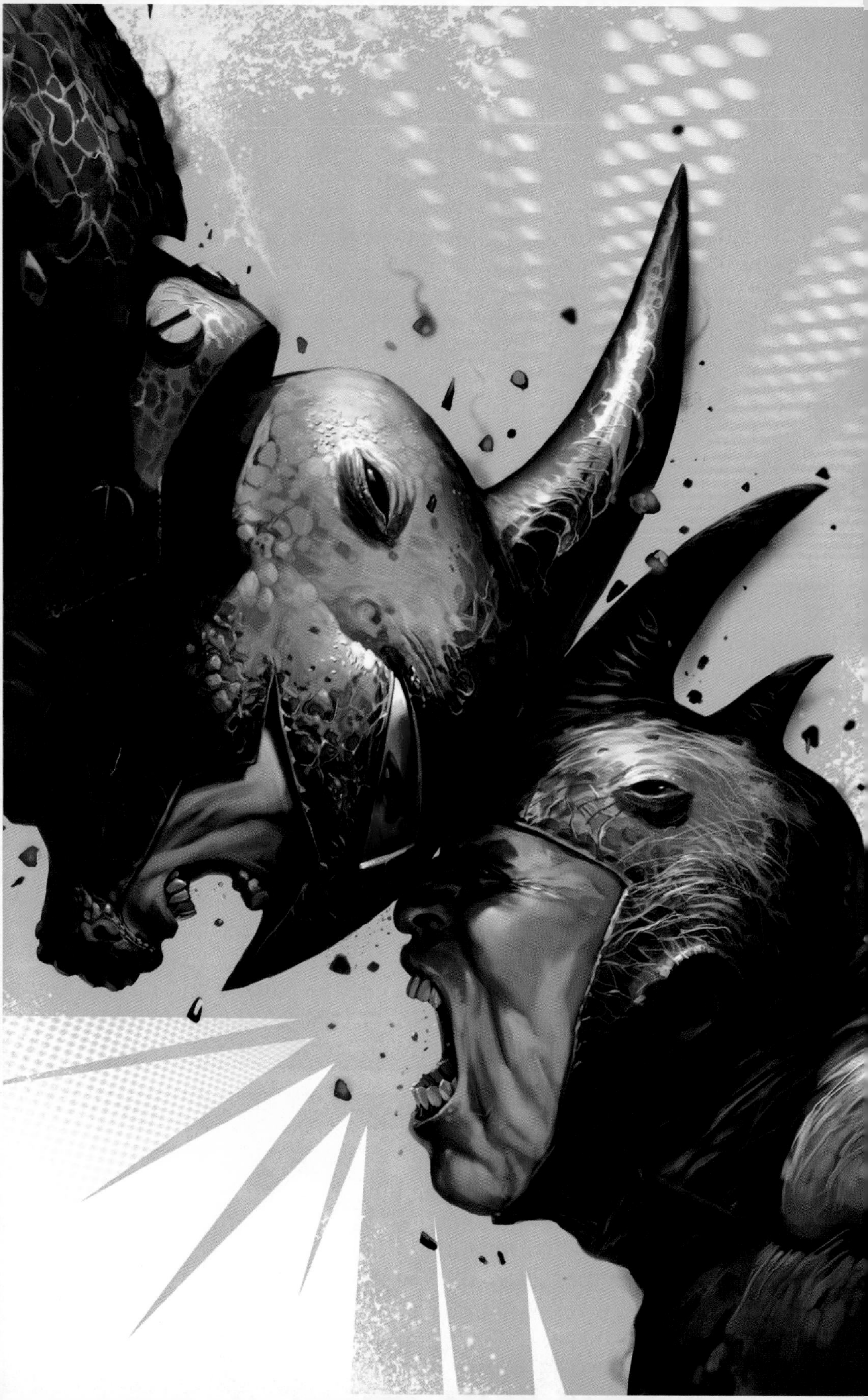

BUGLE GIRL
by
BETTY BRANT

›e Kelly – Writer
lax Fiumara – Art
abio D'Auria – Colorist
C's Joe Caramagna – Letterer
larko Djurdjevic – Cover
›m Brennan – Asst. Editor
tephen Wacker – Editor
›m Brevoort – Executive Editor
›e Quesada – Editor in Chief
›an Buckley – Publisher
lan Fine – Executive Producer

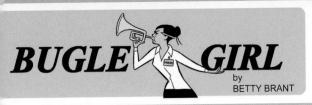

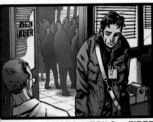

ORGED PHOTO FOILS FIRED HOTOG! The Mayor's personal notographer (and in-law) Peter Parker the most hated guy in town for faking e Mayor...more...

IZ'ONNER DEFENDS HIS HONOR! n the wake of his top aide forging hotographs to exonerate him from rongdoing in the Vulture Fiasco, Mayor ameson is planning "sweeping ethics nvestigation" of his own staff! more...

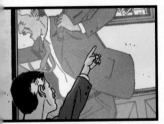

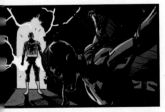

3OLT JOLT! Electro breaks the Vulture ut of jail – with the disappearance f Mysterio and a new Rhino running round town, is something Sinister on he horizon? more...

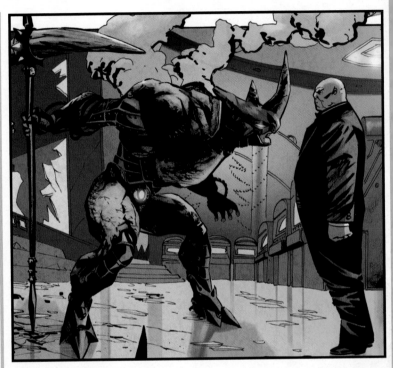

Aleksei Sytsevich was once The Rhino, a true force to be reckoned with in the super villain criminal underworld. With money as his motivation, he became a career criminal known for knocking down his opponents...and frequently being bested by The Amazing Spider-Man. Years of losses to the webhead humbled Sytsevich, and he attempted to reform his ways...

When a new Rhino emerged, a brash and violent, tech-based foe, he called out Sytsevich, who had found a straight job as security at a casino – and a wife named Oksana.

When this new Rhino challenged him, Sytsevich nearly returned to his dark side – until Spider-Man intervened, helping to best the Rhino for the moment – and turning Sytsevich back to his beloved wife.

The new Rhino was put up to his test by the mysterious Kraven family. Their motives are still clouded in shadow – but they've popped up in the lives of tons of Spider-Man's former foes, breaking an amped-up Electro and vicious new Vulture out of prison, all toward some new evil end. Their plans may be unclear, but their ruthless drive may prove unstoppable.

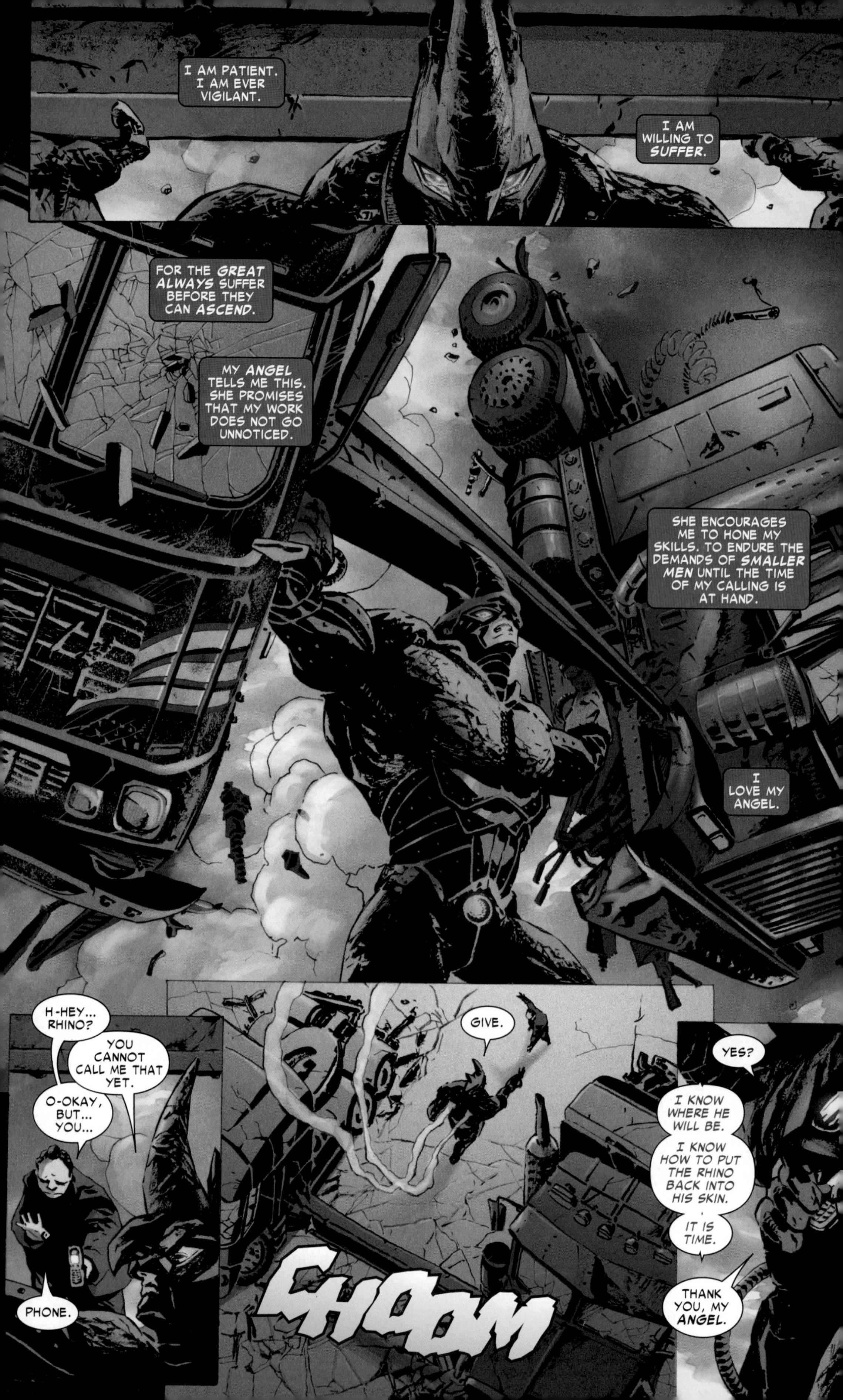

I AM PATIENT. I AM EVER VIGILANT.
I AM WILLING TO SUFFER.
FOR THE GREAT ALWAYS SUFFER BEFORE THEY CAN ASCEND.
MY ANGEL TELLS ME THIS. SHE PROMISES THAT MY WORK DOES NOT GO UNNOTICED.
SHE ENCOURAGES ME TO HONE MY SKILLS. TO ENDURE THE DEMANDS OF SMALLER MEN UNTIL THE TIME OF MY CALLING IS AT HAND.
I LOVE MY ANGEL.
H-HEY... RHINO?
YOU CANNOT CALL ME THAT YET.
O-OKAY, BUT... YOU...
PHONE.
GIVE.
CHOOM
YES?
I KNOW WHERE HE WILL BE.
I KNOW HOW TO PUT THE RHINO BACK INTO HIS SKIN.
IT IS TIME.
THANK YOU, MY ANGEL.

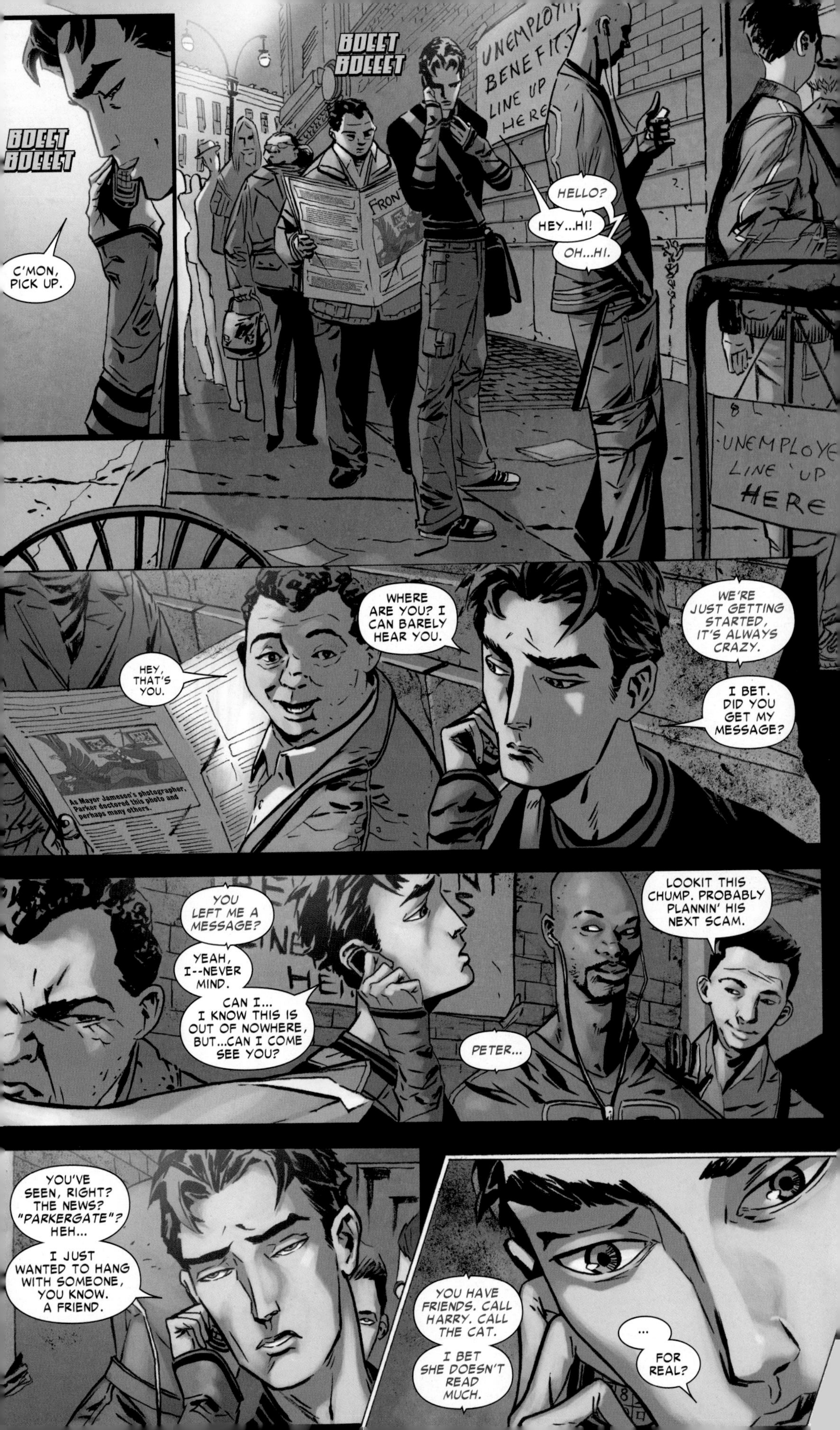
BDEET BDEEET
BDEET BDEEET
C'MON, PICK UP.
UNEMPLOY BENEFITS LINE UP HERE
HELLO?
HEY...HI!
OH...HI.
UNEMPLOYE LINE UP HERE
HEY, THAT'S YOU.
WHERE ARE YOU? I CAN BARELY HEAR YOU.
WE'RE JUST GETTING STARTED, IT'S ALWAYS CRAZY.
I BET. DID YOU GET MY MESSAGE?
As Mayor Jameson's photographer, Parker doctored this photo and perhaps many others.
YOU LEFT ME A MESSAGE?
YEAH, I--NEVER MIND.
CAN I... I KNOW THIS IS OUT OF NOWHERE, BUT...CAN I COME SEE YOU?
PETER...
LOOKIT THIS CHUMP. PROBABLY PLANNIN' HIS NEXT SCAM.
YOU'VE SEEN, RIGHT? THE NEWS? "PARKERGATE"? HEH...
I JUST WANTED TO HANG WITH SOMEONE, YOU KNOW. A FRIEND.
YOU HAVE FRIENDS. CALL HARRY. CALL THE CAT.
I BET SHE DOESN'T READ MUCH.
...
FOR REAL?

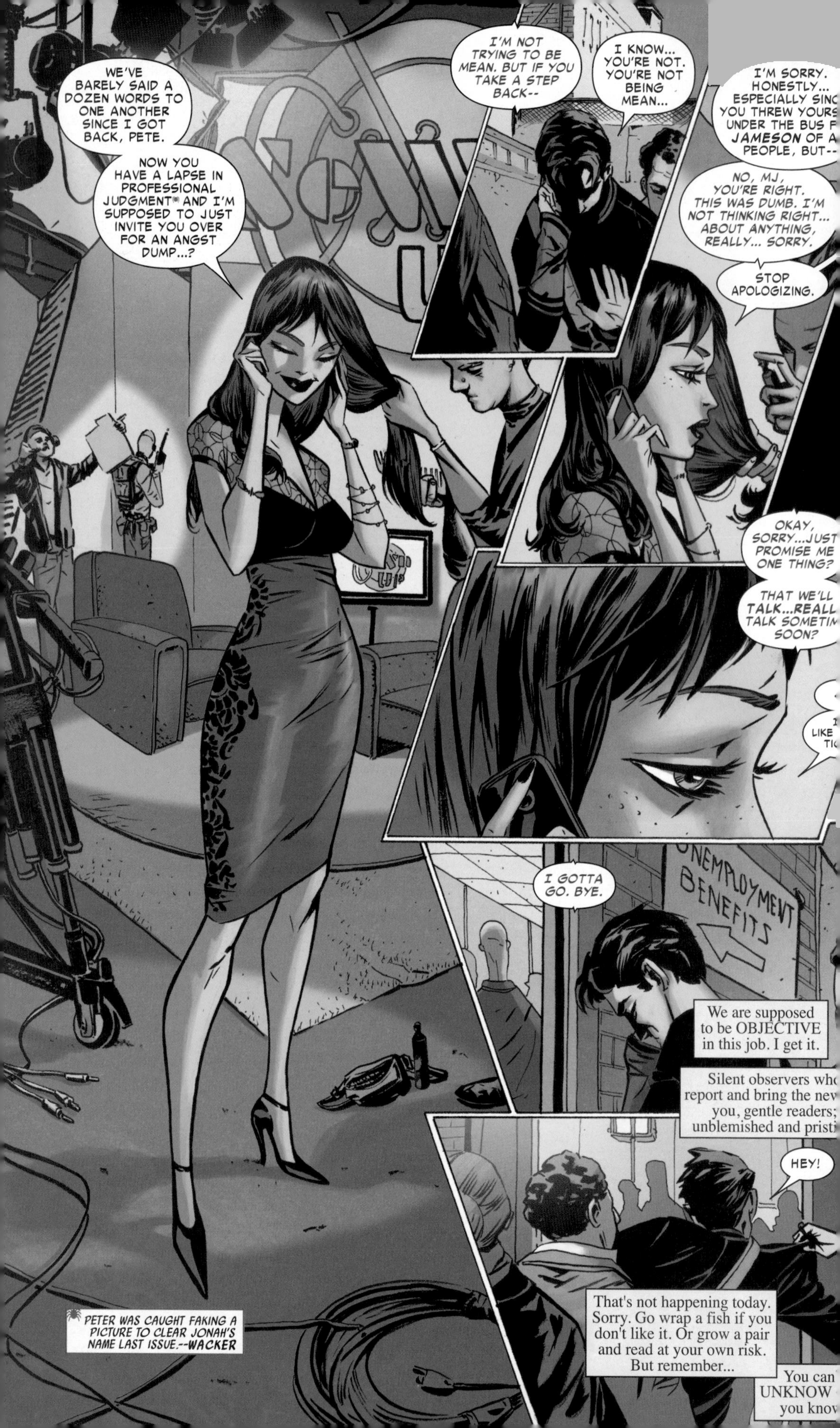
WE'VE BARELY SAID A DOZEN WORDS TO ONE ANOTHER SINCE I GOT BACK, PETE.
NOW YOU HAVE A LAPSE IN PROFESSIONAL JUDGMENT* AND I'M SUPPOSED TO JUST INVITE YOU OVER FOR AN ANGST DUMP...?
PETER WAS CAUGHT FAKING A PICTURE TO CLEAR JONAH'S NAME LAST ISSUE.--WACKER
I'M NOT TRYING TO BE MEAN. BUT IF YOU TAKE A STEP BACK--
I KNOW... YOU'RE NOT. YOU'RE NOT BEING MEAN...
I'M SORRY. HONESTLY... ESPECIALLY SINC YOU THREW YOURS UNDER THE BUS F JAMESON OF A PEOPLE, BUT--
NO, MJ, YOU'RE RIGHT. THIS WAS DUMB. I'M NOT THINKING RIGHT... ABOUT ANYTHING, REALLY... SORRY.
STOP APOLOGIZING.
OKAY, SORRY...JUST PROMISE ME ONE THING?
THAT WE'LL TALK...REALL TALK SOMETIM SOON?
I GOTTA GO. BYE.
UNEMPLOYMENT BENEFITS
We are supposed to be OBJECTIVE in this job. I get it.
Silent observers wh report and bring the nev you, gentle readers; unblemished and pristi
HEY!
That's not happening today. Sorry. Go wrap a fish if you don't like it. Or grow a pair and read at your own risk. But remember...
You can UNKNOW you know

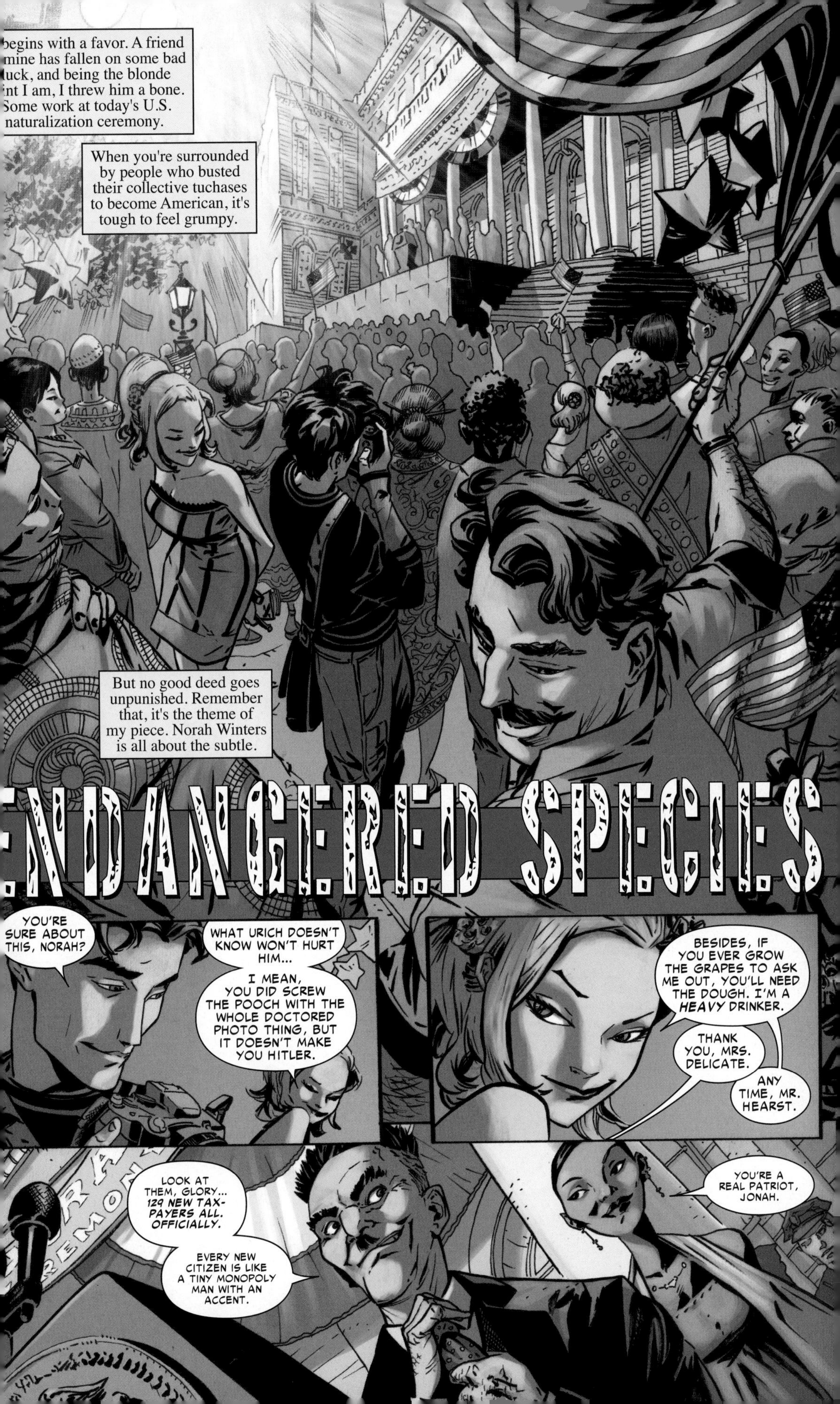

begins with a favor. A friend mine has fallen on some bad luck, and being the blonde nt I am, I threw him a bone. Some work at today's U.S. naturalization ceremony.
When you're surrounded by people who busted their collective tuchases to become American, it's tough to feel grumpy.
But no good deed goes unpunished. Remember that, it's the theme of my piece. Norah Winters is all about the subtle.
ENDANGERED SPECIES
YOU'RE SURE ABOUT THIS, NORAH?
WHAT URICH DOESN'T KNOW WON'T HURT HIM...
I MEAN, YOU DID SCREW THE POOCH WITH THE WHOLE DOCTORED PHOTO THING, BUT IT DOESN'T MAKE YOU HITLER.
BESIDES, IF YOU EVER GROW THE GRAPES TO ASK ME OUT, YOU'LL NEED THE DOUGH. I'M A *HEAVY* DRINKER.
THANK YOU, MRS. DELICATE.
ANY TIME, MR. HEARST.
LOOK AT THEM, GLORY... *129 NEW* TAX-PAYERS ALL. OFFICIALLY.
EVERY NEW CITIZEN IS LIKE A TINY MONOPOLY MAN WITH AN ACCENT.
YOU'RE A REAL PATRIOT, JONAH.

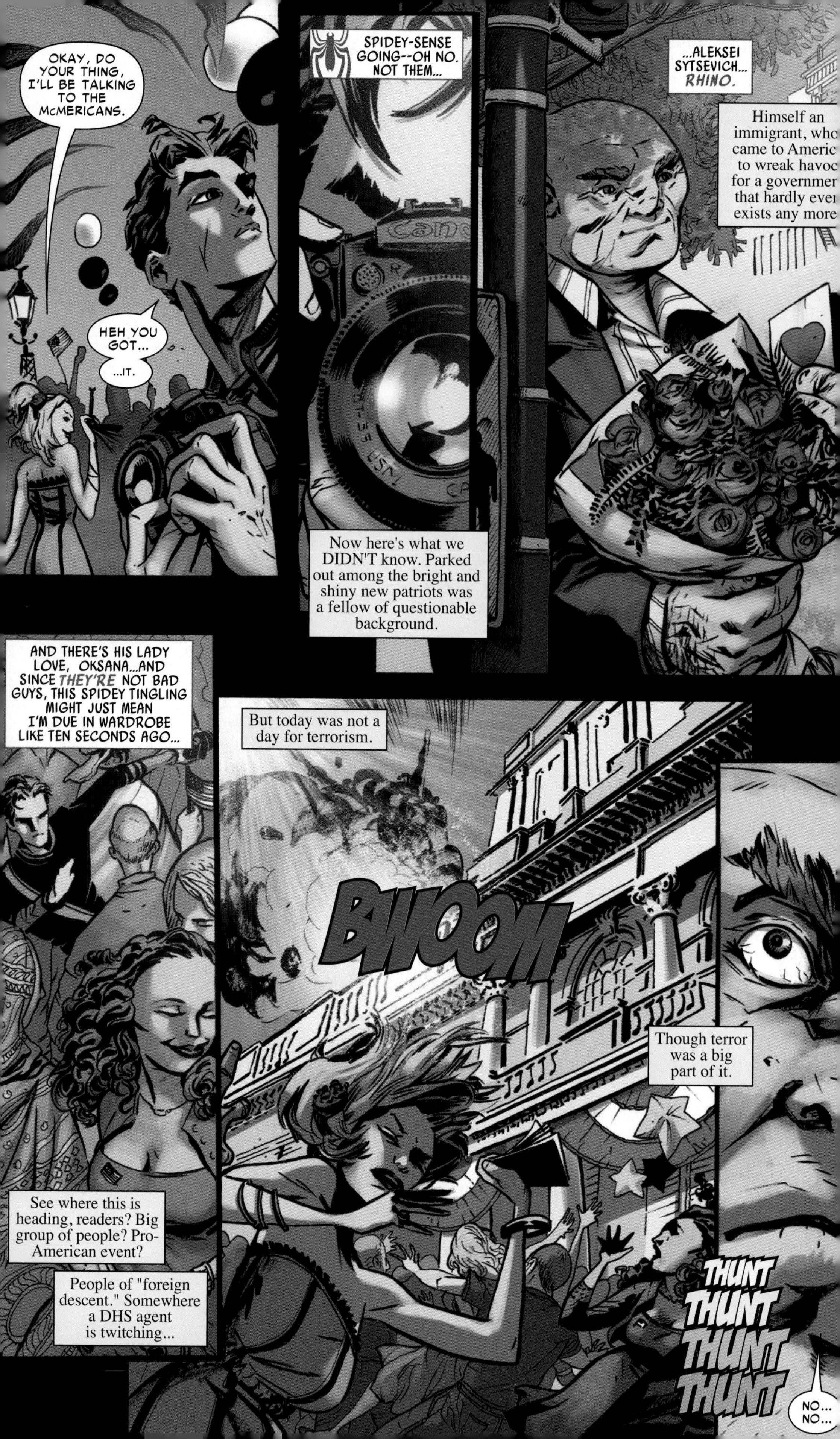

OKAY, DO YOUR THING, I'LL BE TALKING TO THE McMERICANS.
HEH YOU GOT...
...IT.
SPIDEY-SENSE GOING--OH NO. NOT THEM...
Now here's what we DIDN'T know. Parked out among the bright and shiny new patriots was a fellow of questionable background.
...ALEKSEI SYTSEVICH... RHINO.
Himself an immigrant, who came to Americ to wreak havoc for a governmer that hardly ever exists any more
AND THERE'S HIS LADY LOVE, OKSANA...AND SINCE THEY'RE NOT BAD GUYS, THIS SPIDEY TINGLING MIGHT JUST MEAN I'M DUE IN WARDROBE LIKE TEN SECONDS AGO...
See where this is heading, readers? Big group of people? Pro-American event?
People of "foreign descent." Somewhere a DHS agent is twitching...
But today was not a day for terrorism.
BWOOM
Though terror was a big part of it.
THUNT THUNT THUNT THUNT
NO... NO...

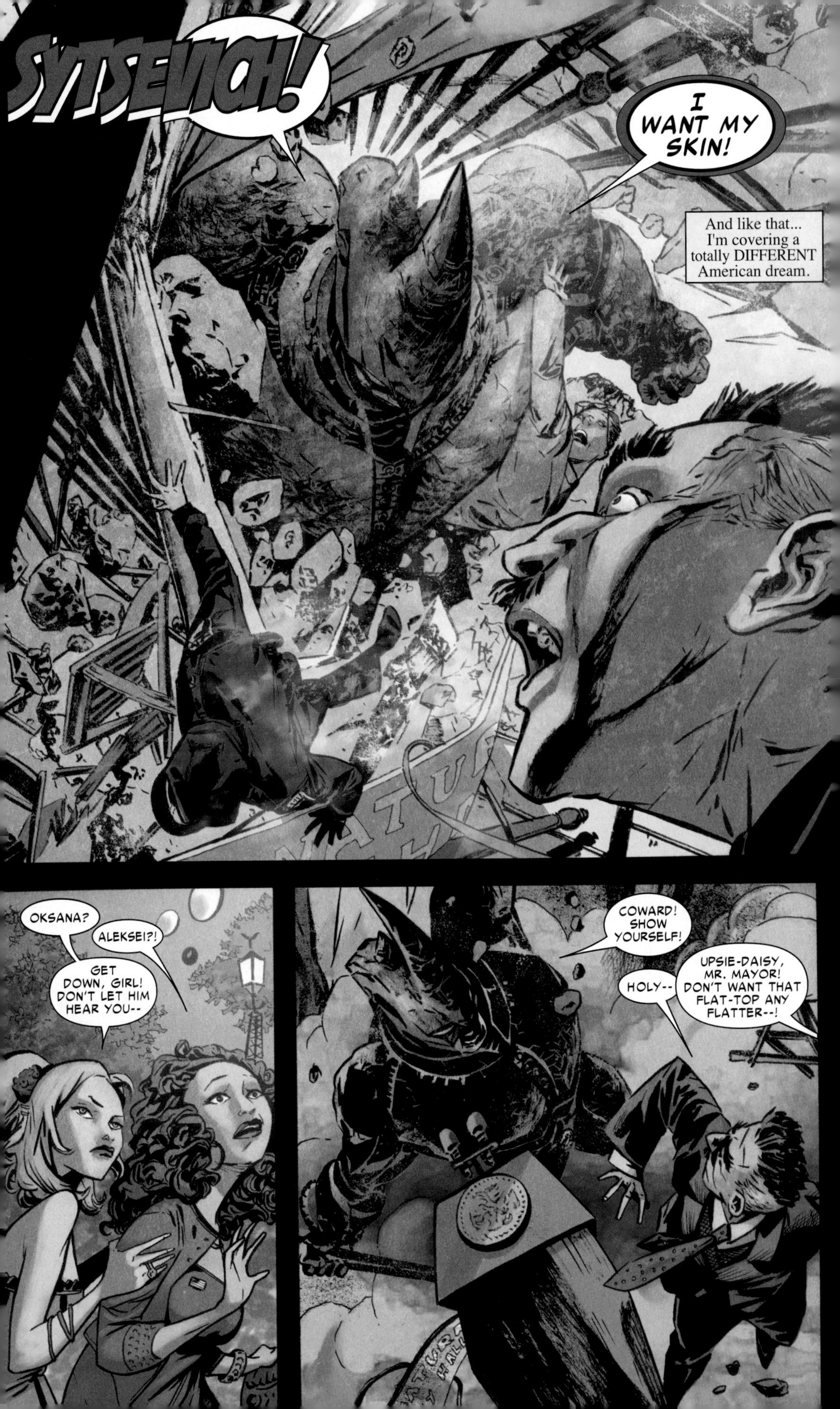
SYTSEVICH!
I WANT MY SKIN!
And like that... I'm covering a totally DIFFERENT American dream.
OKSANA?
ALEKSEI?!
GET DOWN, GIRL! DON'T LET HIM HEAR YOU--
COWARD! SHOW YOURSELF!
HOLY--
UPSIE-DAISY, MR. MAYOR! DON'T WANT THAT FLAT-TOP ANY FLATTER--!

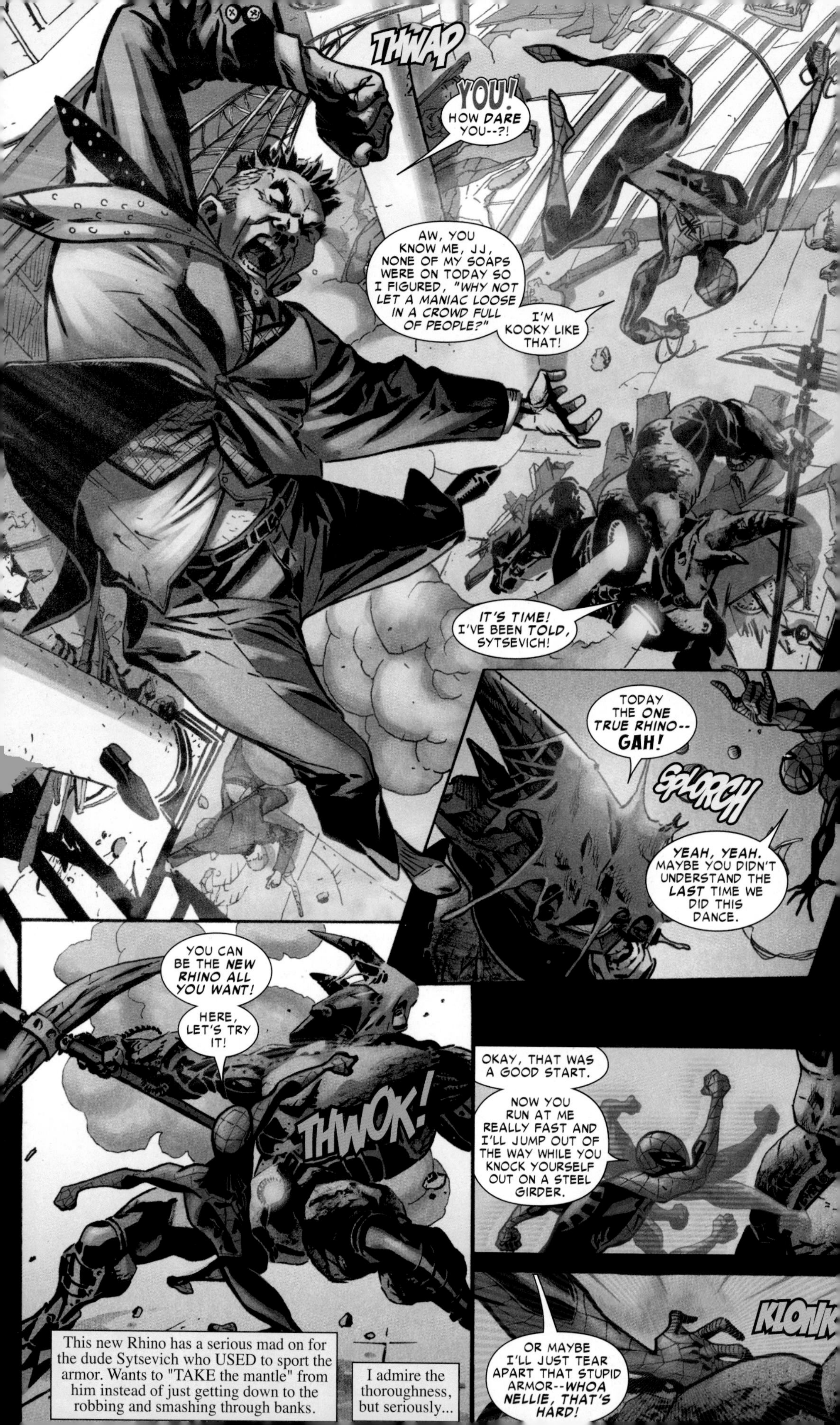
THWAP
YOU! HOW DARE YOU--?!
AW, YOU KNOW ME, JJ, NONE OF MY SOAPS WERE ON TODAY SO I FIGURED, "WHY NOT LET A MANIAC LOOSE IN A CROWD FULL OF PEOPLE?"
I'M KOOKY LIKE THAT!
IT'S TIME! I'VE BEEN TOLD, SYTSEVICH!
TODAY THE ONE TRUE RHINO-- GAH!
SPLORCH
YEAH, YEAH. MAYBE YOU DIDN'T UNDERSTAND THE LAST TIME WE DID THIS DANCE.
YOU CAN BE THE NEW RHINO ALL YOU WANT!
HERE, LET'S TRY IT!
THWOK!
This new Rhino has a serious mad on for the dude Sytsevich who USED to sport the armor. Wants to "TAKE the mantle" from him instead of just getting down to the robbing and smashing through banks.
I admire the thoroughness, but seriously...
OKAY, THAT WAS A GOOD START.
NOW YOU RUN AT ME REALLY FAST AND I'LL JUMP OUT OF THE WAY WHILE YOU KNOCK YOURSELF OUT ON A STEEL GIRDER.
KLONK
OR MAYBE I'LL JUST TEAR APART THAT STUPID ARMOR--WHOA NELLIE, THAT'S HARD!

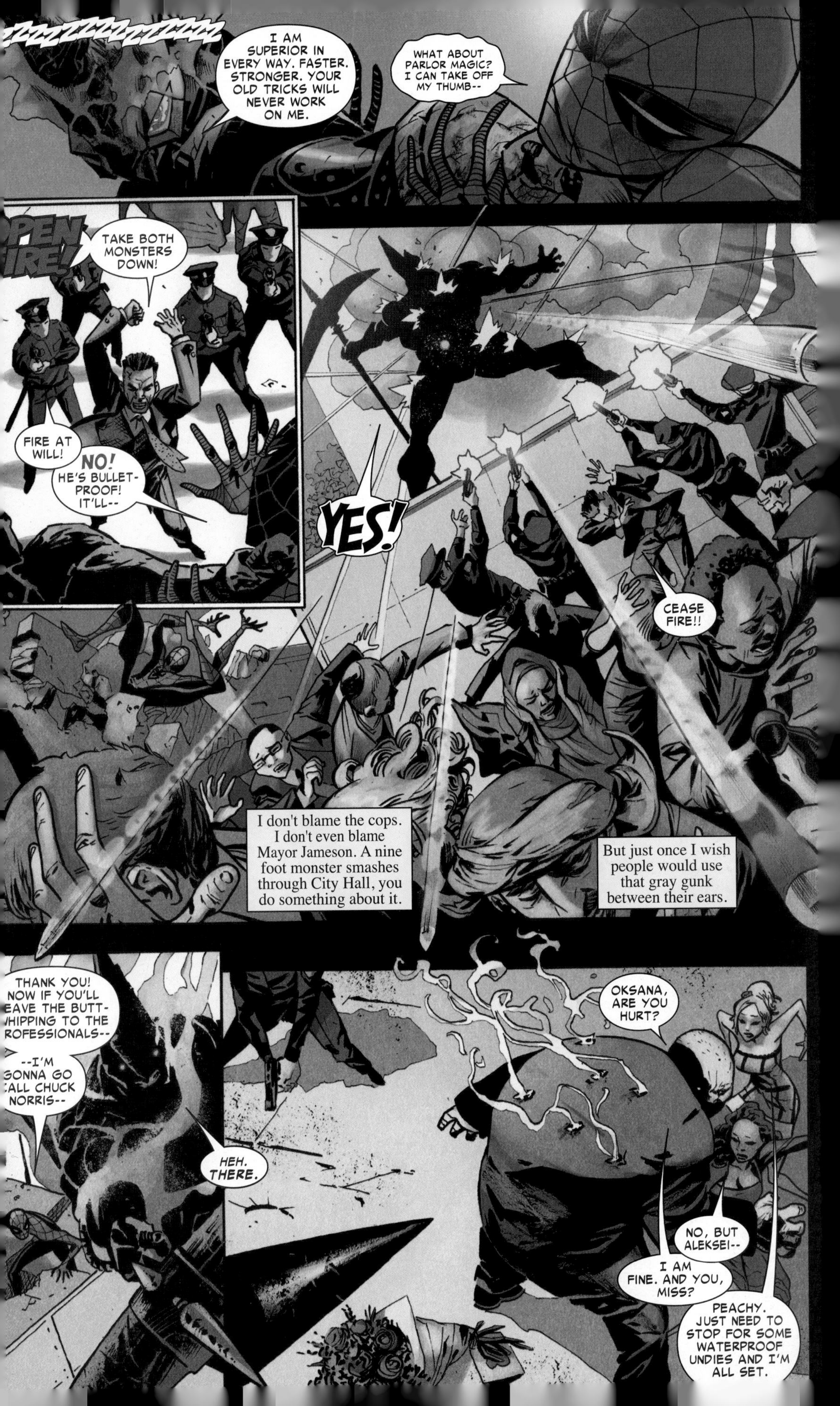
ZZZZZZZZZZZZZZZZZZ
I AM SUPERIOR IN EVERY WAY. FASTER. STRONGER. YOUR OLD TRICKS WILL NEVER WORK ON ME.
WHAT ABOUT PARLOR MAGIC? I CAN TAKE OFF MY THUMB--
OPEN FIRE!
TAKE BOTH MONSTERS DOWN!
FIRE AT WILL!
NO! HE'S BULLET-PROOF! IT'LL--
YES!
CEASE FIRE!!
I don't blame the cops. I don't even blame Mayor Jameson. A nine foot monster smashes through City Hall, you do something about it.
But just once I wish people would use that gray gunk between their ears.
THANK YOU! NOW IF YOU'LL EAVE THE BUTT-WHIPPING TO THE ROFESSIONALS--
--I'M GONNA GO CALL CHUCK NORRIS--
HEH. THERE.
OKSANA, ARE YOU HURT?
NO, BUT ALEKSEI--
I AM FINE. AND YOU, MISS?
PEACHY. JUST NEED TO STOP FOR SOME WATERPROOF UNDIES AND I'M ALL SET.

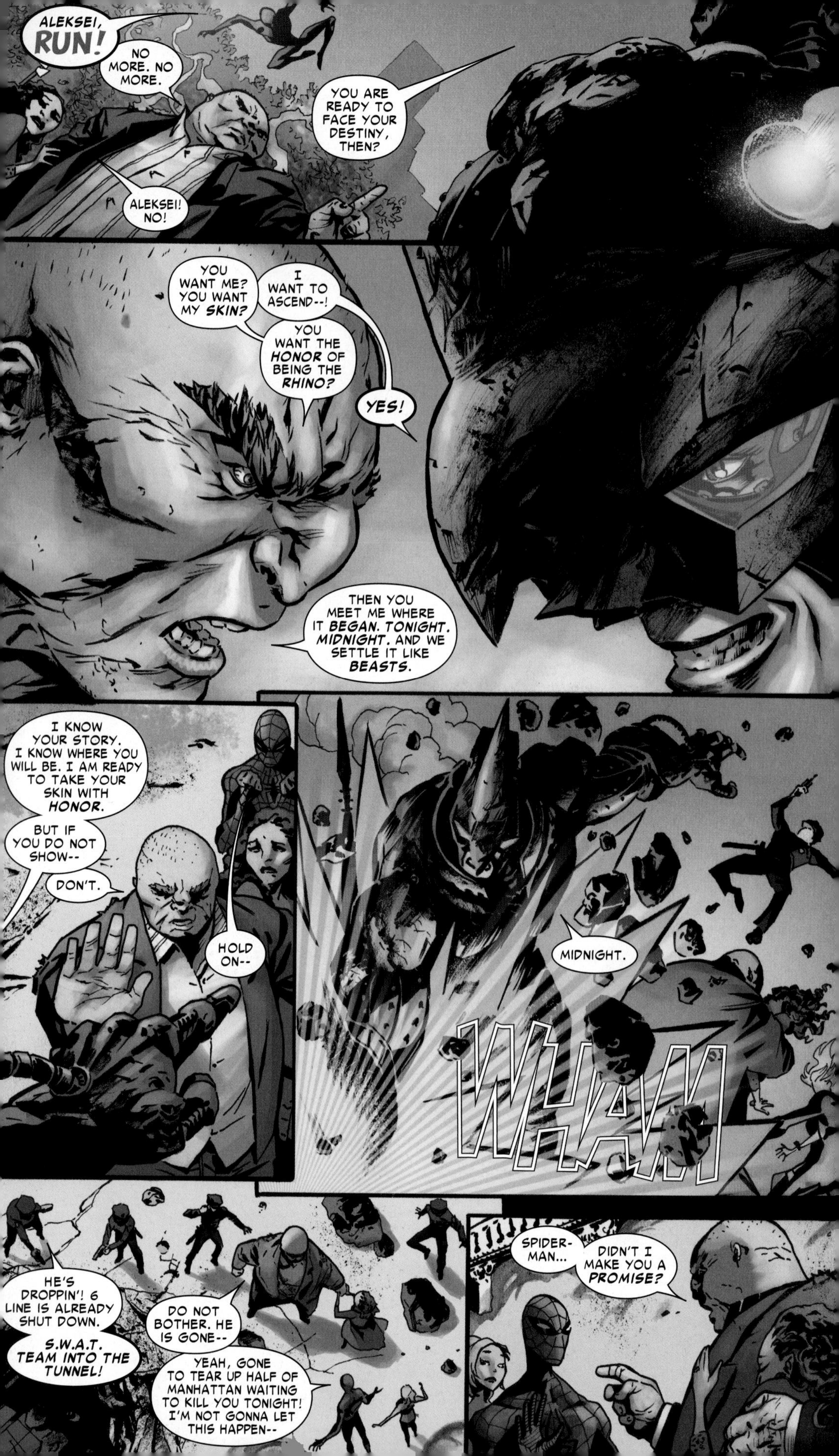

ALEKSEI, RUN!
NO MORE. NO MORE.
YOU ARE READY TO FACE YOUR DESTINY, THEN?
ALEKSEI! NO!
YOU WANT ME? YOU WANT MY SKIN?
I WANT TO ASCEND--!
YOU WANT THE HONOR OF BEING THE RHINO?
YES!
THEN YOU MEET ME WHERE IT BEGAN. TONIGHT. MIDNIGHT. AND WE SETTLE IT LIKE BEASTS.
I KNOW YOUR STORY. I KNOW WHERE YOU WILL BE. I AM READY TO TAKE YOUR SKIN WITH HONOR.
BUT IF YOU DO NOT SHOW--
DON'T.
HOLD ON--
MIDNIGHT.
WHAM
HE'S DROPPIN'! 6 LINE IS ALREADY SHUT DOWN.
S.W.A.T. TEAM INTO THE TUNNEL!
DO NOT BOTHER. HE IS GONE--
YEAH, GONE TO TEAR UP HALF OF MANHATTAN WAITING TO KILL YOU TONIGHT! I'M NOT GONNA LET THIS HAPPEN--
SPIDER-MAN...
DIDN'T I MAKE YOU A PROMISE?

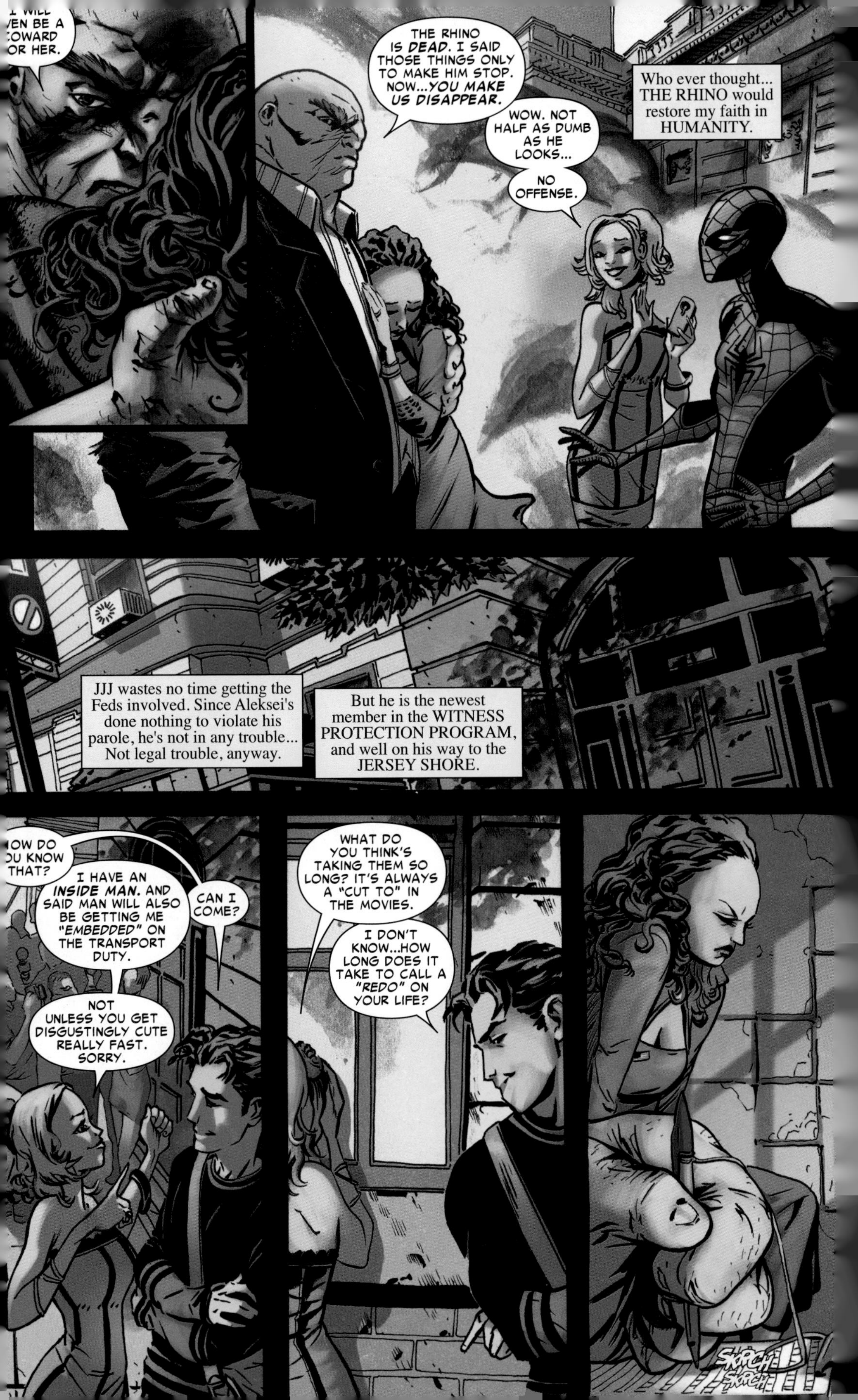

I WILL
EVEN BE A
COWARD
FOR HER.
THE RHINO IS DEAD. I SAID THOSE THINGS ONLY TO MAKE HIM STOP. NOW...YOU MAKE US DISAPPEAR.
WOW. NOT HALF AS DUMB AS HE LOOKS...
NO OFFENSE.
Who ever thought... THE RHINO would restore my faith in HUMANITY.
JJJ wastes no time getting the Feds involved. Since Aleksei's done nothing to violate his parole, he's not in any trouble... Not legal trouble, anyway.
But he is the newest member in the WITNESS PROTECTION PROGRAM, and well on his way to the JERSEY SHORE.
HOW DO YOU KNOW THAT?
I HAVE AN INSIDE MAN. AND SAID MAN WILL ALSO BE GETTING ME "EMBEDDED" ON THE TRANSPORT DUTY.
CAN I COME?
NOT UNLESS YOU GET DISGUSTINGLY CUTE REALLY FAST. SORRY.
WHAT DO YOU THINK'S TAKING THEM SO LONG? IT'S ALWAYS A "CUT TO" IN THE MOVIES.
I DON'T KNOW...HOW LONG DOES IT TAKE TO CALL A "REDO" ON YOUR LIFE?
SKRCH
SKRCH

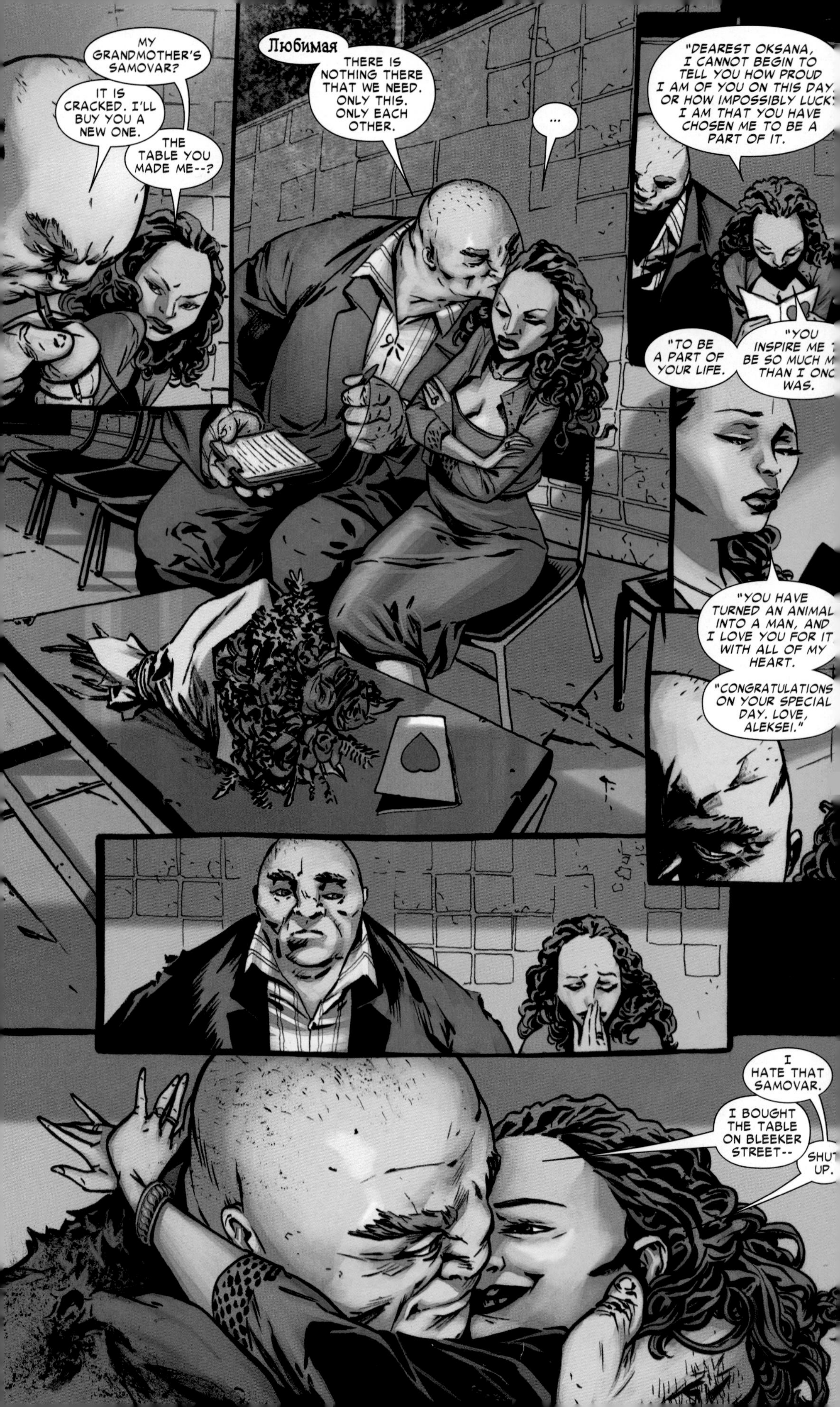

MY GRANDMOTHER'S SAMOVAR?
IT IS CRACKED. I'LL BUY YOU A NEW ONE.
THE TABLE YOU MADE ME--?
Любимая
THERE IS NOTHING THERE THAT WE NEED. ONLY THIS. ONLY EACH OTHER.
...
"DEAREST OKSANA, I CANNOT BEGIN TO TELL YOU HOW PROUD I AM OF YOU ON THIS DAY, OR HOW IMPOSSIBLY LUCKY I AM THAT YOU HAVE CHOSEN ME TO BE A PART OF IT.
"TO BE A PART OF YOUR LIFE.
"YOU INSPIRE ME TO BE SO MUCH MORE THAN I ONCE WAS.
"YOU HAVE TURNED AN ANIMAL INTO A MAN, AND I LOVE YOU FOR IT WITH ALL OF MY HEART.
"CONGRATULATIONS ON YOUR SPECIAL DAY. LOVE, ALEKSEI."
I HATE THAT SAMOVAR.
I BOUGHT THE TABLE ON BLEEKER STREET--
SHUT UP.

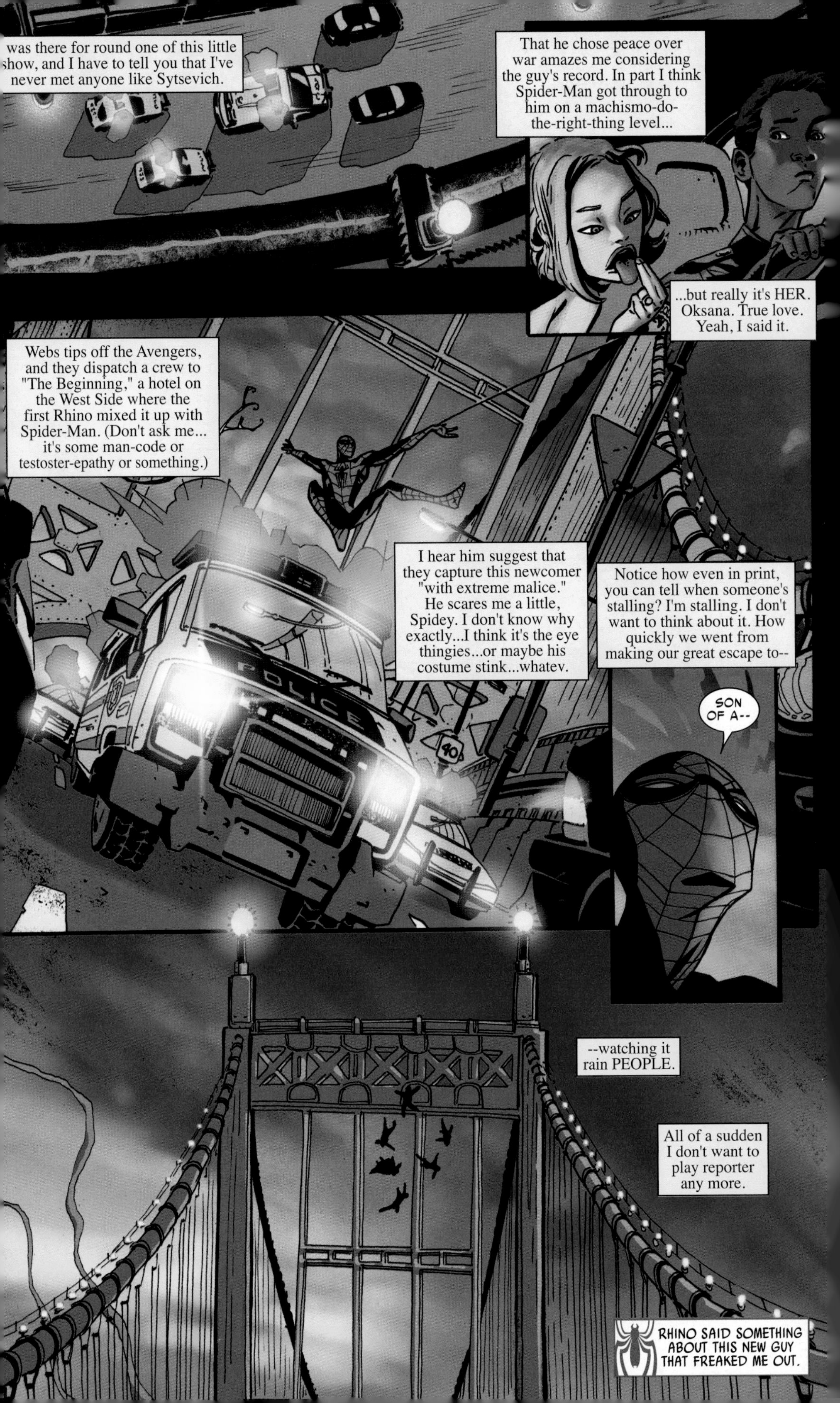

was there for round one of this little show, and I have to tell you that I've never met anyone like Sytsevich.
That he chose peace over war amazes me considering the guy's record. In part I think Spider-Man got through to him on a machismo-do-the-right-thing level...
...but really it's HER. Oksana. True love. Yeah, I said it.
Webs tips off the Avengers, and they dispatch a crew to "The Beginning," a hotel on the West Side where the first Rhino mixed it up with Spider-Man. (Don't ask me... it's some man-code or testoster-epathy or something.)
I hear him suggest that they capture this newcomer "with extreme malice." He scares me a little, Spidey. I don't know why exactly...I think it's the eye thingies...or maybe his costume stink...whatev.
POLICE
Notice how even in print, you can tell when someone's stalling? I'm stalling. I don't want to think about it. How quickly we went from making our great escape to--
SON OF A--
--watching it rain PEOPLE.
All of a sudden I don't want to play reporter any more.
RHINO SAID SOMETHING ABOUT THIS NEW GUY THAT FREAKED ME OUT.

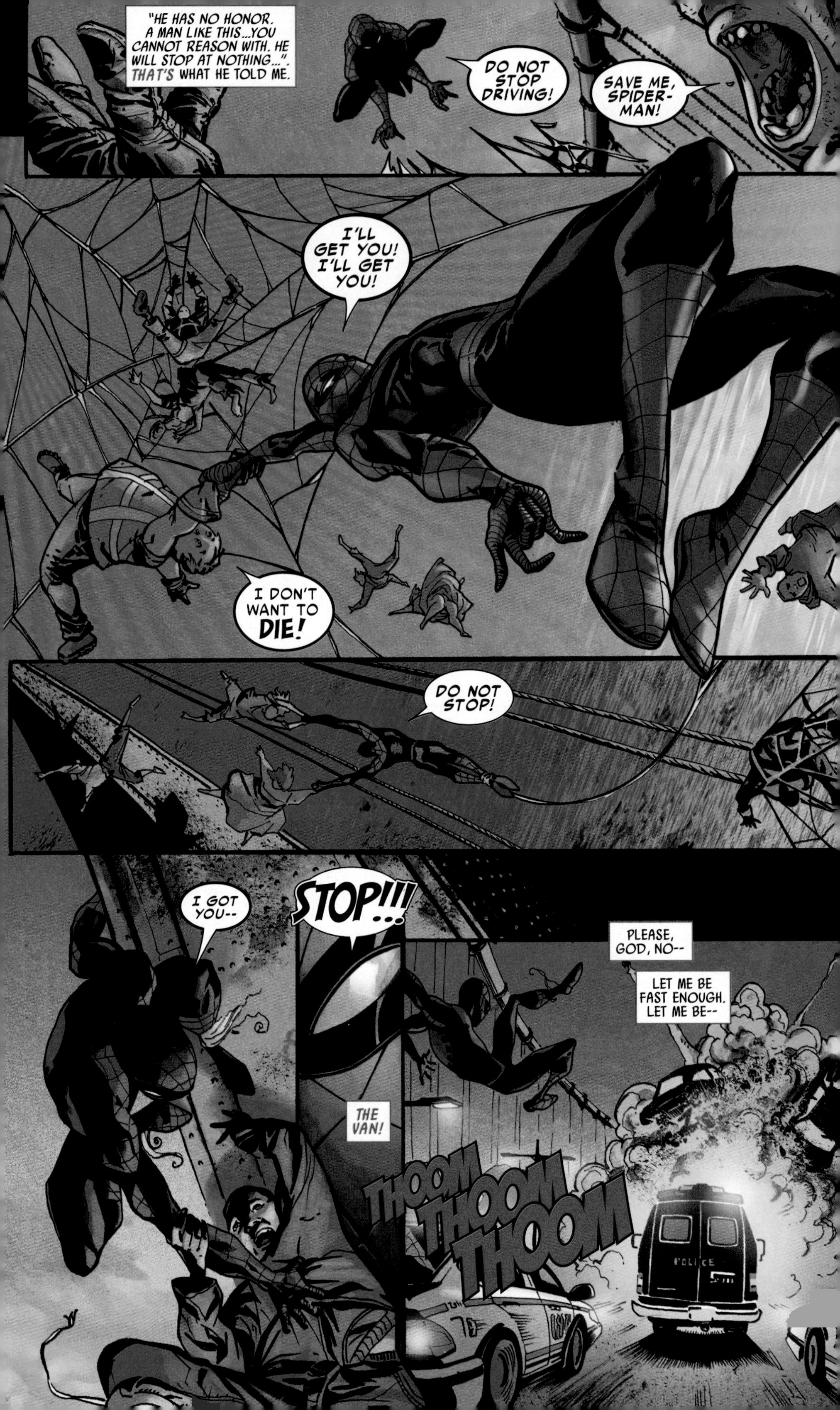
"HE HAS NO HONOR. A MAN LIKE THIS...YOU CANNOT REASON WITH. HE WILL STOP AT NOTHING...". THAT'S WHAT HE TOLD ME.
DO NOT STOP DRIVING!
SAVE ME, SPIDER-MAN!
I'LL GET YOU! I'LL GET YOU!
I DON'T WANT TO DIE!
DO NOT STOP!
I GOT YOU--
STOP!!!
PLEASE, GOD, NO--
LET ME BE FAST ENOUGH. LET ME BE--
THE VAN!
THOOM THOOM THOOM
POLICE

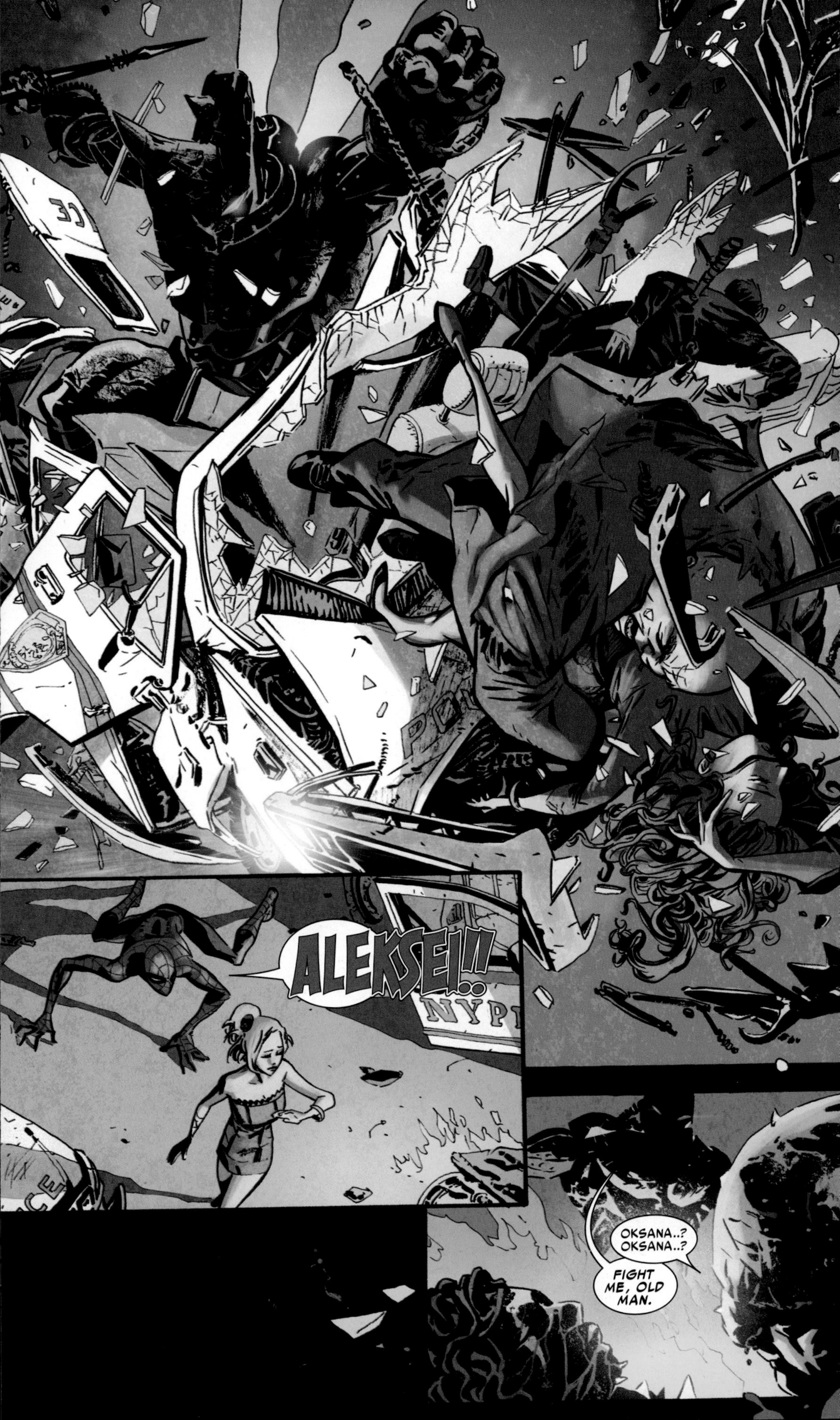
ALEKSEI!!
OKSANA..? OKSANA..?
FIGHT ME, OLD MAN.

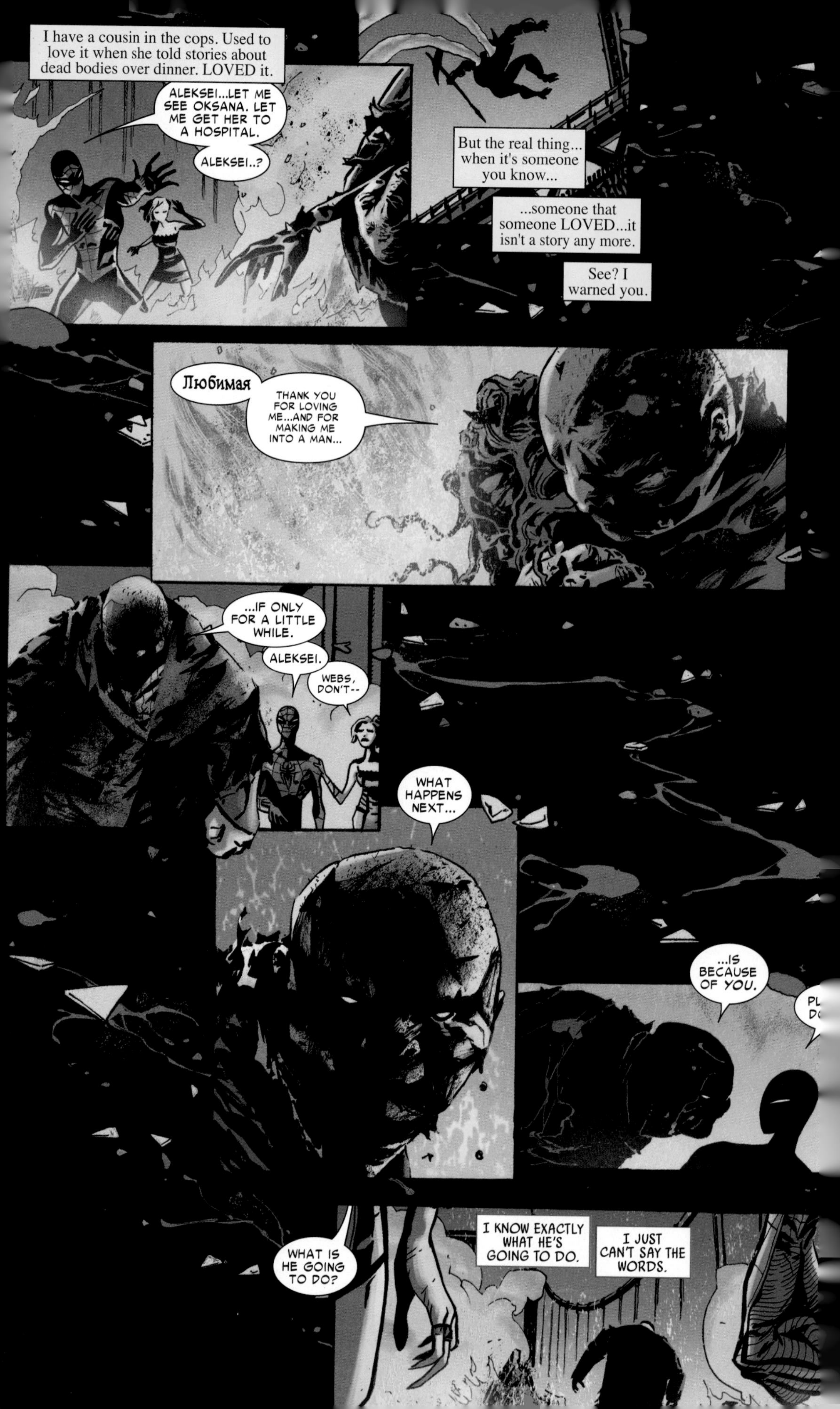
I have a cousin in the cops. Used to love it when she told stories about dead bodies over dinner. LOVED it.
ALEKSEI...LET ME SEE OKSANA. LET ME GET HER TO A HOSPITAL.
ALEKSEI..?
But the real thing... when it's someone you know...
...someone that someone LOVED...it isn't a story any more.
See? I warned you.
Любимая
THANK YOU FOR LOVING ME...AND FOR MAKING ME INTO A MAN...
...IF ONLY FOR A LITTLE WHILE.
ALEKSEI.
WEBS, DON'T--
WHAT HAPPENS NEXT...
...IS BECAUSE OF *YOU*.
WHAT IS HE GOING TO DO?
I KNOW EXACTLY WHAT HE'S GOING TO DO.
I JUST CAN'T SAY THE WORDS.

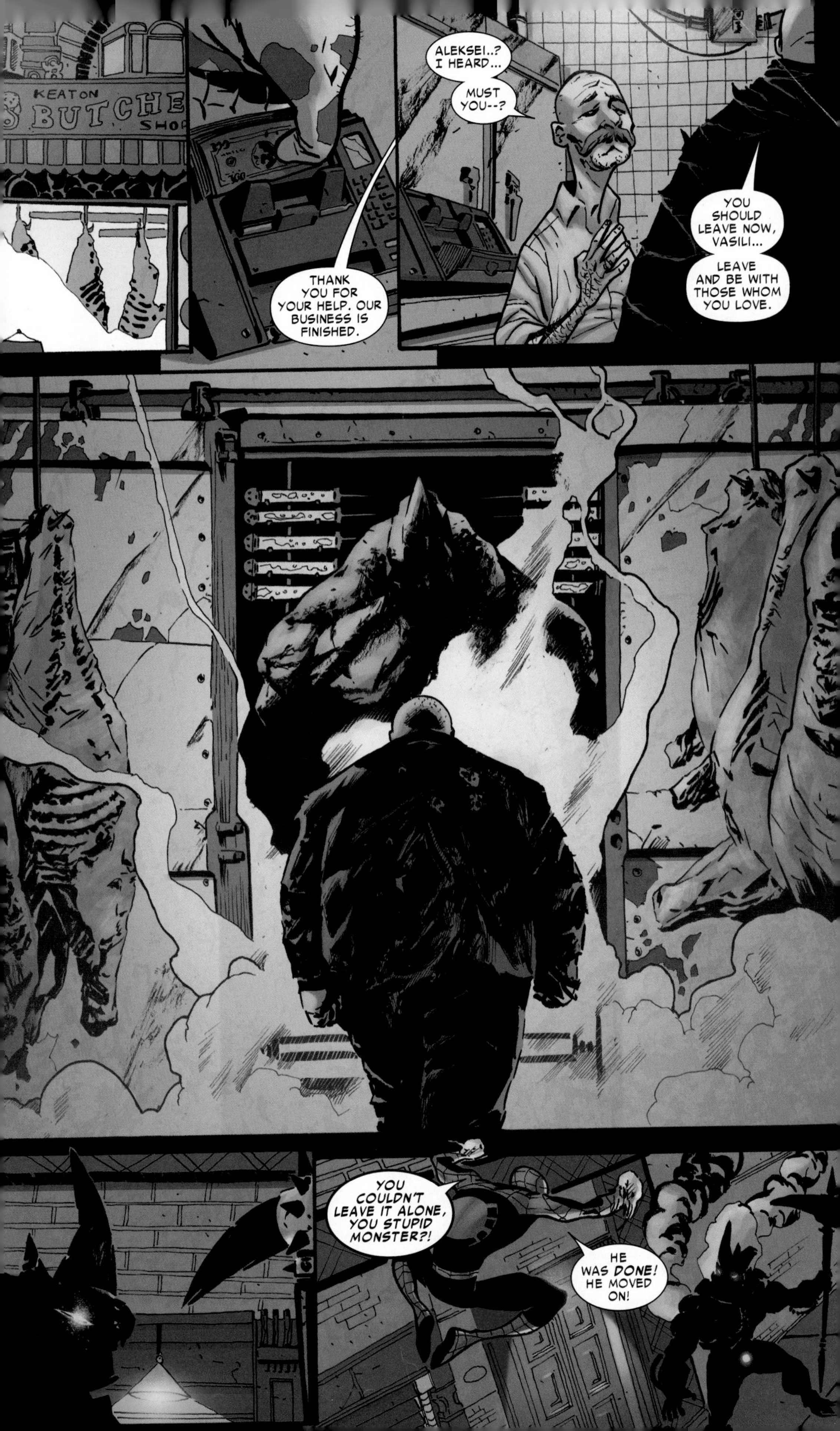
KEATON
BUTCHE
SHOP
ALEKSEI..? I HEARD...
MUST YOU--?
THANK YOU FOR YOUR HELP. OUR BUSINESS IS FINISHED.
YOU SHOULD LEAVE NOW, VASILI...
LEAVE AND BE WITH THOSE WHOM YOU LOVE.
YOU COULDN'T LEAVE IT ALONE, YOU STUPID MONSTER?!
HE WAS DONE! HE MOVED ON!

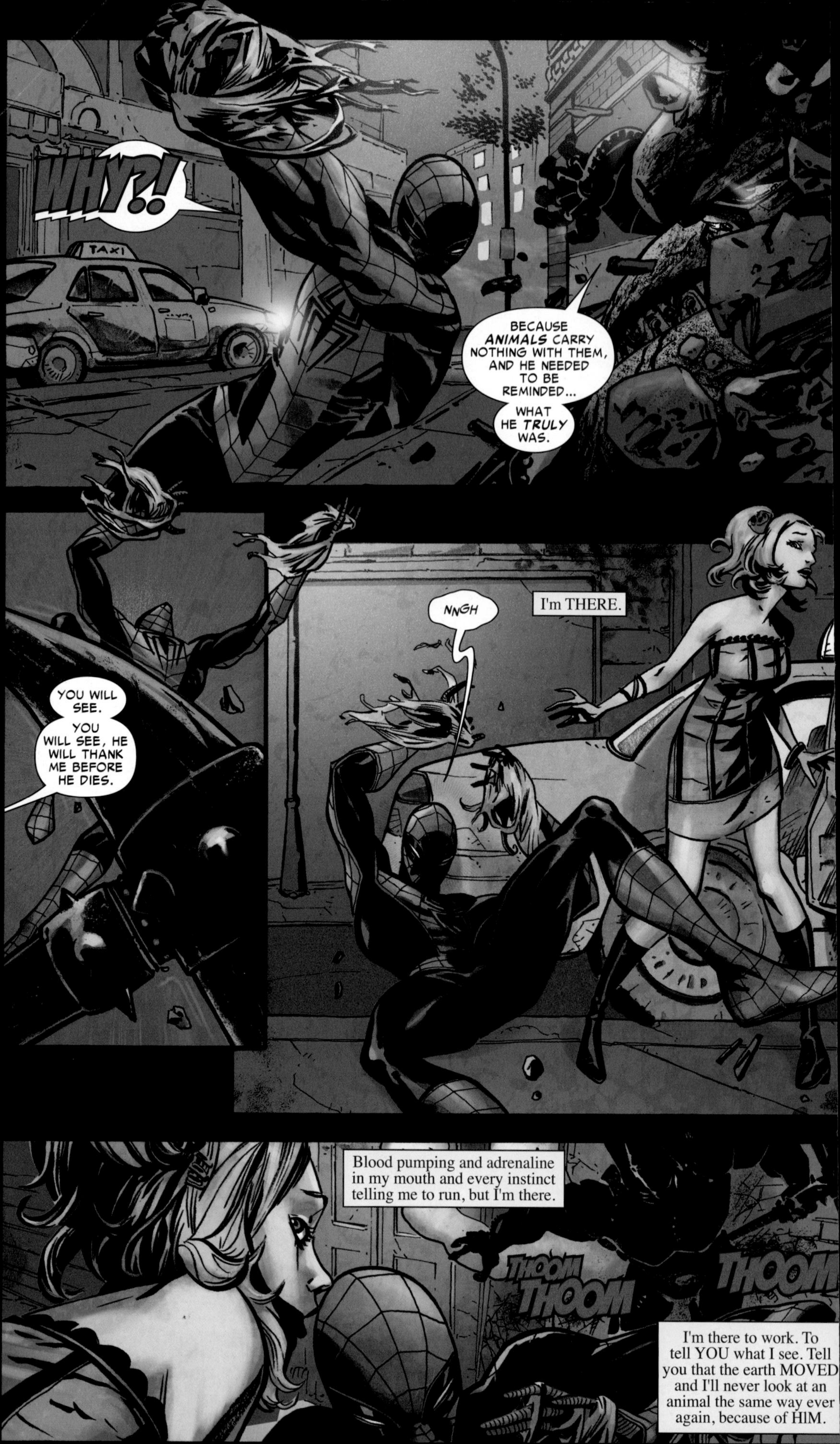

WHY?!
BECAUSE ANIMALS CARRY NOTHING WITH THEM, AND HE NEEDED TO BE REMINDED...
WHAT HE TRULY WAS.
YOU WILL SEE.
YOU WILL SEE, HE WILL THANK ME BEFORE HE DIES.
NNGH
I'm THERE.
Blood pumping and adrenaline in my mouth and every instinct telling me to run, but I'm there.
THOOM THOOM
THOOM
I'm there to work. To tell YOU what I see. Tell you that the earth MOVED and I'll never look at an animal the same way ever again, because of HIM.

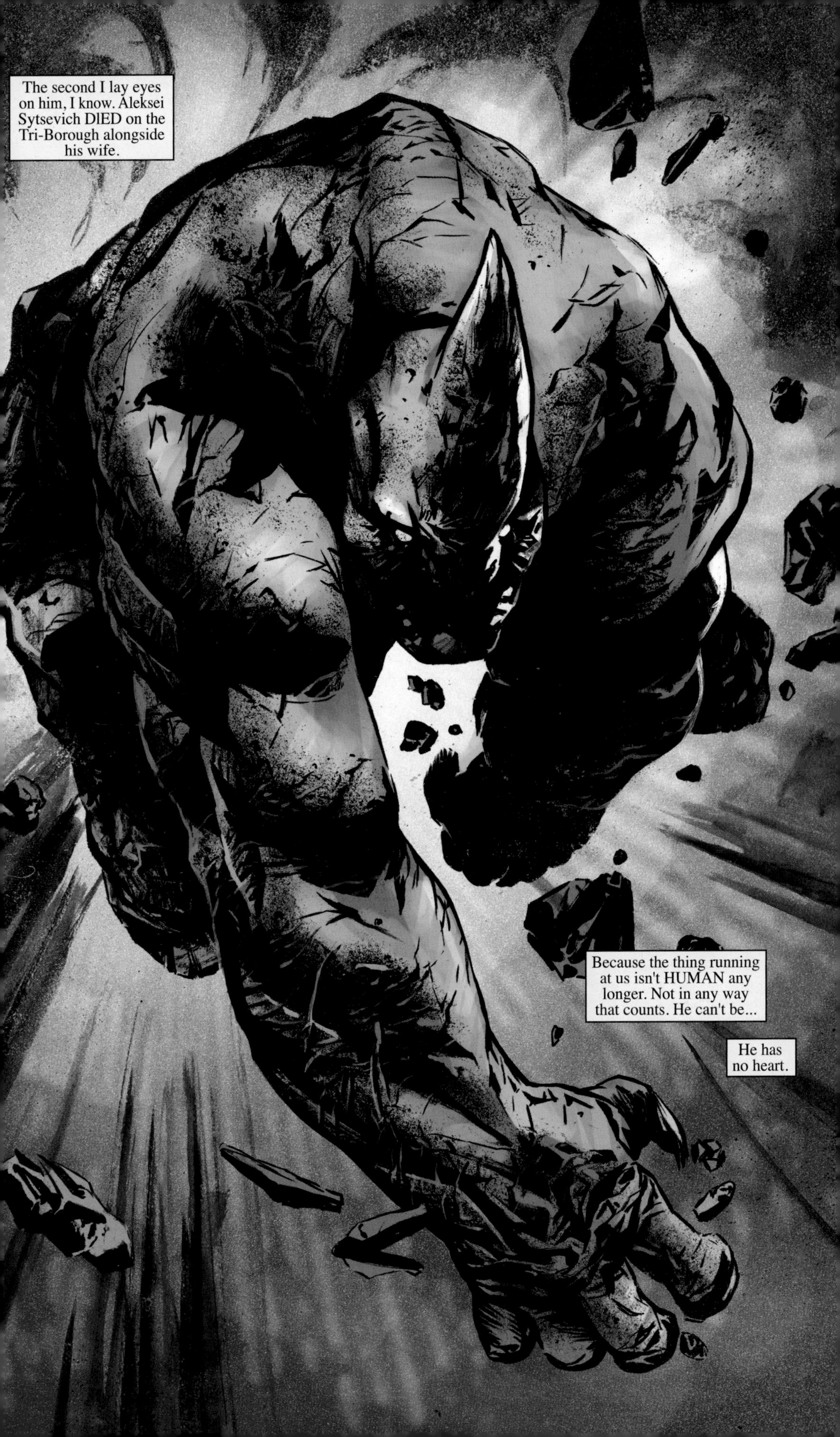
The second I lay eyes on him, I know. Aleksei Sytsevich DIED on the Tri-Borough alongside his wife.
Because the thing running at us isn't HUMAN any longer. Not in any way that counts. He can't be...
He has no heart.

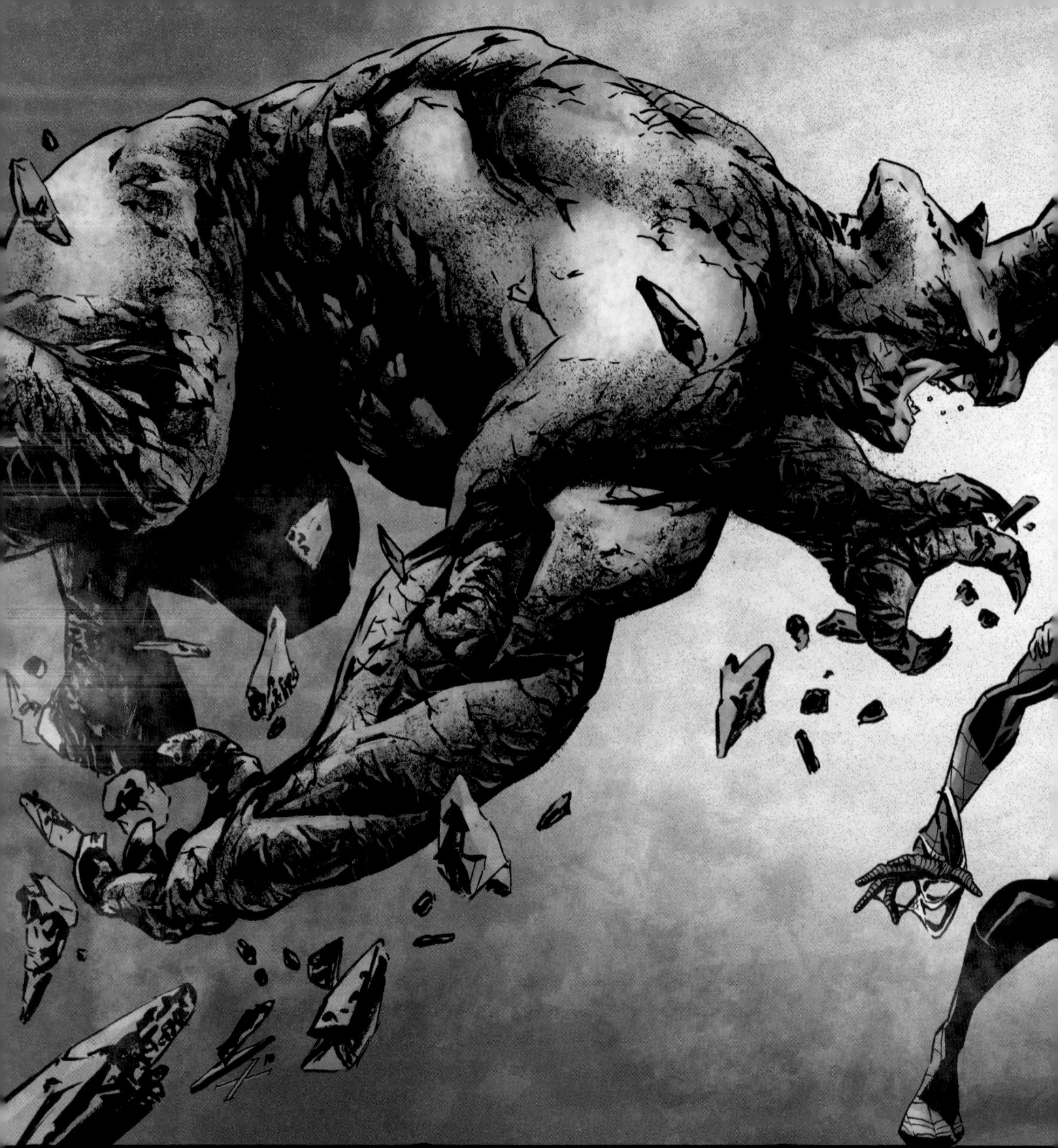

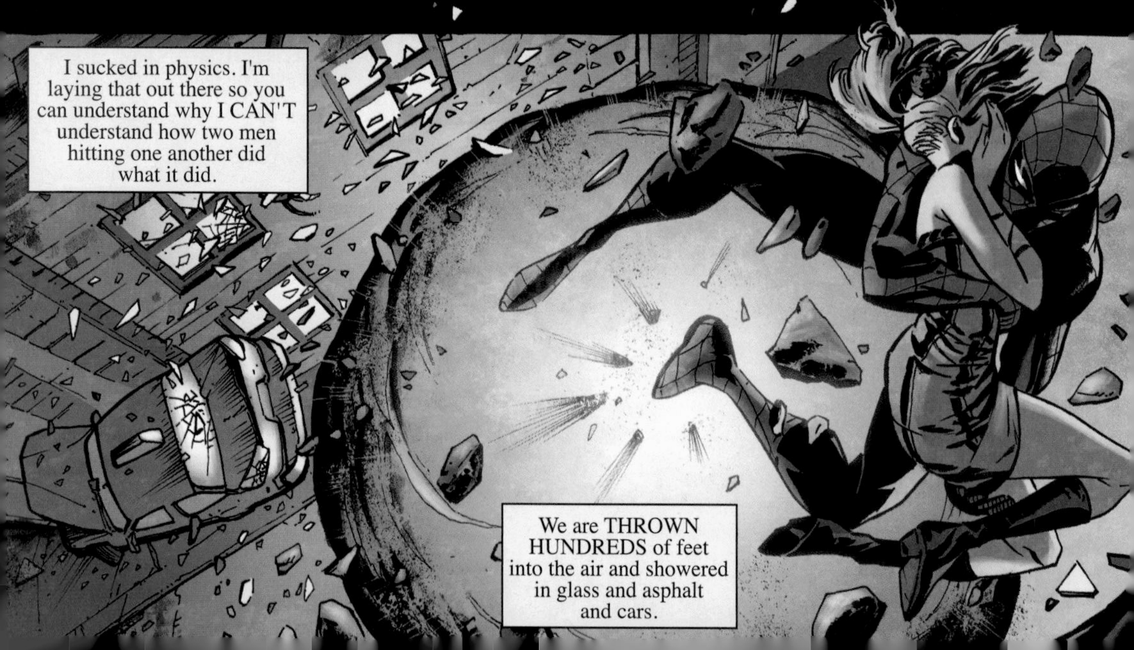
I sucked in physics. I'm laying that out there so you can understand why I CAN'T understand how two men hitting one another did what it did.
We are THROWN HUNDREDS of feet into the air and showered in glass and asphalt and cars.

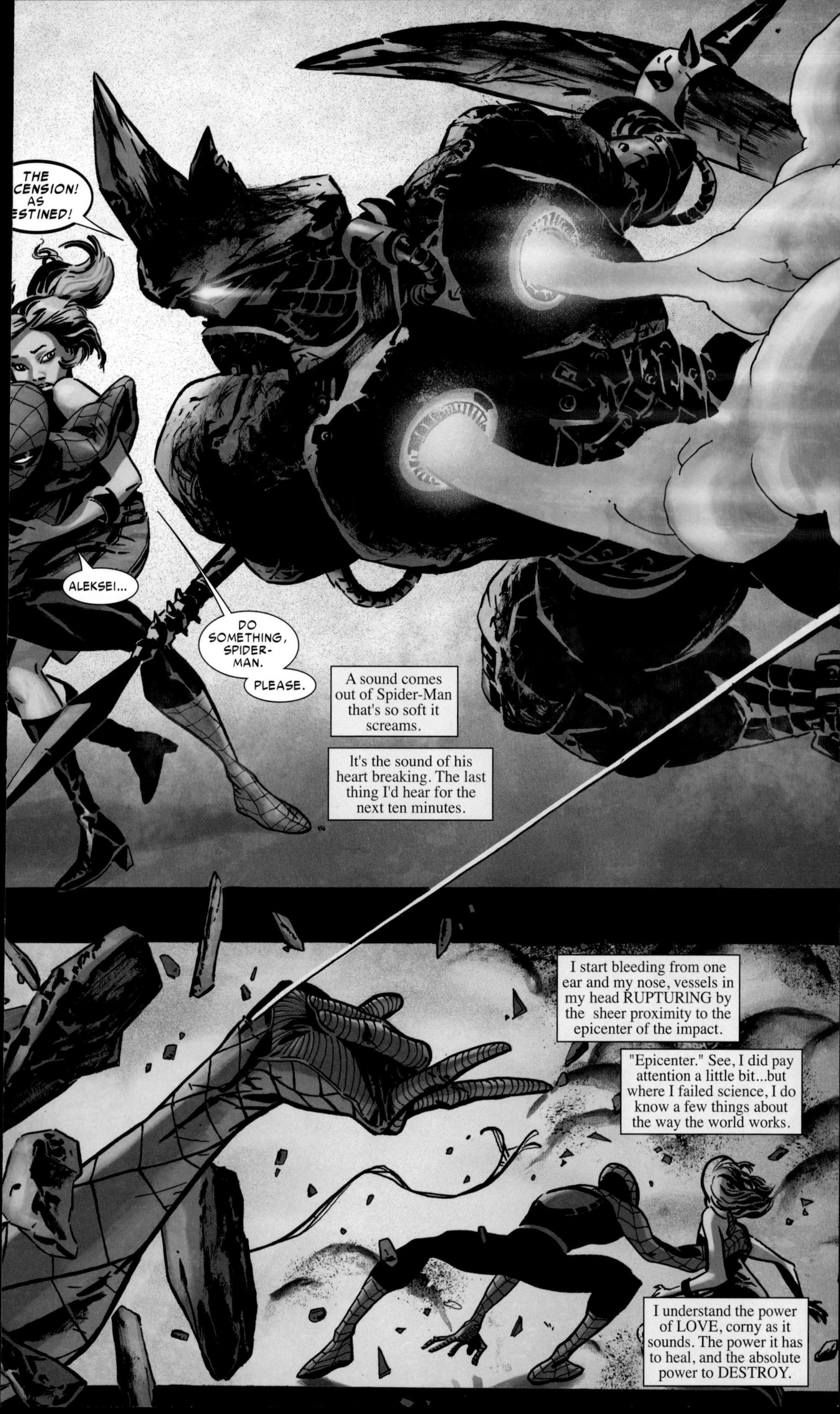
THE
CENSION! AS
ESTINED!
ALEKSEI...
DO SOMETHING, SPIDER-MAN.
PLEASE.
A sound comes out of Spider-Man that's so soft it screams.
It's the sound of his heart breaking. The last thing I'd hear for the next ten minutes.
I start bleeding from one ear and my nose, vessels in my head RUPTURING by the sheer proximity to the epicenter of the impact.
"Epicenter." See, I did pay attention a little bit...but where I failed science, I do know a few things about the way the world works.
I understand the power of LOVE, corny as it sounds. The power it has to heal, and the absolute power to DESTROY.

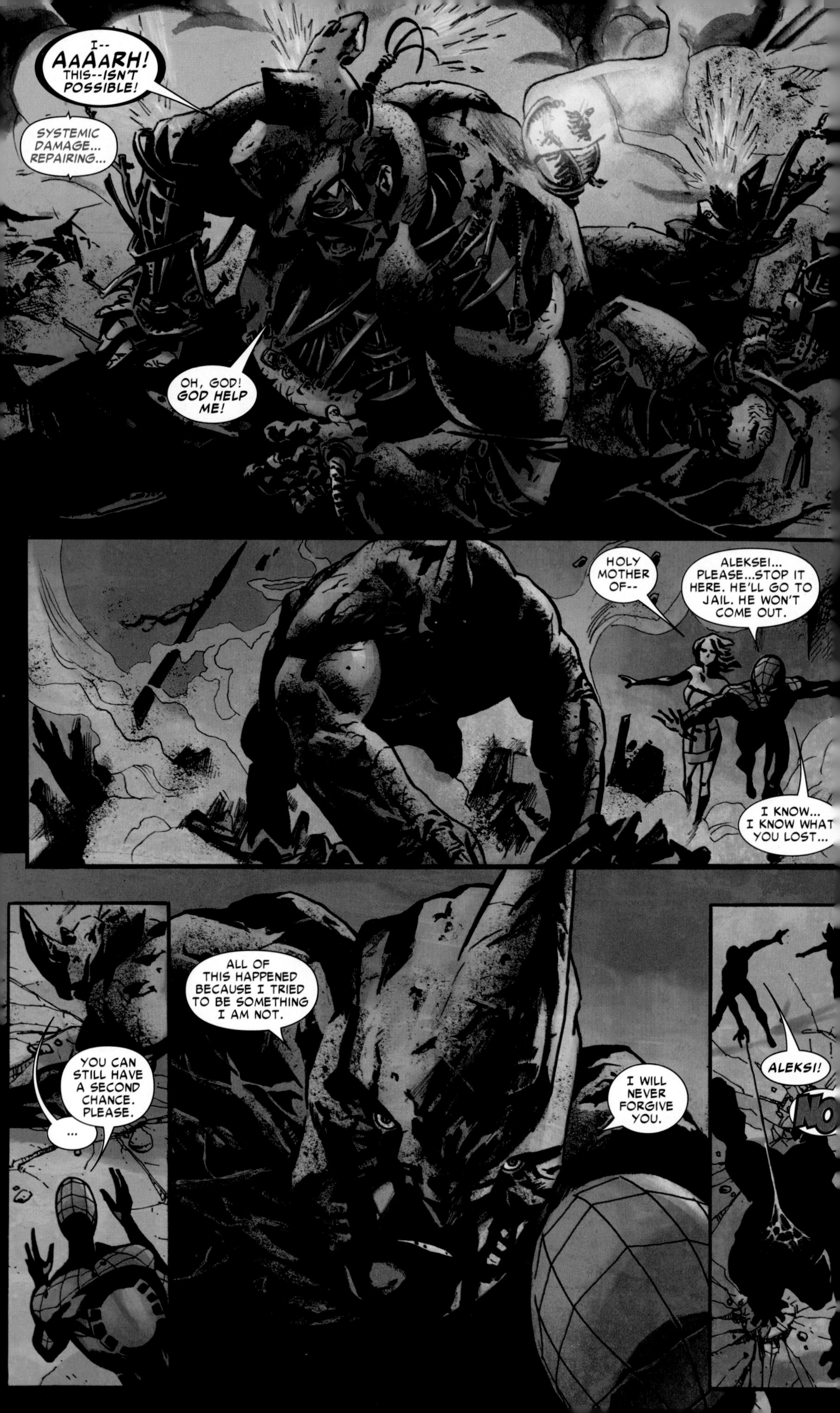
I-- AAAARH! THIS--ISN'T POSSIBLE!
SYSTEMIC DAMAGE... REPAIRING...
OH, GOD! GOD HELP ME!
HOLY MOTHER OF--
ALEKSEI... PLEASE...STOP IT HERE. HE'LL GO TO JAIL. HE WON'T COME OUT.
I KNOW... I KNOW WHAT YOU LOST...
ALL OF THIS HAPPENED BECAUSE I TRIED TO BE SOMETHING I AM NOT.
YOU CAN STILL HAVE A SECOND CHANCE. PLEASE.
...
I WILL NEVER FORGIVE YOU.
ALEKSI!
NO

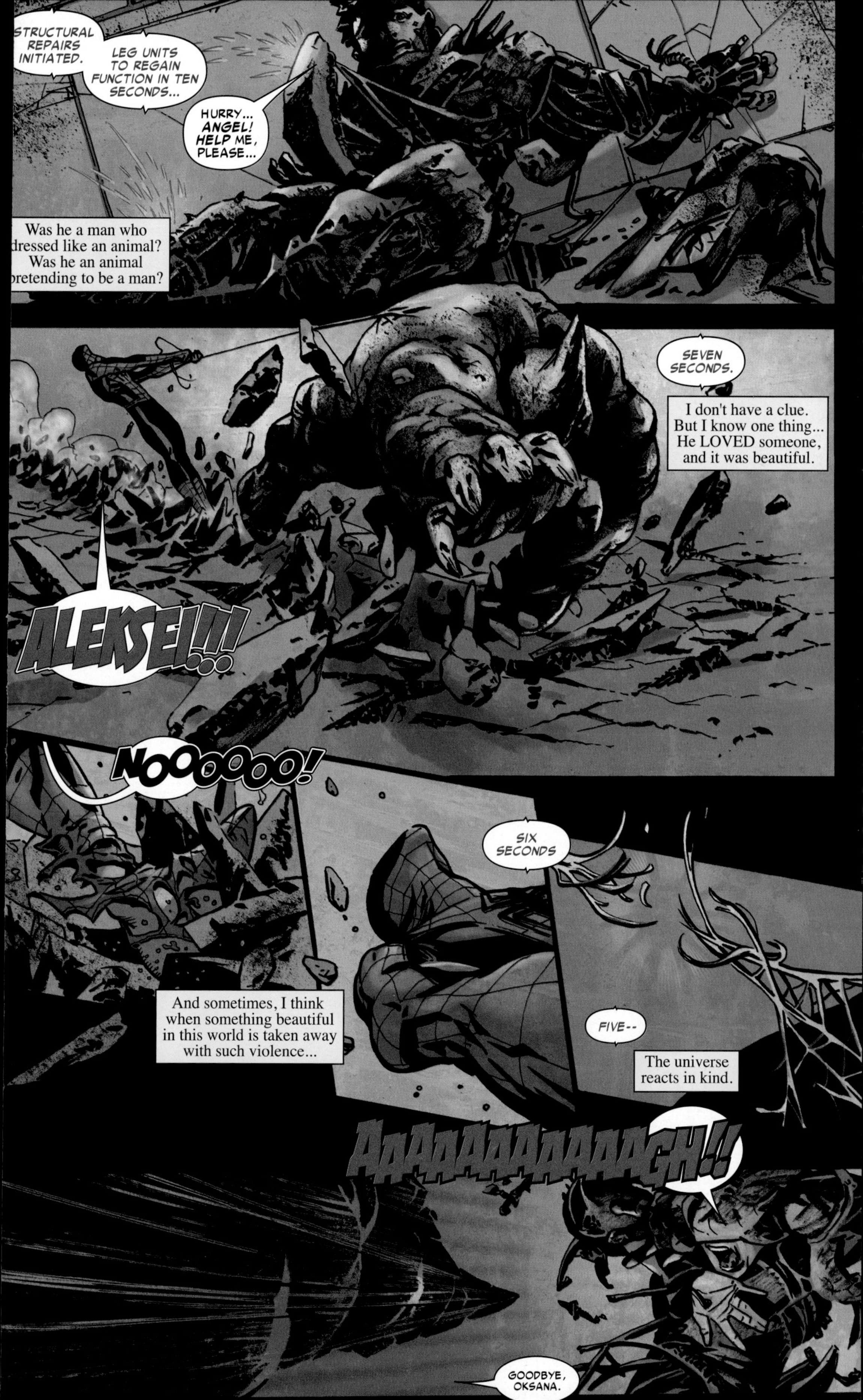
STRUCTURAL REPAIRS INITIATED.
LEG UNITS TO REGAIN FUNCTION IN TEN SECONDS...
HURRY... ANGEL! HELP ME, PLEASE...
Was he a man who dressed like an animal? Was he an animal pretending to be a man?
SEVEN SECONDS.
I don't have a clue. But I know one thing... He LOVED someone, and it was beautiful.
ALEKSEI!!!...
NOOOOOO!
SIX SECONDS
And sometimes, I think when something beautiful in this world is taken away with such violence...
FIVE--
The universe reacts in kind.
AAAAAAAAAAAGH!!
GOODBYE, OKSANA.

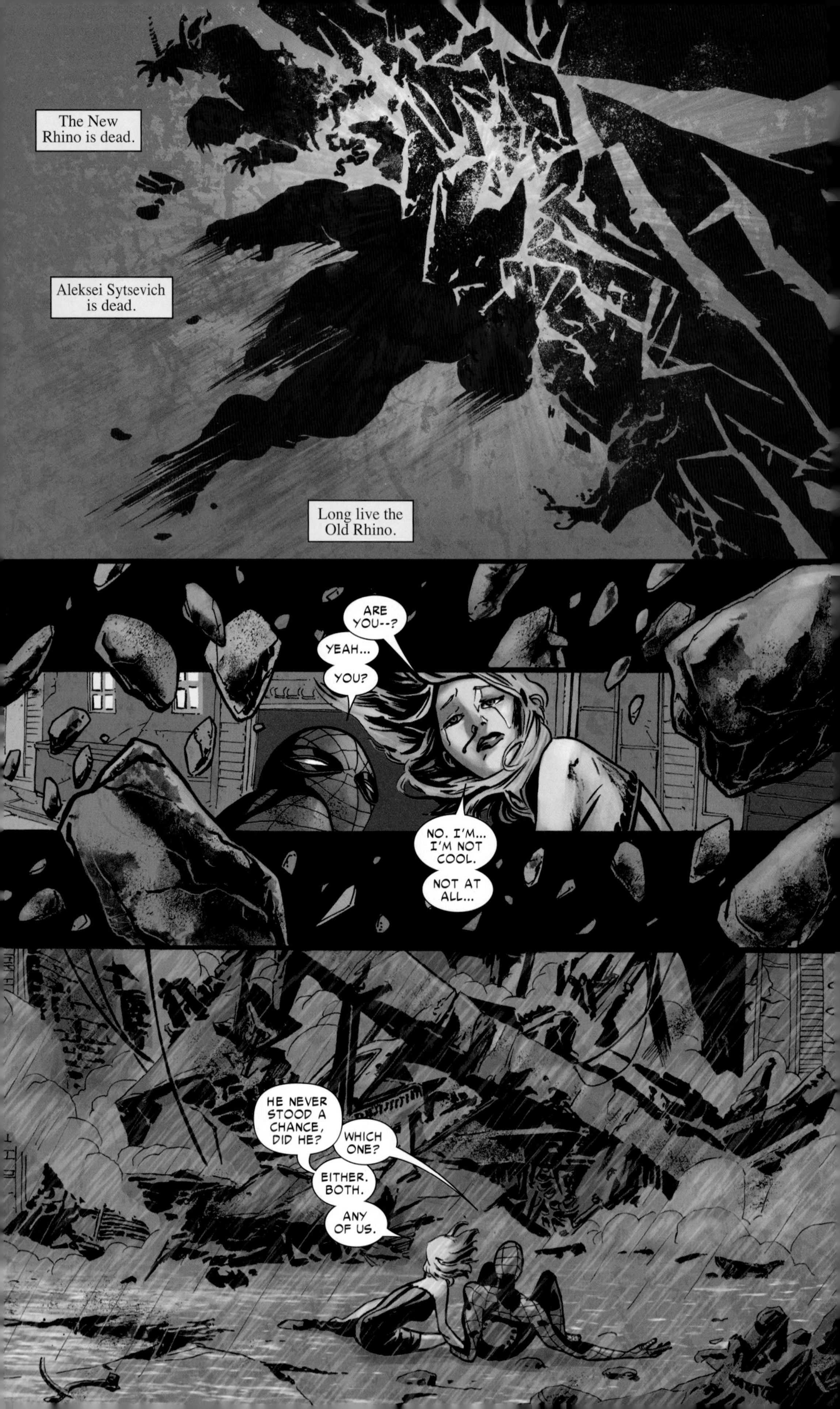

The New Rhino is dead.
Aleksei Sytsevich is dead.
Long live the Old Rhino.
ARE YOU--?
YEAH...
YOU?
NO. I'M... I'M NOT COOL.
NOT AT ALL...
HE NEVER STOOD A CHANCE, DID HE?
WHICH ONE?
EITHER. BOTH.
ANY OF US.

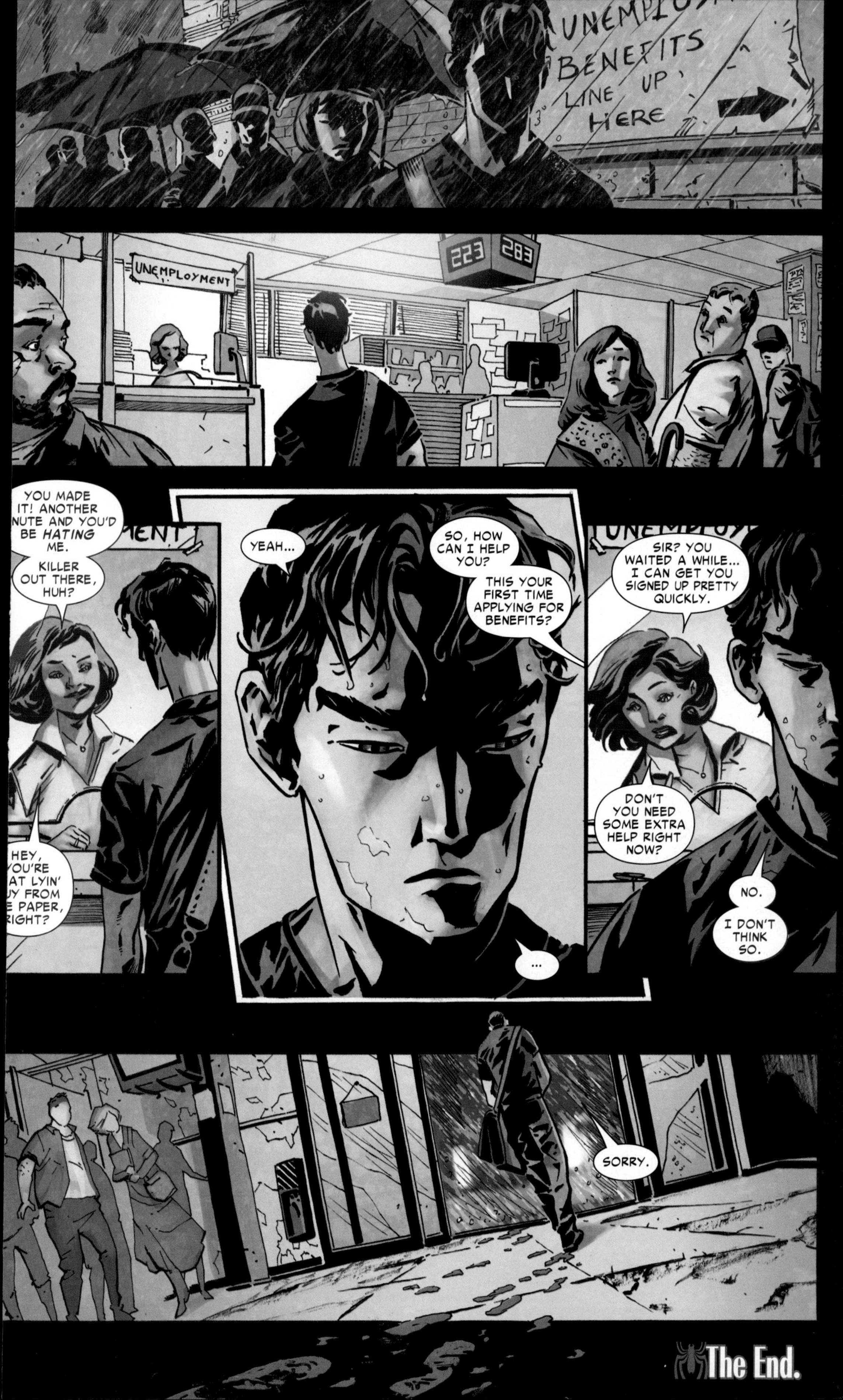
UNEMPLO...
BENEFITS
LINE UP
HERE
UNEMPLOYMENT
223
283
YOU MADE IT! ANOTHER ...NUTE AND YOU'D BE *HATING* ME.
KILLER OUT THERE, HUH?
HEY, ...YOU'RE ...AT LYIN' ...UY FROM ...E PAPER, ...RIGHT?
YEAH...
SO, HOW CAN I HELP YOU?
THIS YOUR FIRST TIME APPLYING FOR BENEFITS?
...
SIR? YOU WAITED A WHILE... I CAN GET YOU SIGNED UP PRETTY QUICKLY.
DON'T YOU NEED SOME EXTRA HELP RIGHT NOW?
NO.
I DON'T THINK SO.
SORRY.
The End.

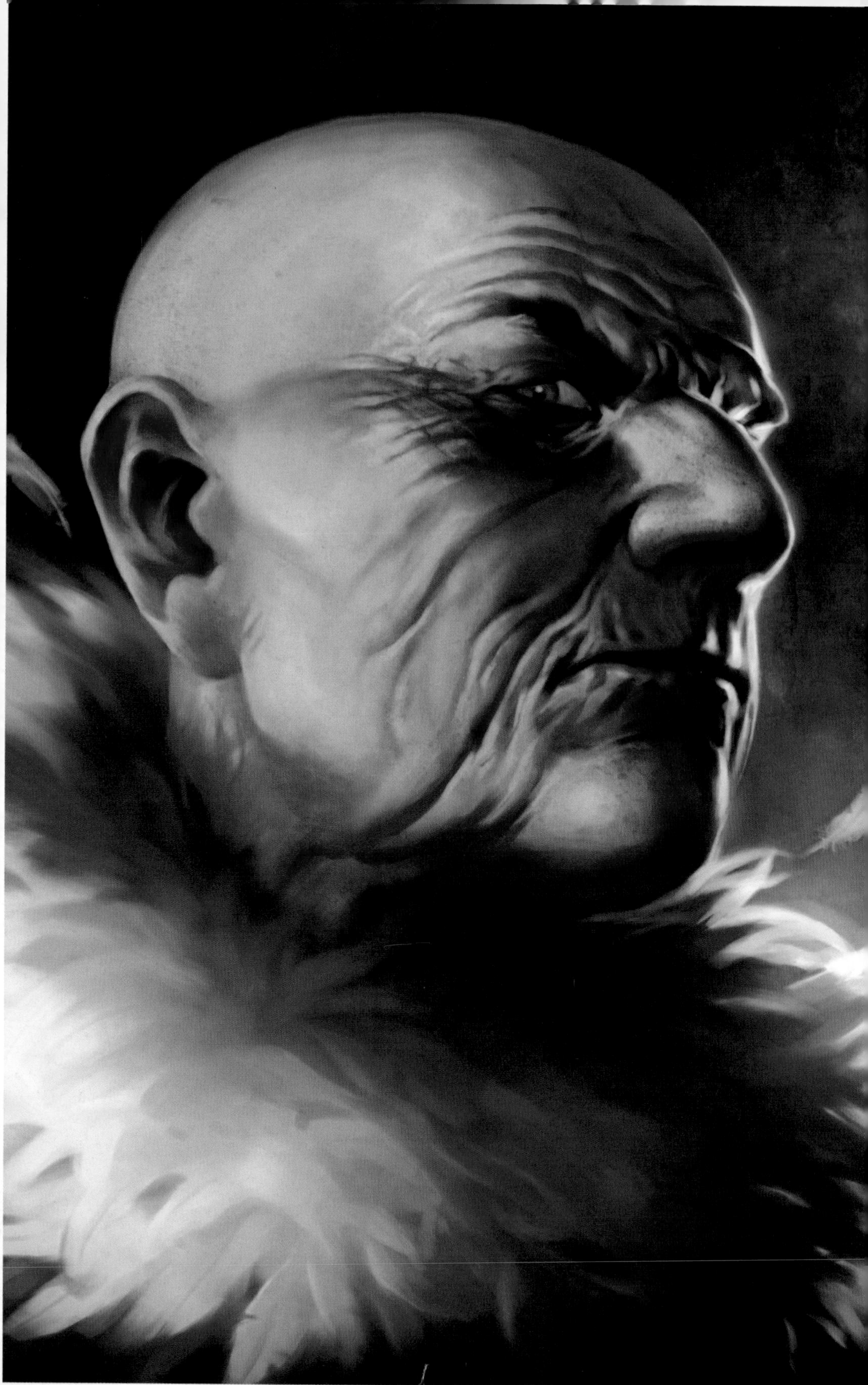

WEB OF SPIDER-MAN #5 – "GAUNTLET ORIGINS: VULTURE"

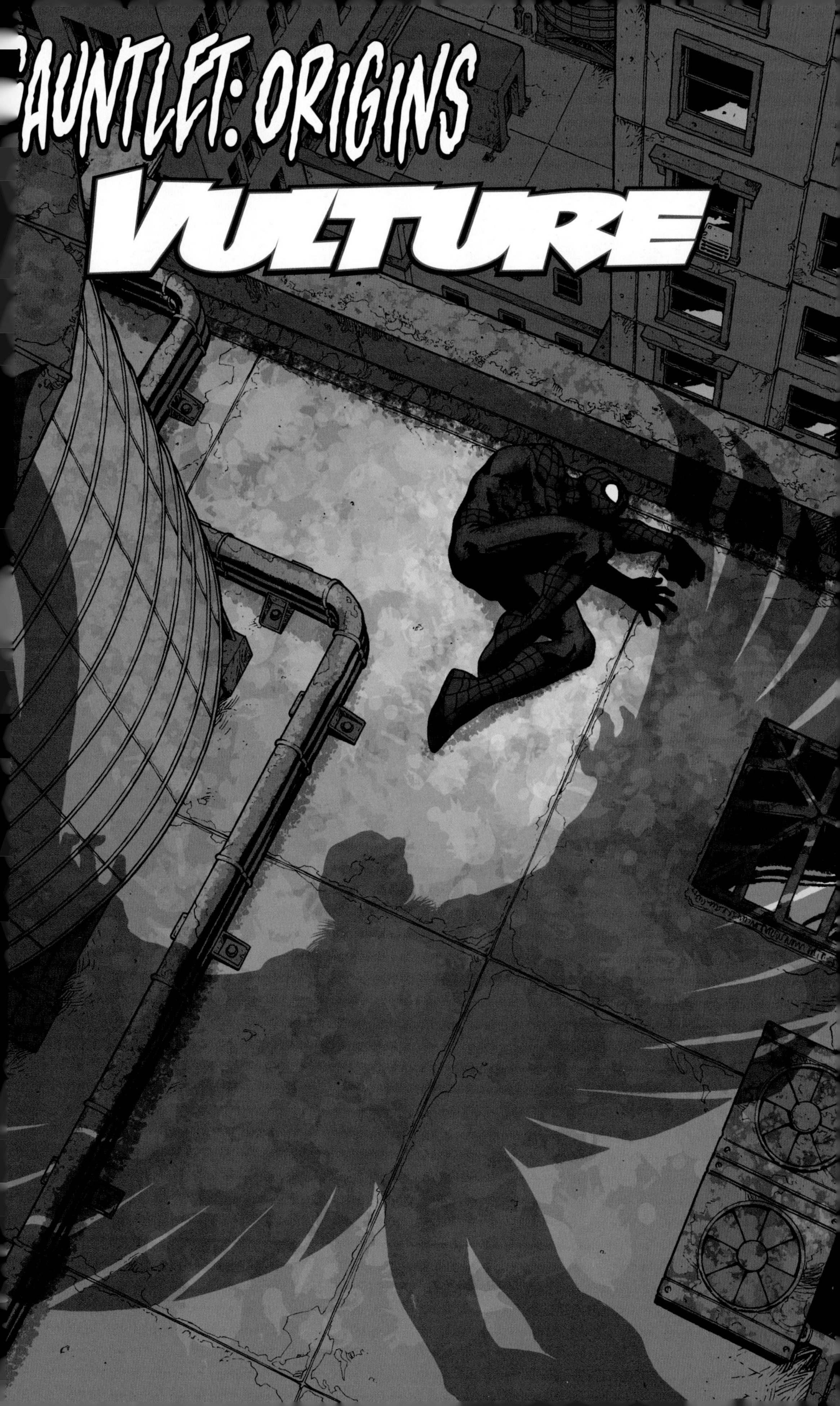
GAUNTLET: ORIGINS
VULTURE

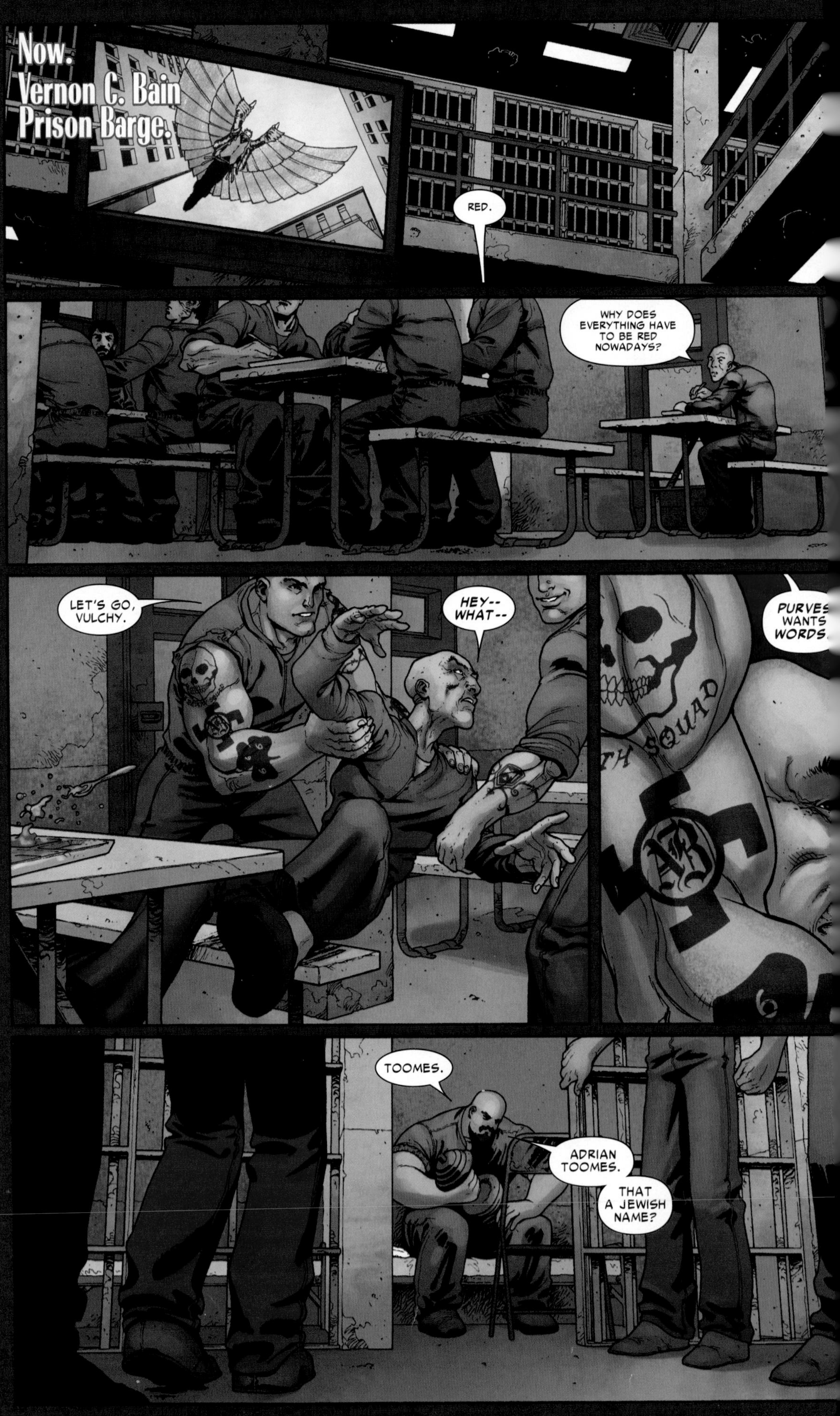
Now.
Vernon C. Bain
Prison Barge.
RED.
WHY DOES EVERYTHING HAVE TO BE RED NOWADAYS?
LET'S GO, VULCHY.
HEY-- WHAT--
PURVES WANTS WORDS.
TOOMES.
ADRIAN TOOMES.
THAT A JEWISH NAME?

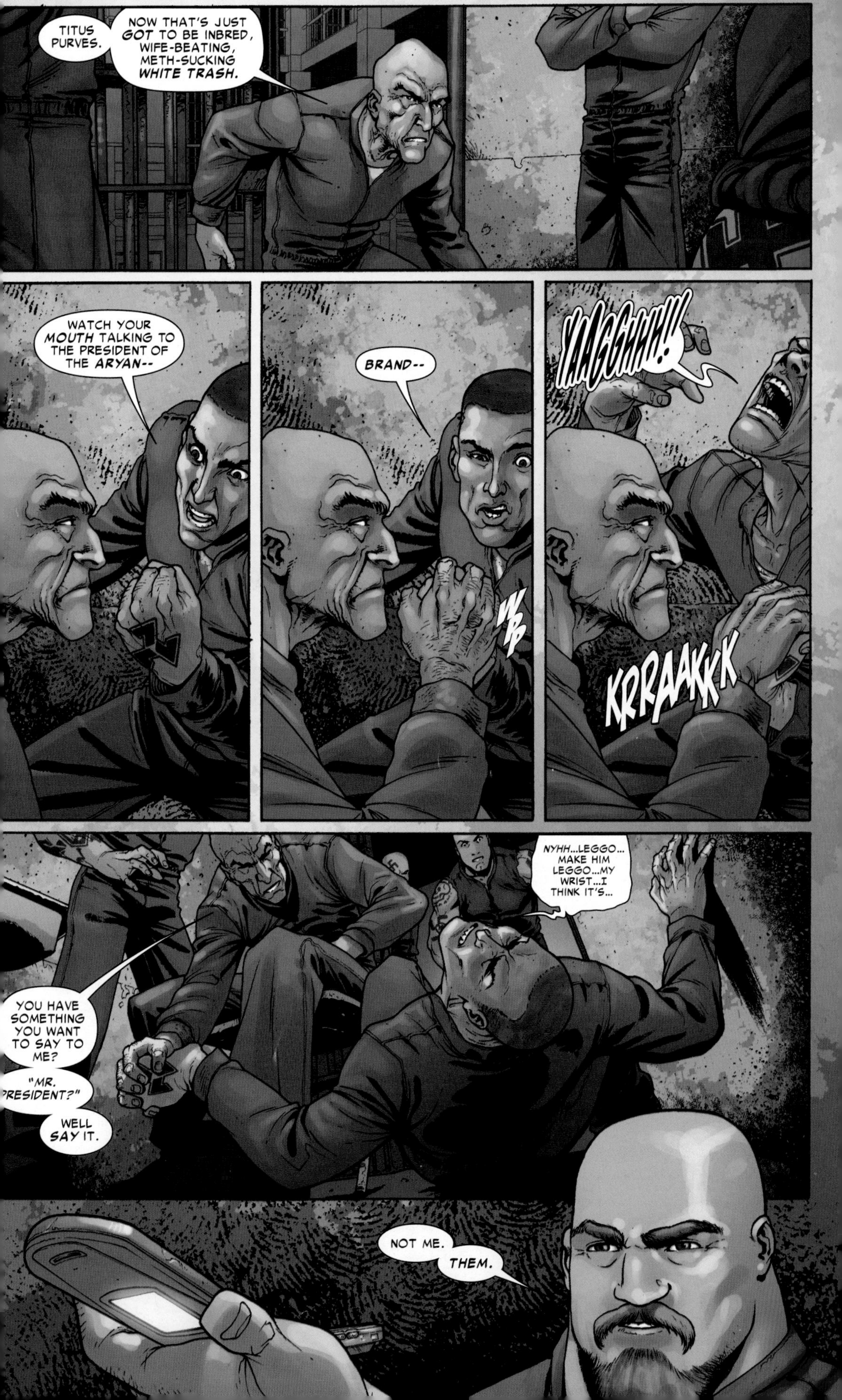
TITUS PURVES.
NOW THAT'S JUST GOT TO BE INBRED, WIFE-BEATING, METH-SUCKING WHITE TRASH.
WATCH YOUR MOUTH TALKING TO THE PRESIDENT OF THE ARYAN--
BRAND--
YAAGGHHH!!
KRRAAKKK
NYHH...LEGGO... MAKE HIM LEGGO...MY WRIST...I THINK IT'S...
YOU HAVE SOMETHING YOU WANT TO SAY TO ME?
"MR. PRESIDENT?"
WELL SAY IT.
NOT ME.
THEM.

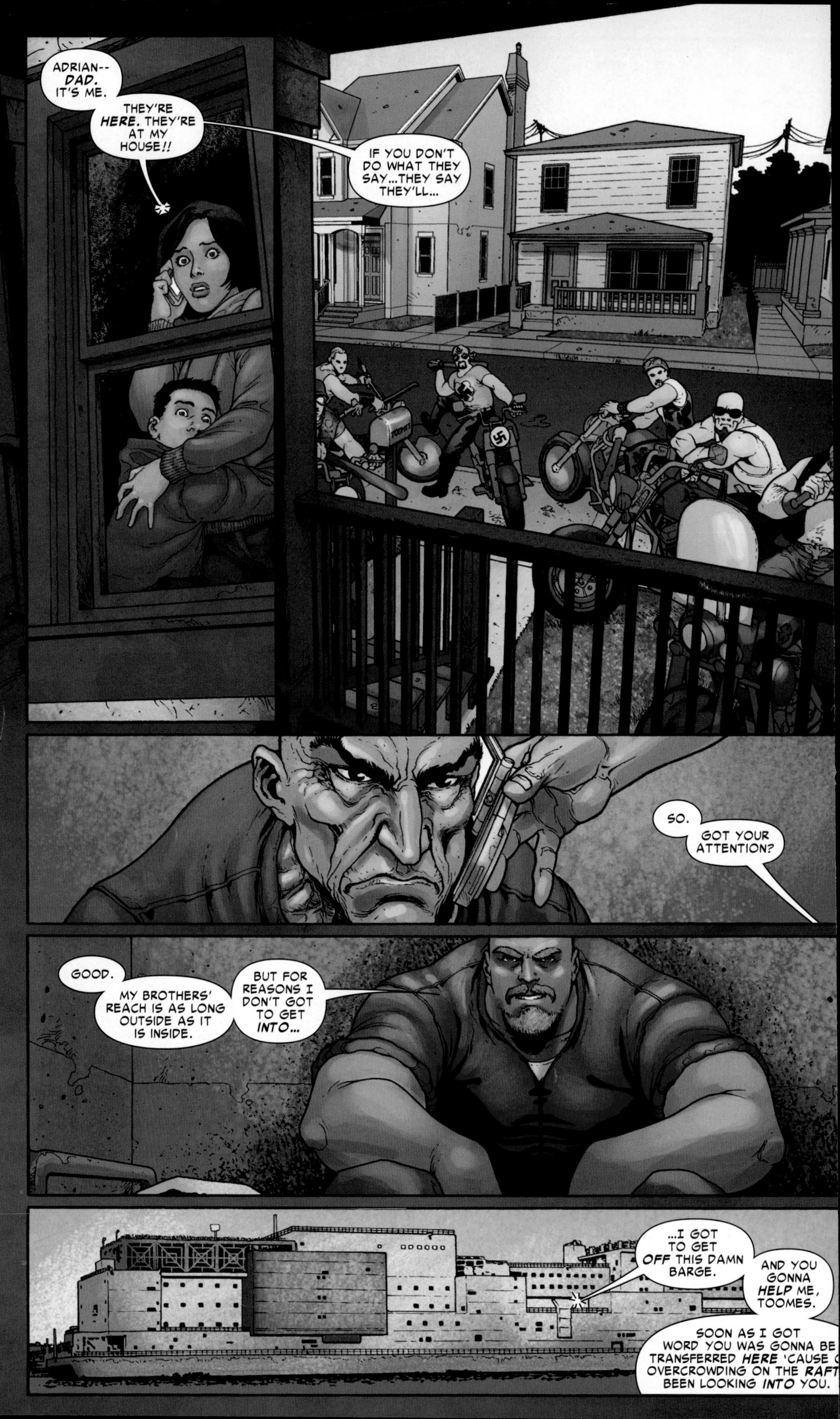

ADRIAN-- DAD. IT'S ME.
THEY'RE HERE. THEY'RE AT MY HOUSE!!
IF YOU DON'T DO WHAT THEY SAY...THEY SAY THEY'LL...
TOOMES
SO.
GOT YOUR ATTENTION?
GOOD.
MY BROTHERS' REACH IS AS LONG OUTSIDE AS IT IS INSIDE.
BUT FOR REASONS I DON'T GOT TO GET INTO...
...I GOT TO GET OFF THIS DAMN BARGE.
AND YOU GONNA HELP ME, TOOMES.
SOON AS I GOT WORD YOU WAS GONNA BE TRANSFERRED HERE 'CAUSE O OVERCROWDING ON THE RAFT BEEN LOOKING INTO YOU.

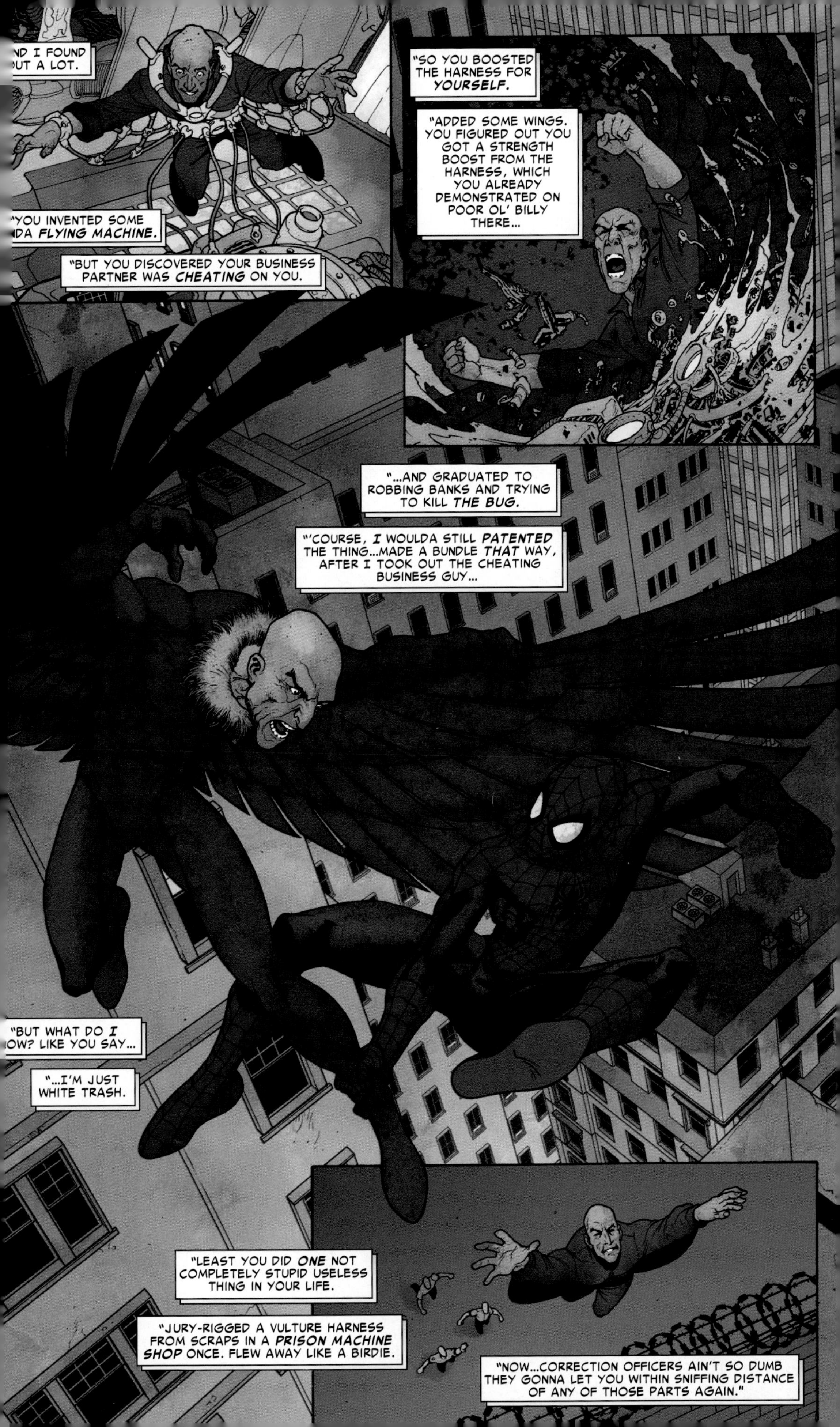
ND I FOUND
UT A LOT.
"YOU INVENTED SOME
NDA *FLYING MACHINE.*
"BUT YOU DISCOVERED YOUR BUSINESS PARTNER WAS *CHEATING* ON YOU.
"SO YOU BOOSTED THE HARNESS FOR *YOURSELF.*
"ADDED SOME WINGS. YOU FIGURED OUT YOU GOT A STRENGTH BOOST FROM THE HARNESS, WHICH YOU ALREADY DEMONSTRATED ON POOR OL' BILLY THERE...
"...AND GRADUATED TO ROBBING BANKS AND TRYING TO KILL *THE BUG.*
"'COURSE, *I* WOULDA STILL *PATENTED* THE THING...MADE A BUNDLE *THAT* WAY, AFTER I TOOK OUT THE CHEATING BUSINESS GUY...
"BUT WHAT DO *I*
OW? LIKE YOU SAY...
"...I'M JUST WHITE TRASH.
"LEAST YOU DID *ONE* NOT COMPLETELY STUPID USELESS THING IN YOUR LIFE.
"JURY-RIGGED A VULTURE HARNESS FROM SCRAPS IN A *PRISON MACHINE SHOP* ONCE. FLEW AWAY LIKE A BIRDIE.
"NOW...CORRECTION OFFICERS AIN'T SO DUMB THEY GONNA LET YOU WITHIN SNIFFING DISTANCE OF ANY OF THOSE PARTS AGAIN."

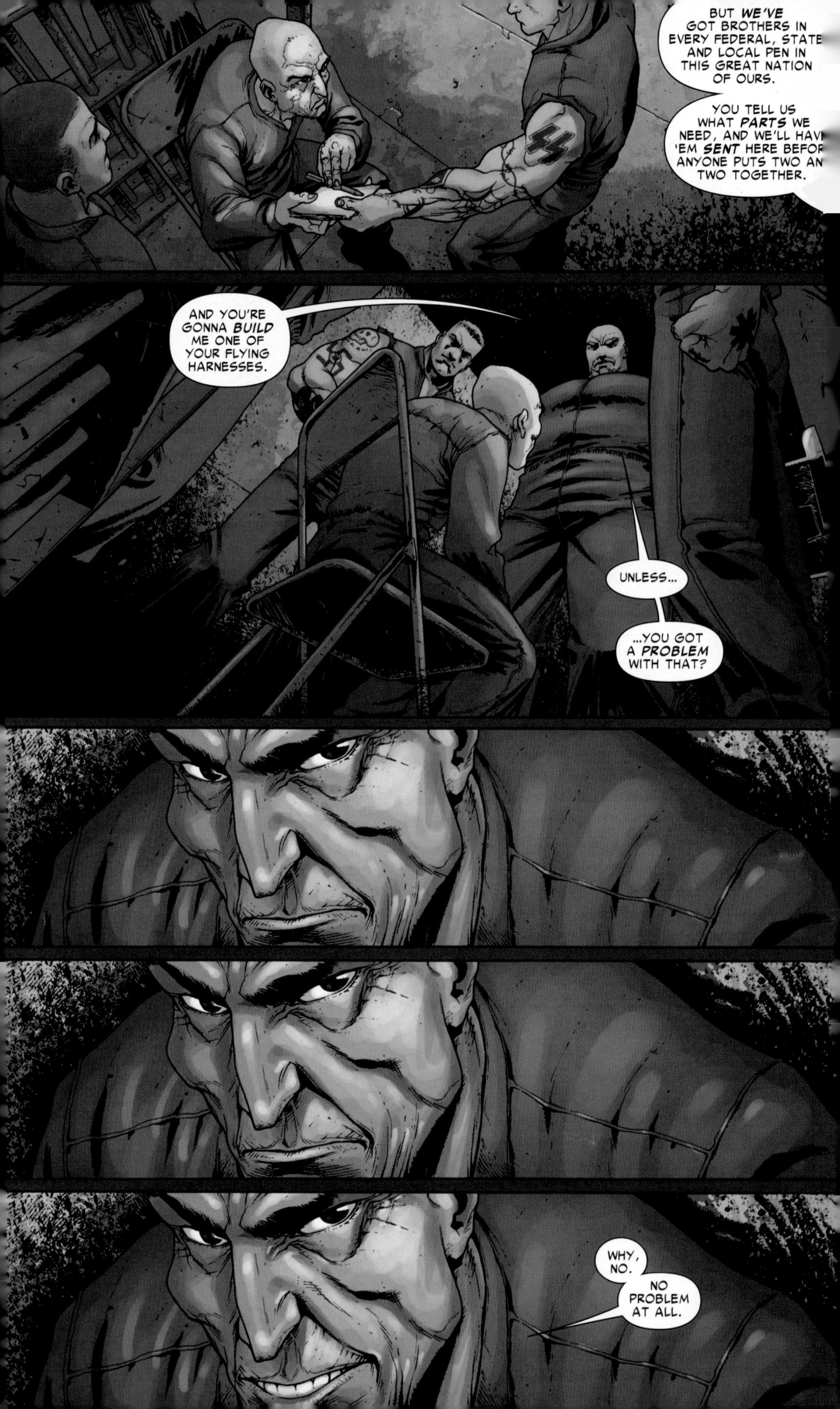
BUT WE'VE GOT BROTHERS IN EVERY FEDERAL, STATE AND LOCAL PEN IN THIS GREAT NATION OF OURS.
YOU TELL US WHAT PARTS WE NEED, AND WE'LL HAV 'EM SENT HERE BEFOR ANYONE PUTS TWO AN TWO TOGETHER.
AND YOU'RE GONNA BUILD ME ONE OF YOUR FLYING HARNESSES.
UNLESS...
...YOU GOT A PROBLEM WITH THAT?
WHY, NO.
NO PROBLEM AT ALL.

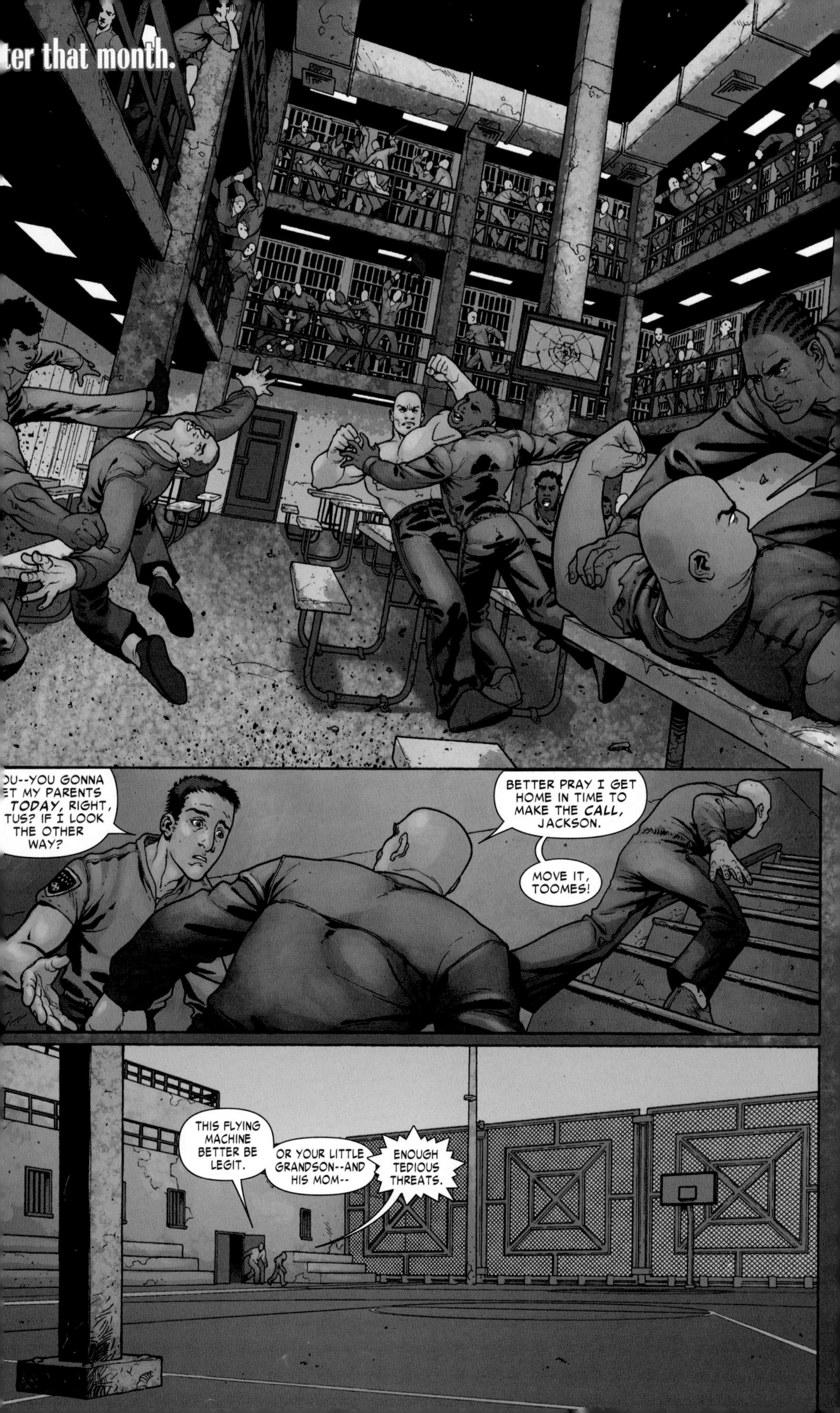
ter that month.
OU--YOU GONNA
ET MY PARENTS
TODAY, RIGHT,
TUS? IF I LOOK
THE OTHER
WAY?
BETTER PRAY I GET HOME IN TIME TO MAKE THE CALL, JACKSON.
MOVE IT, TOOMES!
THIS FLYING MACHINE BETTER BE LEGIT.
OR YOUR LITTLE GRANDSON--AND HIS MOM--
ENOUGH TEDIOUS THREATS.

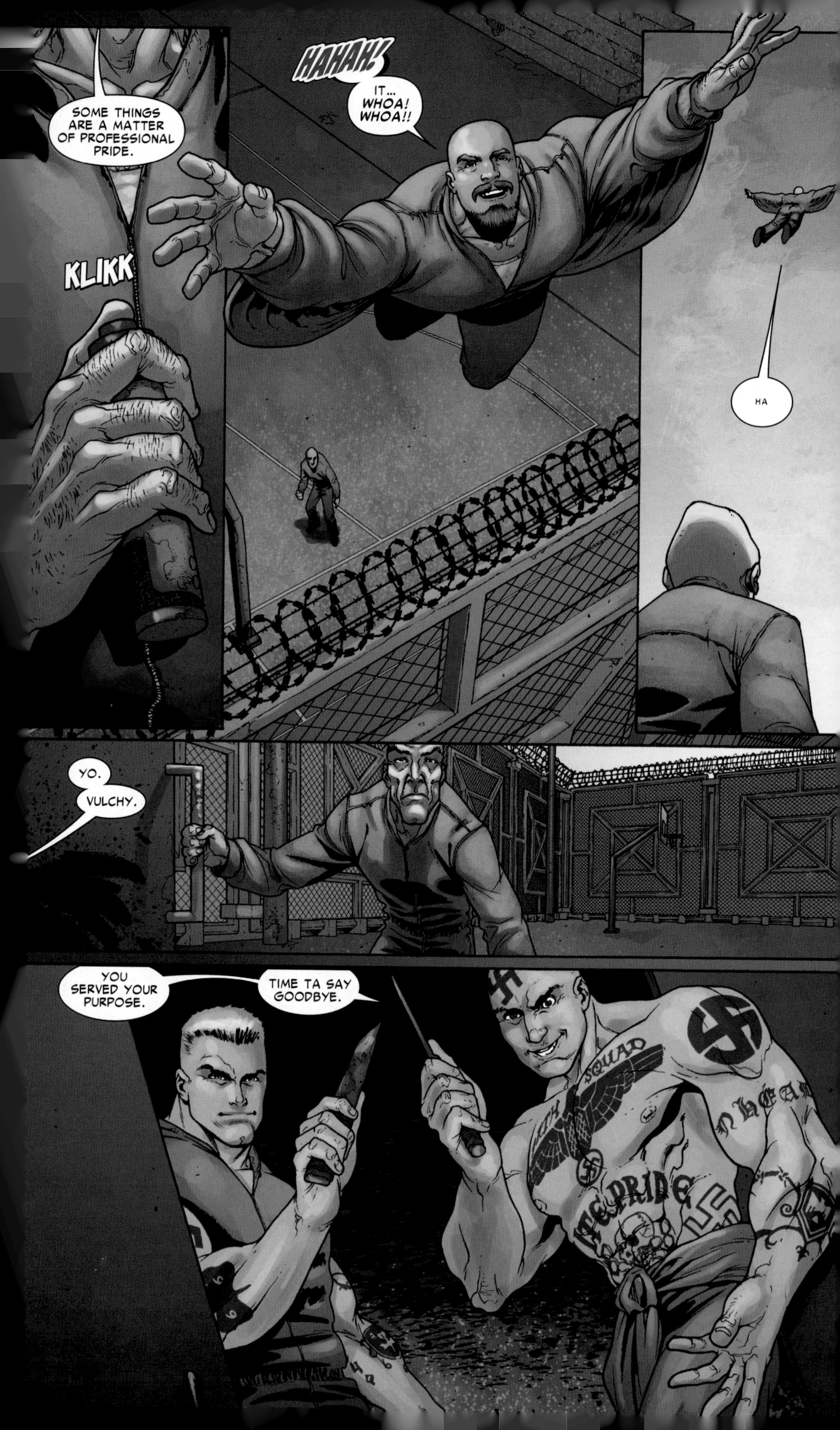
SOME THINGS ARE A MATTER OF PROFESSIONAL PRIDE.
KLIKK
HAHAH!
IT... WHOA! WHOA!!
HA
YO.
VULCHY.
YOU SERVED YOUR PURPOSE.
TIME TA SAY GOODBYE.

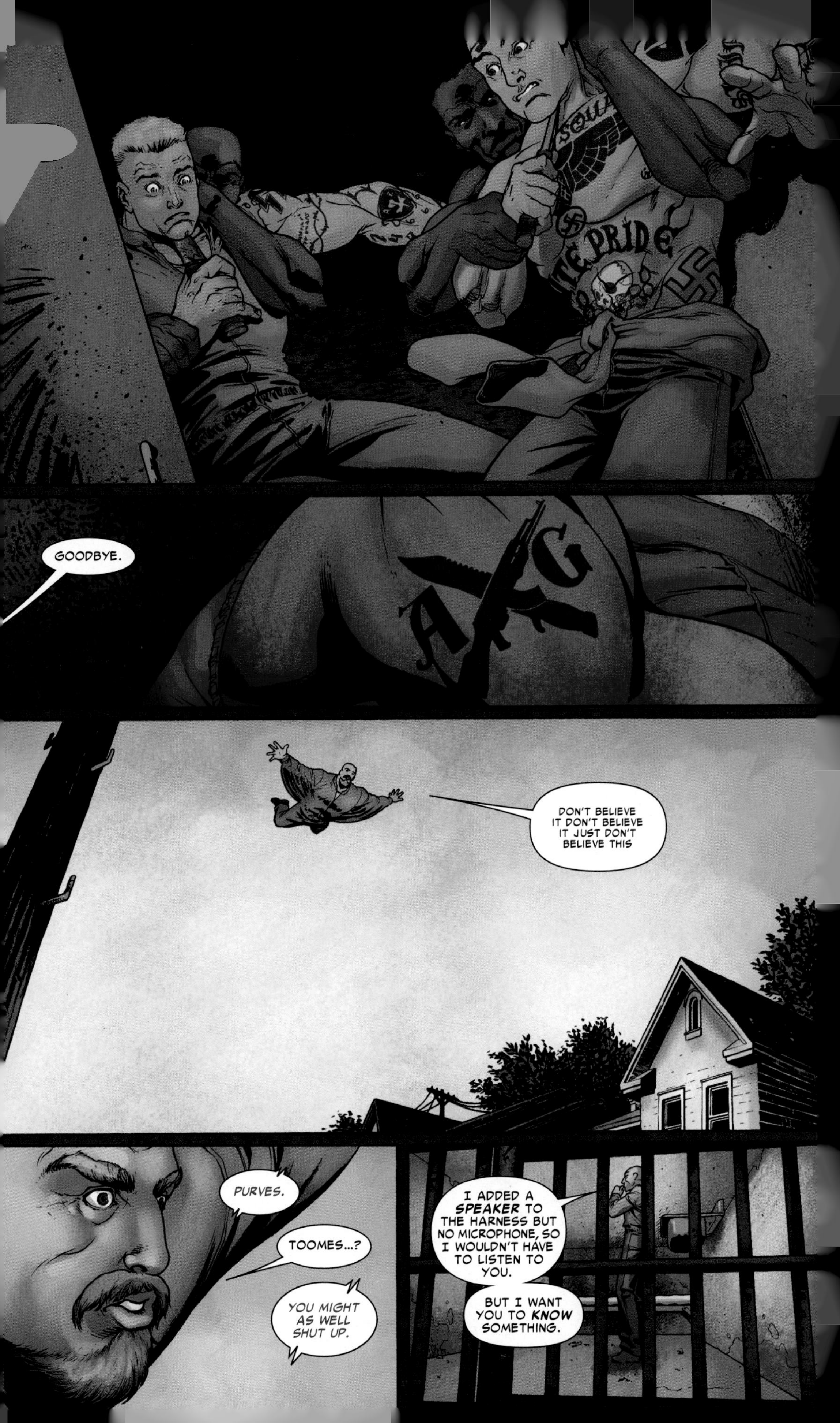
GOODBYE.
DON'T BELIEVE IT DON'T BELIEVE IT JUST DON'T BELIEVE THIS
PURVES.
TOOMES...?
YOU MIGHT AS WELL SHUT UP.
I ADDED A *SPEAKER* TO THE HARNESS BUT NO MICROPHONE, SO I WOULDN'T HAVE TO LISTEN TO YOU.
BUT I WANT YOU TO *KNOW* SOMETHING.

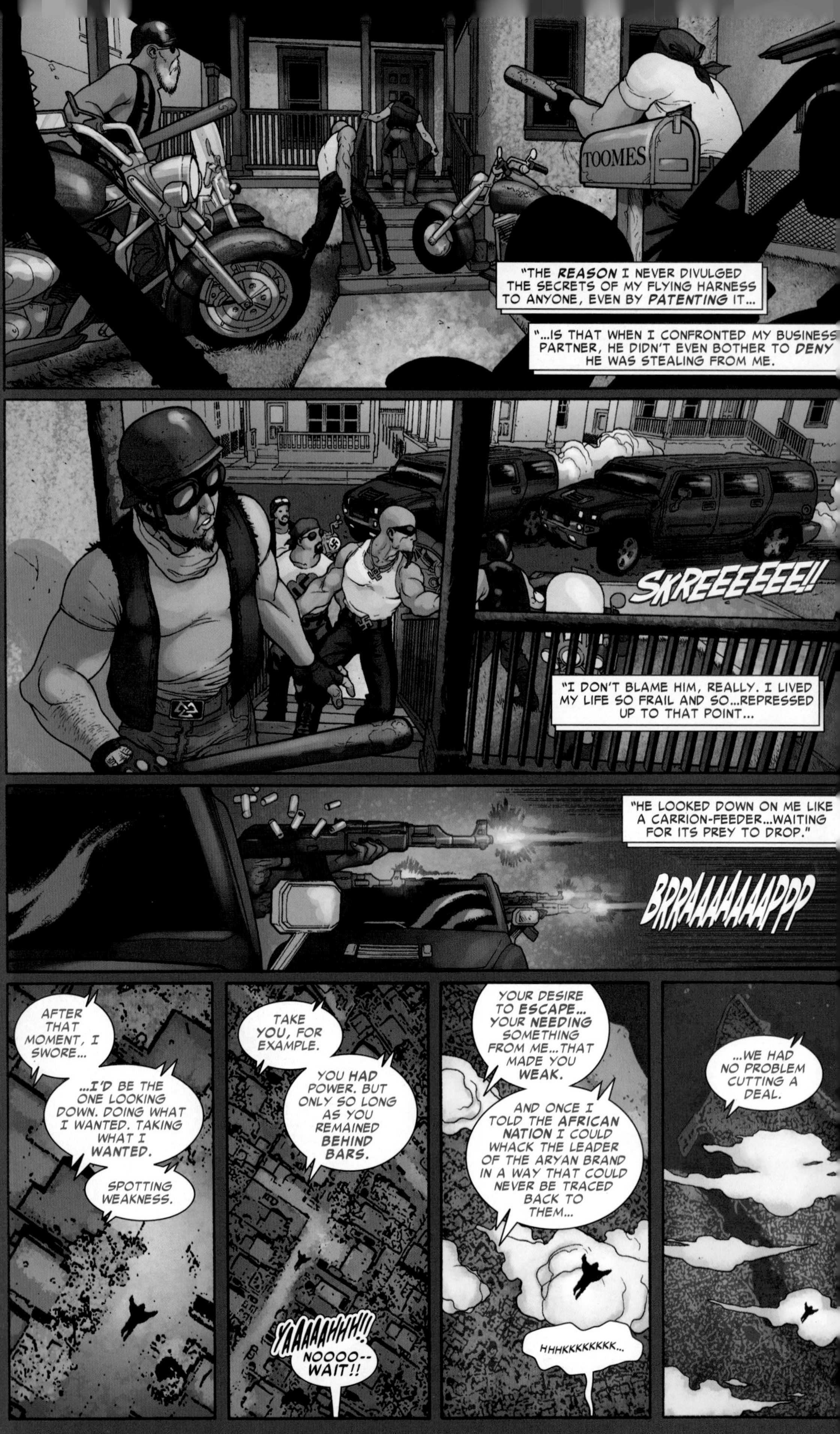
TOOMES
"THE REASON I NEVER DIVULGED THE SECRETS OF MY FLYING HARNESS TO ANYONE, EVEN BY PATENTING IT...
"...IS THAT WHEN I CONFRONTED MY BUSINESS PARTNER, HE DIDN'T EVEN BOTHER TO DENY HE WAS STEALING FROM ME.
SKREEEEEE!!
"I DON'T BLAME HIM, REALLY. I LIVED MY LIFE SO FRAIL AND SO...REPRESSED UP TO THAT POINT...
"HE LOOKED DOWN ON ME LIKE A CARRION-FEEDER...WAITING FOR ITS PREY TO DROP."
BRRAAAAAAPPP
AFTER THAT MOMENT, I SWORE...
...I'D BE THE ONE LOOKING DOWN. DOING WHAT I WANTED. TAKING WHAT I WANTED.
SPOTTING WEAKNESS.
TAKE YOU, FOR EXAMPLE.
YOU HAD POWER. BUT ONLY SO LONG AS YOU REMAINED BEHIND BARS.
YAAAAAHHH!! NOOOO--WAIT!!
YOUR DESIRE TO ESCAPE... YOUR NEEDING SOMETHING FROM ME...THAT MADE YOU WEAK.
AND ONCE I TOLD THE AFRICAN NATION I COULD WHACK THE LEADER OF THE ARYAN BRAND IN A WAY THAT COULD NEVER BE TRACED BACK TO THEM...
HHHKKKKKKKK...
...WE HAD NO PROBLEM CUTTING A DEAL.

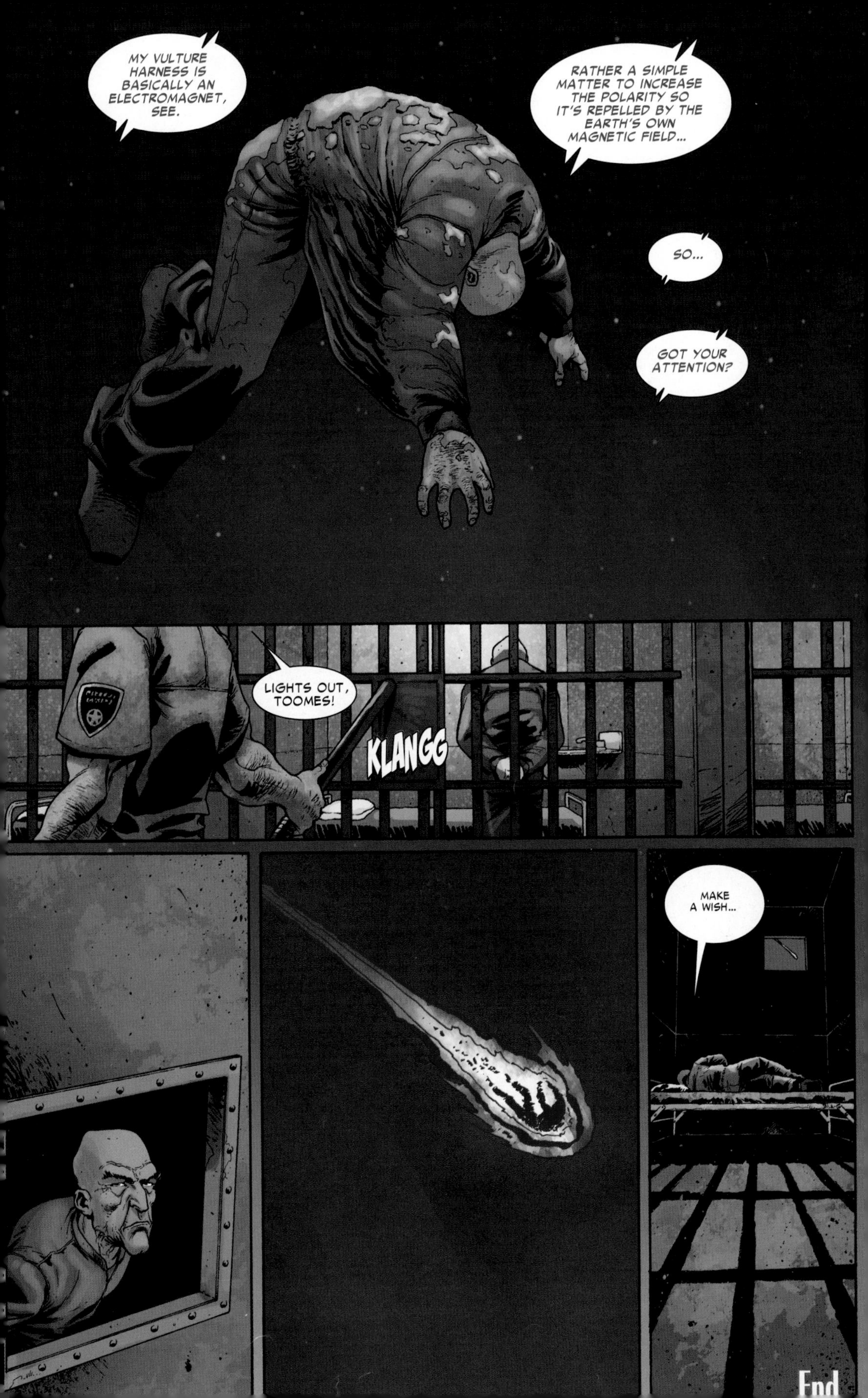
MY VULTURE HARNESS IS BASICALLY AN ELECTROMAGNET, SEE.
RATHER A SIMPLE MATTER TO INCREASE THE POLARITY SO IT'S REPELLED BY THE EARTH'S OWN MAGNETIC FIELD...
SO...
GOT YOUR ATTENTION?
LIGHTS OUT, TOOMES!
KLANGG
MAKE A WISH...
End

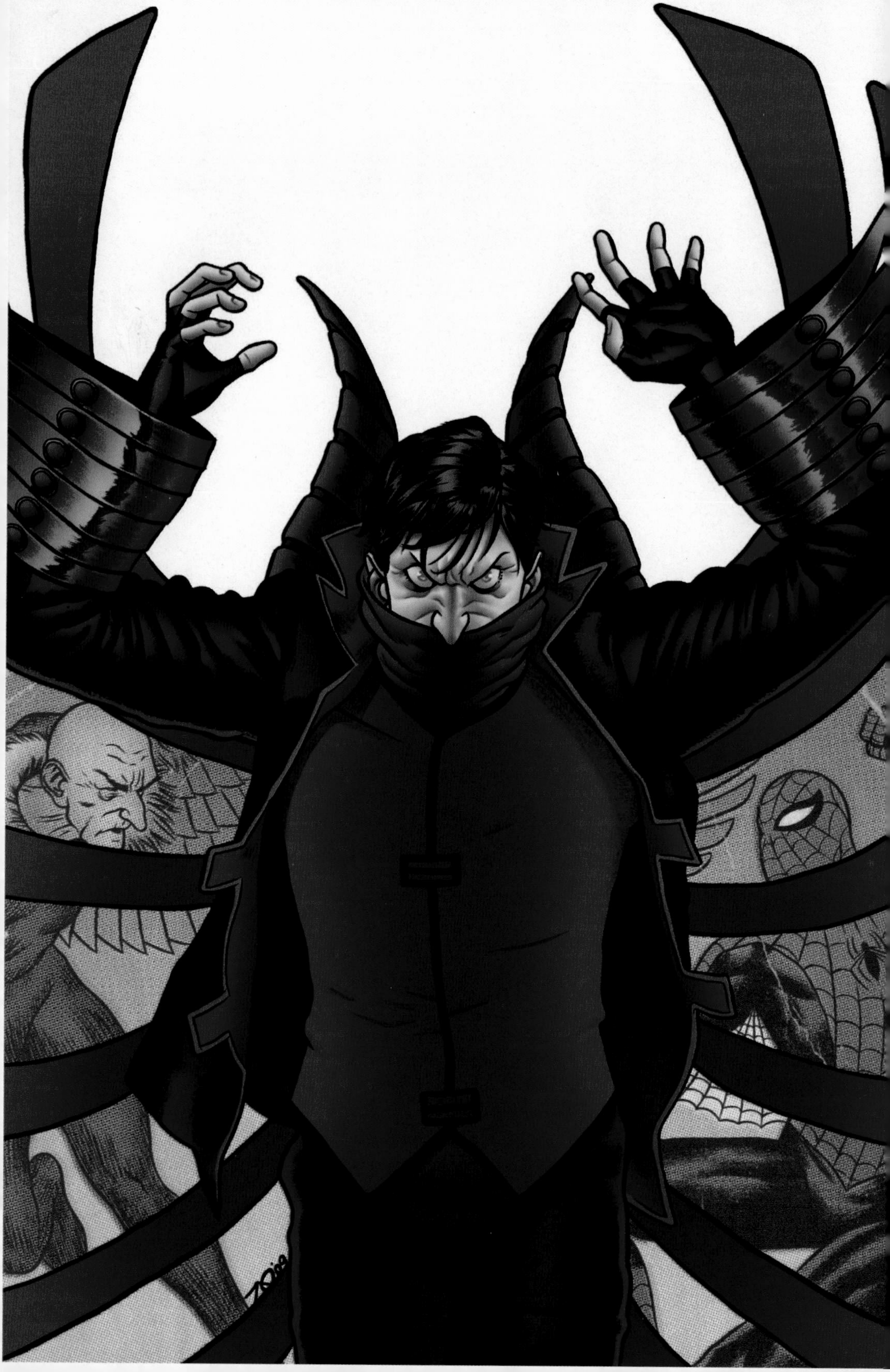

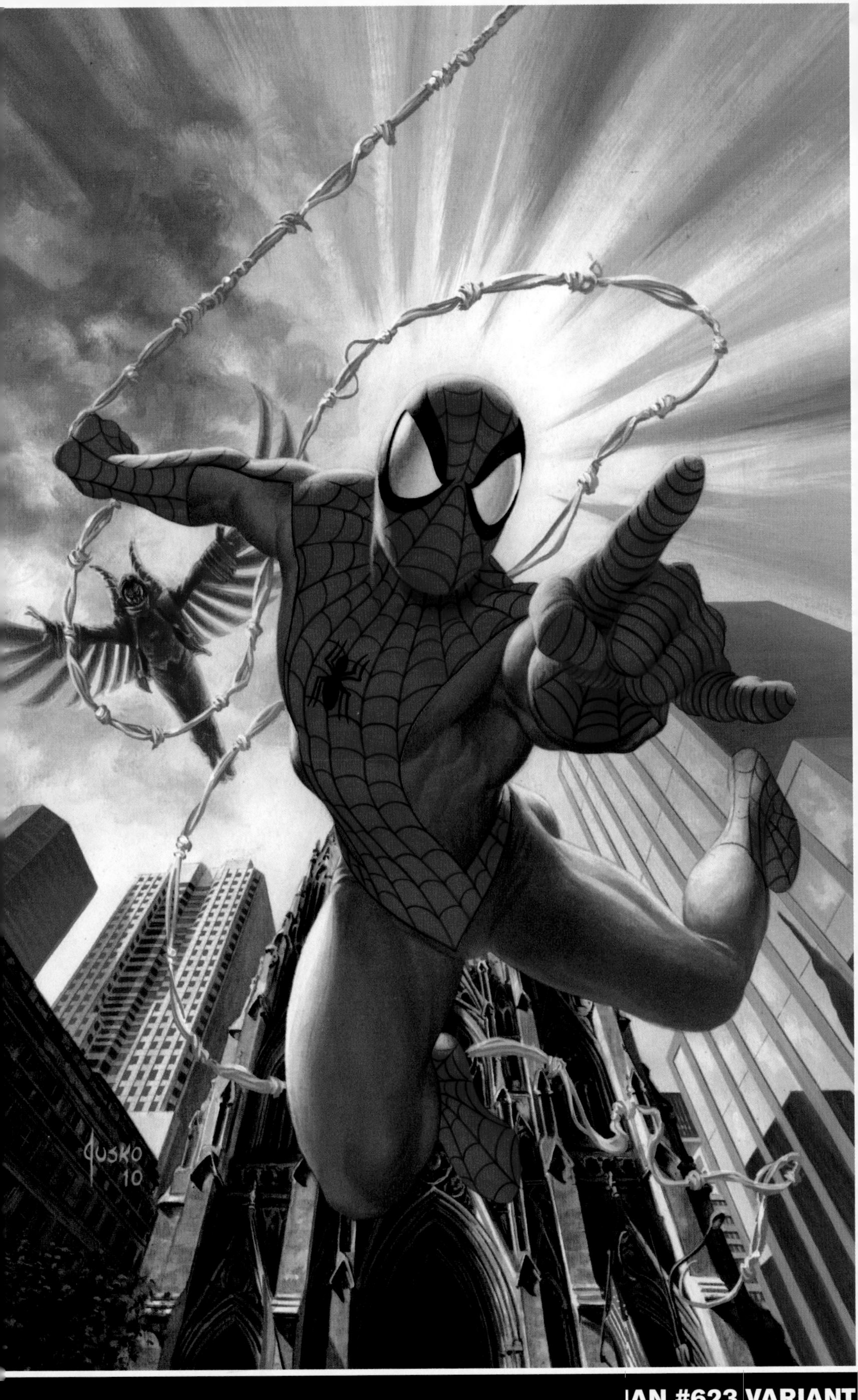
JUSKO
10

IAN #623 VARIANT

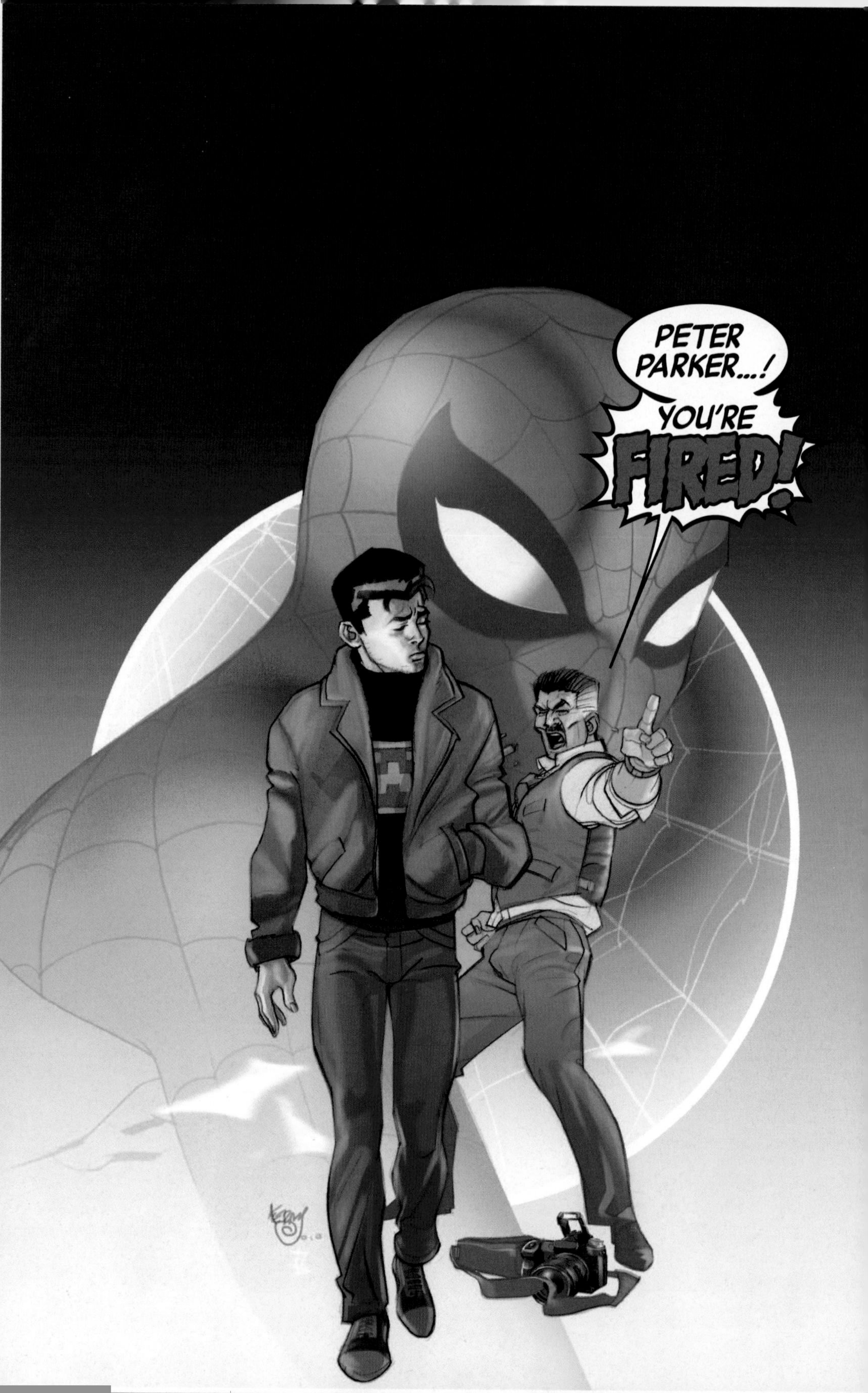
PETER PARKER...!
YOU'RE FIRED!

G SPIDER
Y PASQUAL

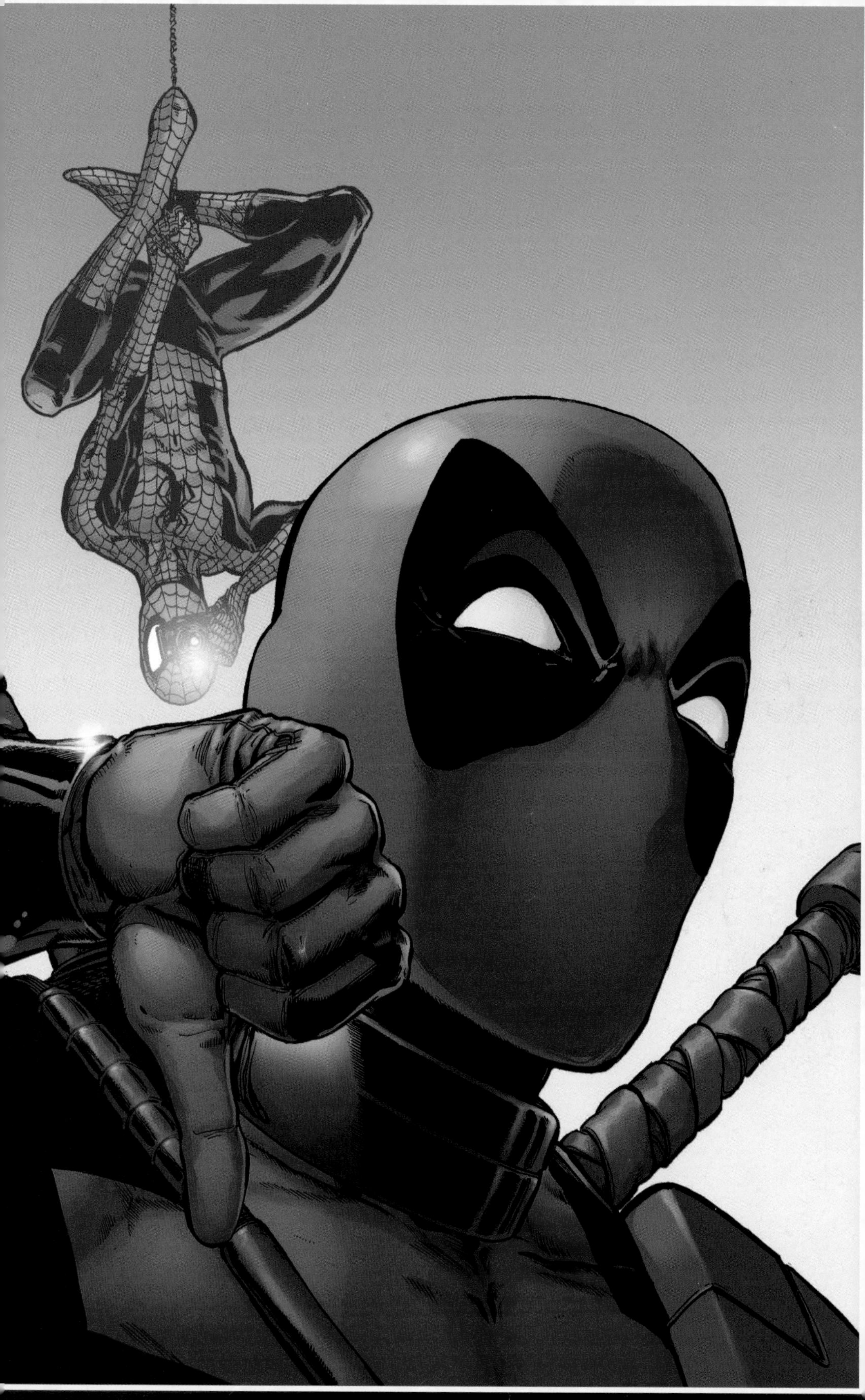

WEB OF SPIDER-MAN #5 DEADPOOL VARIANT

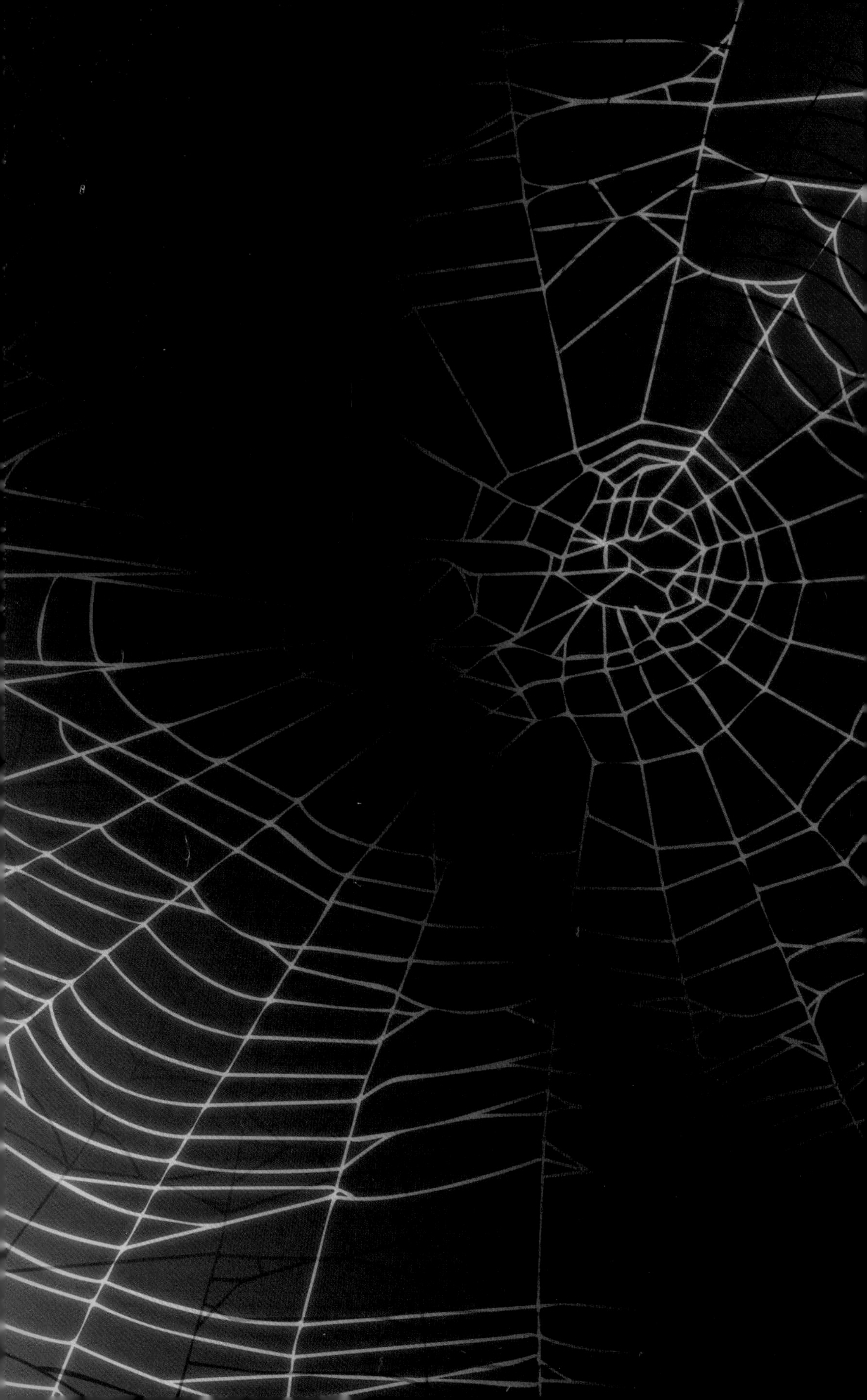